D0649224

The Just King

The Just King

The Tibetan Buddhist Classic on Leading an Ethical Life

Jamgön Mipham

TRANSLATED BY

José Ignacio Cabezón

LIBRARY OF
CONGRESS
SURPLUS
DUPLICATE

SNOW LION
BOULDER
2017

Snow Lion
An imprint of Shambhala Publications, Inc.
4720 Walnut Street
Boulder, Colorado 80301
www.shambhala.com

© 2017 by José Ignacio Cabezón

All rights reserved. No part of this book may be reproduced
in any form or by any means, electronic or mechanical, including
photocopying, recording, or by any information storage and retrieval
system, without permission in writing from the publisher.

9 8 7 6 5 4 3 2 1

First Edition
Printed in the United States of America

♾This edition is printed on acid-free paper that meets
the American National Standards Institute Z39.48 Standard.
♻This book is printed on 30% postconsumer recycled paper.
For more information please visit www.shambhala.com.

Distributed in the United States by Penguin Random House LLC
and in Canada by Random House of Canada Ltd

LIBRARY OF CONGRESS CATALOGING-IN-PUBLICATION DATA

Names: Mi-pham-rgya-mtsho, 'Jam-mgon 'Ju, 1846–1912, author. |
Cabezón, José Ignacio, 1956– translator.
Title: The just king: the Tibetan Buddhist classic on leading an ethical life /
Mipham; translated by José Ignacio Cabezón.
Other titles: Rgyal po lugs kyi bstan bcos sa gzhi skyong ba'i rgyan. English
Description: First edition. | Boulder: Snow Lion, 2017. | Includes bibliographical references.
Identifiers: LCCN 2016044914 | ISBN 9781611804966 (pbk.: alk. paper)
Subjects: LCSH: Buddhism and politics. | Kings and rulers—Duties. | Political ethics.
Classification: LCC BQ4570.S7 M5413 2017 | DDC 172/.2—dc23
LC record available at https://lccn.loc.gov/2016044914

In memory of Michael Hahn and Jim Blumenthal,
who devoted their lives to the study of the literature
and ideals found in this book.

All people are my children. What I desire for my own children, that I desire for everyone.

There is no better work than promoting the welfare of all the people, and whatever efforts I make is to repay the debt I owe to all beings to assure their happiness in this life, and the attainment of heaven in the next.

I, King Piyadasi (Aśoka), desire that all religions should exist everywhere, for all of them desire self-control and purity of heart.

Dhamma is good, but what does Dhamma mean? It means doing little evil and much good, and practicing kindness, generosity, truthfulness, and purity. . . . It means proper behavior towards servants and employees, respect for teachers, restraint towards living beings, and generosity towards ascetics and brahmins.

There is no gift like the gift of the Dhamma, no acquaintance like acquaintance with Dhamma, no distribution like distribution of Dhamma, and no kinship like kinship through Dhamma.

—From the Aśokan edicts (third century BCE)
Adapted from the translation by Ven. S. Dhammika

Contents

Introduction

> They rule who are truly rich, not in silver and gold, but in virtue and wisdom, which are the true blessings of life.
>
> —Plato, *The Republic*

SIDDHĀRTHA GAUTAMA WAS born a prince, heir to the throne of the small North Indian kingdom of Kapilavastu. His biographies tell us that when he was an infant, he was brought before the sage Asita, who predicted that he would one day become either a universal monarch, or else "an awakened one," a Buddha. Leaving home and adopting a religious path, he achieved enlightenment, and among his many epithets was "King of the Dharma" (*dharmarāja*). Buddhist texts through the ages are filled with allusions to kingship, employing a plethora of both royal images and metaphors of kingly conquest. As Peter Skilling notes, "The victorious king mirrors the Buddha; and the victorious Buddha mirrors the king."[1] Many of the Buddha's monks and nuns came from royal families.

The sūtras or scriptures tell us that the Buddha himself enjoyed cordial relations with the most important North Indian monarchs of his day: Prasenajit, the king of Kosala; the Magadhan ruler Bimbisāra and his parricide son Ajātaśatru; Udāyana, ruler of Vatsa; and of course his own father Śuddhodana. Two centuries after the Buddha, the Mauryan monarch Aśoka (d. 232 BCE), arguably the greatest of all Indian kings, is said to have converted to Buddhism after witnessing the devastation caused by one of his military campaigns. Fast forward another century and we see Buddhist monks serving as advisors or interlocutors to other Indian rulers, like the Indo-Greek king Menander (d. 135 BCE), and the Kushan king Kaniṣka

1. Peter Skilling, "King, *Sangha*, and Brahmans: Ideology, Ritual, and Power in Pre-modern Siam," in Ian Harris, *Buddhism, Power and Political Order*, 192.

(ca. 127–163 ce). Beginning in the first centuries of the common era, various foreign rulers started to play an important role in the spread of Buddhism throughout Asia. Is it any wonder then that Buddhist authors through the ages have had a lot to say about kings?

This book is a translation of a Tibetan work on the theory and practice of Buddhist kingship and political ethics, perhaps the longest premodern work on the subject. It was written by one of Tibet's greatest luminaries, Ju Mipham Namgyal Gyatso (1846–1912). Mipham composed *A Treatise on Ethics for Kings: An Ornament for Rulers*[2] in 1895 at the behest of Ngawang Jampel Rinchen, a prince of the kingdom of Dergé in Kham in eastern Tibet. Although written in the form of advice to a Buddhist monarch, Mipham touts the work's relevance to anyone who is in a position of authority, and even to people who live a solitary life.

> Even those who live alone without companions
> should engage in self-cultivation based on the Dharma of kings.
> When one trains one's mind to care for living beings,
> one eventually becomes a Dharma king oneself.
>
> Therefore, even when those who study these texts
> are not of royal blood,
> their good qualities will definitely give them dominion
> over a royal kingdom.

According to Mipham, the work is meant as a guide to living an ethical life, but also a cause for achieving temporal power. Tibetans have taught and studied Mipham's *Treatise* for over one hundred years, seeing it as an excellent practical resource for navigating day-to-day life. We have evidence that the work was being taught at Dergé Gönchen, the monastery of the capital of the Dergé kingdom in Kham, in the 1940s.[3] It is still used at the Larung Gar Buddhist Academy, the largest Buddhist monastery in the world, located in Sertar, Kham.

In this introduction we present an overview of the *Treatise*, and a brief

2. The Tibetan title is *Rgyal po lugs kyi bstan bcos sa gzhi skyong ba'i rgyan*. The editions of the work consulted in this translation are discussed later in this introduction.
3. Namkhai Norbu Rinpoche studied the text there under his uncle Khyentse Chökyi Wangchug in 1945; see "Asian Scholars at IsMEO," 89.

sketch of Mipham's life and of the political situation in Kham during the period that Mipham wrote the *Treatise*. The introduction concludes with some remarks on the Tibetan text and its translation.

MIPHAM'S *TREATISE*: AN OVERVIEW

Mipham's work belongs to two interrelated verse genres of Indian and Tibetan literature. The first of these, the *nīti* treatises, are works on worldly ethics. Although they often allude to religious ideals, they do not deal with complex doctrinal issues, focusing instead on practical concerns like wealth, power, and the material aspects of human flourishing. From the earliest times, some of the *nīti* literature, called *rājanīti*, or "ethics for kings," dealt with governance and statecraft: how kings should lead their lives to be effective and just rulers. The other genre is called *subhāṣita*, "well-spoken" or "well-turned" verses—wise sayings or adages that set forth fundamental truths about life and offer practical moral advice. The interested reader will find a more thorough explanation of the *nīti* and *subhāṣita* literature in appendix 1.

Although written principally for rulers, Mipham's *Treatise* has been a source of inspiration and ethical guidance for Tibetan Buddhists—kings and citizens alike—for over a century. How relevant is the *Treatise* to us today? The principles that Mipham advocates—the importance of cultivating virtue and avoiding evil, of *ahiṃsa* or "non-harm," of justice for the poor and downtrodden of society, of the equality of all people before the law—are just as important in the twenty-first century as they were in ancient times.

With some exceptions, noted below, most of the ethical principles found in these pages could be easily adopted as the basis for Buddhist social justice—as the foundation of what today we call Engaged Buddhism. As Mipham states, rulers and politicians have a special responsibility to uphold high moral standards, to serve as an example for others, and to protect society and the environment. It would require a bit of thought to translate all of the *Treatise*'s concerns to our own time, but the world would undoubtedly be a much better place if these ethical guidelines found their way into contemporary political life. It is true that Mipham did not know about nuclear weapons, or drones, or the ravages of modern mass warfare, but he writes eloquently about war as a last resort, about the need to avoid civilian casualties, destruction of cultural treasures, and harm to the environment. Buddhism, as Mipham shows, has a lot to say to the issues confronting our world today, but the *Treatise* is also meant as an ethical guide for ordinary individuals. Its principles apply not only to those in power, but to everyone.

That said, the *Treatise* is a work of the *nīti* genre, and as such it presumes a very specific form of government: monarchy. This is the only type of government that Mipham writes about, and his presumed audience is the Buddhist king. Since the sovereign is at the center of the *Treatise*, it might be useful to present a brief synopsis of what that king was supposed to be like—what was expected of him in this context.

The king belongs to a royal line, inheriting his position from his father. He is extremely powerful, the master of the royal court in the capital and the ruler of the people throughout the kingdom. He is responsible for making all appointments—ministers, district governors, judges, and the like. He also oversees the administration of the law. He is the leader of the army and makes all major military decisions. The king also controls the treasury, both how it is augmented and how it is spent. But despite his great power, the king is not all powerful, nor is he a god, nor infallible. His royal blood is no guarantee of his success as a ruler, nor does it assure a lengthy reign.

Some classical Indian texts advocated the divinity of the king—that the sovereign was a god incarnate—but Buddhist Indian sources generally reject this. According to the *Aggañña Sutta*, the first Buddhist king was elected from among men. An alternative vision of Buddhist kingship is that of the cakravartin or "wheel-turner," an extraordinary man who conquers the world by his charisma and the power of a magical wheel (*cakra*) that he alone possesses. Even the cakravartin, however, is not a god, but a human being who has accrued vast amounts of merit. Texts like the *Sūtra of Golden Light* (*Suvarṇaprabhāsa*), to which Mipham devotes an entire chapter, imply a close connection between the king and the gods, but these works claim only that the sovereign is "appointed" by the gods and not that he *is* a god. In his summary of the *Suvarṇaprabhāsa*'s theory and practice of kingship, Mipham states that "when the appointed king is a wastrel . . . the gods stop supporting him. . . . They abandon that evil king and his kingdom quickly collapses." Elsewhere, Mipham states that despots—rulers who control their subjects using violence—"end up being destroyed, even if they are of royal blood." In short, despite the king's unique social position and tremendous power, his status as a ruler is never guaranteed, either by the gods or by his royal pedigree. Kings can be defeated by other kingdoms, be overthrown by their own subjects, and they can lose the support of heaven or the gods. When kings are evil, this is in fact to be expected.

Being human and fallible, monarchs need to be educated. They have to engage in a program of self-cultivation that will give them the intellectual and ethical wherewithal to be effective rulers. The program of self-fashioning elaborated in the *nīti* literature is no easy thing. Kings must study the classical texts, associate with wise and upright people, and distance themselves from the wicked. They must learn to distinguish right from wrong, cultivate a long list of virtues, eschew an equally long list of sins, and have the will to act in accordance with what is right and just. Note that the "technologies of self" elaborated in Buddhist *nīti* works like Mipham's are wholly directed at the ruler. This is not a "subjectivation" of the masses—a process of individualization and identity formation that, according to Michel Foucault, serves (in modernity) as the precondition to their being governed—but rather a subjectivation of the ruler, the creation of the king as an ethical subject that makes it possible for him to successfully rule.

The *nīti* treatises and the Buddhist sūtras and commentaries form the basis for this program of moral self-cultivation, mediated, of course, by the explanations of the teacher or guru, who serves as a guide. Lists of kingly virtues and vices are found in both Buddhist canonical works and in the *nīti* literature. In his *Treatise*, Mipham especially focuses on a list of thirty-five kingly duties taught in the *Sūtra on Establishing Recollection* (*Smṛtyupasthāna Sūtra*). I have listed these in appendix 2.

This list as well as the *Treatise* as a whole give one a sense of how much is expected of the ideal king. First, he should be well versed in Buddhist doctrine, especially the doctrine of karmic cause and effect. Elsewhere, Mipham states that the sovereign must sometimes adjudicate doctrinal or clerical disputes that might arise in his kingdom, so a strong foundation in the Dharma is essential. The king must also engage in a variety of religious practices: worshipping the local gods, supporting holy beings, propagating the Dharma, and even meditating on wisdom.

Regarding his demeanor, the king must be energetic, truthful, humble, patient, even-keeled, compassionate, sweet-spoken, and charitable. He is self-controlled and restrained in the pursuit of sense pleasures. He practices moderation in food and sleep. He does not procrastinate and sees his plans through to completion. He is a good judge of character and a steadfast friend.

Once these personal qualities have been perfected through education, they must be "exteriorized" and put into practice in the real world. When administering the law, the king is fair and impartial, but also committed to stamping out unrighteousness (animal sacrifice, insolence toward elders, nihilistic views, crime, and so forth), and punishing or banishing the wicked when necessary.

In matters of governance, he protects his subjects and works for their welfare. His timing is always impeccable, knowing exactly when and when not to act. He is not credulous, but rather possesses a keen and critical intellect that investigates things from different perspectives before coming to a conclusion. Once he decides on a course of action, however, he is resolute and acts independently, remaining aloof from the petty politics of the court and not allowing himself to come under others' sway.

Realizing the horrors of war, he is not quick to take up arms against his adversaries; when he does, it is only as a last resort. In warfare, he tries to minimize loss of life and damage to property, especially cultural treasures. In the economic sphere, he does not renege on the financial promises made by his ancestors, he does not impose excessive taxes on his subjects, he provides for his family both materially and spiritually, he helps the poor, and he ensures that resources are properly distributed among his dependents (servants, serfs, and so forth).

By ruling his kingdom in this way, the gods show him favor, sending timely rains, providing abundant harvests, and so forth. His cities flourish; he garners vast wealth and enjoys a good reputation in the world. Other kingdoms rarely rise up against him, and if they do, they are quickly defeated; his subjects neither criticize him nor revolt against him; his reign is long-lasting. "And when his body is no more, he is reborn in heaven, and becomes a ruler of the gods."

The Buddhist king is not a god, but his relationship to the gods is important to his success. Western scholars of Buddhist kingship have stressed the "horizontal" relationship of the monarch with the feudal states that lie on the periphery of his kingdom. This theory of kingship emphasizes the king's position at the center of a maṇḍala over which he rules. Without denying the validity of this model, the Indian and Tibetan *nīti* literature is arguably more concerned with the king's "vertical" relationship with the nonhuman world. A king must have the gods' support if his kingdom is to flourish, but gods only assist virtuous and righteous sovereigns, withholding their support from evil kings. In the absence of such support—or worse, when a king incurs the wrath of the gods—it is not long before his kingdom collapses. This vertical dimension of kingship is extremely important to understanding Buddhist ideas of sovereignty. In one of Aśoka's inscriptions at Girnar, the Mauryan emperor, whose epithet was "Beloved of the Gods," rejoices at the fact that he has "replaced the sound of the drum [of war] with the sound of the Dharma" throughout his kingdom. As a result:

> The sighting of heavenly carriages, auspicious elephants, bodies of fire, and other divine sightings that have not been witnessed for many hundreds of years have increased because Beloved of the Gods, King Piyadasi, promotes restraint in the killing and harming of living beings, proper behavior toward relatives, brahmins, and ascetics, and respect for parents and elders.[4]

Virtue brings the gods' support, and this support can be adduced from various heavenly signs. Contrariwise, natural disasters are sometimes also seen as godsend, as signs that something is amiss in the kingdom or in the court. It is not unusual for such events to be used to challenge a king's authority, and even his right to rule. This is not unique to Buddhism. Tibetan historians tell us that when Buddhism was first introduced into Tibet, a series of natural catastrophes were interpreted by those non-Buddhist priests and ministers who were antagonistic to Buddhism as signs that the gods were displeased with the king's decision to adopt a new religion.

In a worldview that sees the king as divine, infallible, and all powerful, the king's word comes to be equated with the law. Michel Foucault has argued that in medieval Europe the king and the lawbreaker are antipodal; that the king's "other" is the condemned criminal: "In the darkest region of the political field the condemned man represents the inverted figure of the king."[5] This is because a violation of the law was seen as a violation of the king's word, and even as an affront to the king himself. "Crime," says Foucault, "attacks the sovereign; it attacks him personally since the law represents the will of the sovereign."[6] When the king's word is the law, and his power is absolute, then penalties for legal infractions have no limits. Criminals are then subjected to the most horrific punishments—torture and even death—because crime, the violation of the law, offends and threatens the person of the king. In this case, punishment is, in Foucault's words, an act of "the dissymmetry between the subject who has dared to violate

4. S. Dhammika, "Kalinga Rock Edicts," *The Edicts on King Ashoka*, www.cs.colostate.edu/~malaiya/ashoka.html#KALINGA.
5. Michel Foucault, *Discipline and Punish*, 29.
6. Ibid., 47.

the law and the all-powerful sovereign who displays its strength."[7] I would go one step further by claiming that the severity of punishment in a monarchical tradition is in direct proportion to the perceived divinity, power, and infallibility of the sovereign.

Mipham, as we have seen, does not subscribe to the view that kings are divine or infallible.[8] It is true that the king is very powerful, "more powerful," he says, "than all the commanders combined,"[9] but he is not all-powerful. Nor is the law, in Mipham's understanding, coterminous with the king's word or will. Having been laid down "by former Dharma kings," the royal laws exist prior to any given monarch. And the religious laws found in the universal ethical code of restraint from the ten nonvirtues of Buddhism—not killing, not stealing, and so on—are eternal. Mipham discusses these extensively in chapter 16.

The sovereign is the "custodian of the laws." What is more, both sets of laws apply as much to the king as to his subjects. "Follow accepted principles," Mipham advises the monarch. "If you act according to your whims, you violate the rule of law; this is unprincipled." "When a king transgresses the law," he states elsewhere, "how can it be appropriate for him to sit in judgment of others?" The laws are not, therefore, whatever the king decrees; rather, they are a pre-existent ethical code. The king is subject to those laws, both "secular" and religious. Even though the sovereign can pardon convicts, he does not have the right to simply punish someone on a whim.

The accused has the right to a fair and impartial trial, and if convicted, punishment has to be proportionate to the offense. Moreover, "whoever violates the law should receive the same punishment regardless of his or her social standing." "The royal laws," Mipham states, "are not lighter for the powerful

7. Ibid., 49.

8. Skilling ("King, *Sangha*, and Brahmans," 194–95) suggests that the same may not be true in Thailand since, among other things, Thai monarchs often adopted the names of gods—Rāma, Indra, and so on. But the fact that kings bore such names, or that they were addressed in a special language, or were said to "go to heaven" after they die, does not strike me as proof of the fact that they were considered divine.

9. It is precisely for this reason that Mipham places so much emphasis on the king learning self-control (*apramāda, bag yod*), which is the subject of the first chapter of his work. Since a king enjoys great power, it is incumbent upon him to learn to control it, especially in matters of pleasure seeking. Not to do so leads to a wanton and dissolute life, the opposite of self-control. The king's practice of self-control is also the moral of a story found at the end of the *Meeting of Father and Son* (*Pitāputrasamāgama*), an important Mahāyāna scripture (Lha sa ed., from fol. 346b).

and wealthy, and not heavier for the humble and poor. Instead, everyone is equal in the eyes of the law, just as in a brothel all men are the same."

Mipham follows the *Sūtra of the (Bodhisattva) Truth-Teller* (*Satyaka Sūtra*) in prohibiting the death penalty, the severing of limbs, and other forms of cruel and excessive punishment that "cannot be reversed or remedied." When neither the king nor the courts are infallible, mistakes can occur, and there has to be room in the system for reversing these errors.

While in this respect Mipham's legal views are progressive, it would be a mistake to conceive of him as a progressive or liberal in the contemporary sense. For example, Mipham follows the *Satyaka Sūtra* in permitting "beating and striking" (i.e., torture) when prisoners, having been admonished, refuse to change their ways. Nor does he challenge the misogyny prevalent in many of the *nīti* texts, which see women as scheming, divisive, and in need of being controlled by men, through corporal punishment if necessary. These aspects of Mipham's thought notwithstanding, by comparison to the legal traditions that saw no limits to the punishment that could be meted out to criminals—traditions that, I have argued, go hand in hand with a notion of an all-powerful king whose word is the law—the Buddhist theory of punishment espoused by Mipham is indeed more progressive. The decoupling of the law from the will of the king, and the recognition of the fallibility of both the king and courts of law, opened a space for the possibility of error in the law's implementation, and for forms of punishment that were comparatively more humane.

One final set of observations: In chapter 5 of the *Treatise*, Mipham describes the other members of society and their duties—the nobility, the king's ministers and advisors, the functionaries (district governors, judges, clerks, and so on), the palace staff (guards, eunuchs, workers, and so on), and the king's subjects. Mipham urges the king to be cautious in making appointments, since the welfare of the state depends on having noble and ethical people administering it.

Corruption, of course, is always a danger in all ranks of government, but Mipham is especially critical of the nobility, who "do as they please . . . bringing grief to both themselves and others . . . with no interest in doing good." Nobles or the aristocracy see ordinary people as chattel to be used or as fodder to be consumed. Mipham compares them to the offspring of scorpions, "who see their mother as food and eat her." It is the king's responsibility to protect his subjects from such unscrupulous people. "Those who persist, regardless of your attempt to reform them," Mipham says, "should be banished."

In contrast to this negative portrayal of the aristocracy, the common people are mostly portrayed throughout the *Treatise* in a positive light. Even when they make mistakes, the king is encouraged to practice patience and cultivate compassion for them. A monarch who lacks compassion for the most vulnerable members of a society—the elderly, children, the sick, the poor, and so forth—"is inhuman." Although the king has the right to collect taxes, he should always do so in moderation and should never threaten his subjects' livelihood. People work hard for what little they have, barely able to make ends meet. The king should therefore only "collect small amounts of taxes from each of his subjects . . . with a sense of pity for his people." The common people never find happiness in any kingdom in which there is too much inequality. People's different karmic pasts may make it impossible to ever achieve complete equality in the world, but this should not stop the king from trying to lessen inequality. Moderation in collecting taxes is just one of the ways in which the king cares for the people.

It is also the duty of the king to protect his subjects from hostile kingdoms, criminals, and corrupt officials; to help them in the time of famine, plague, and natural disasters; and to ensure their ongoing well-being by setting up hospitals, schools, markets, parks, and temples. The sovereign is even responsible for providing entertainment to the masses by supporting artists, dancers, and musicians.

Although the sovereign of Mipham's *Treatise* is presumed to be Buddhist, he is the king of all his subjects, no matter what religion they practice. Without trying to create a single pastiche out of all the religions in his land, the sovereign not only practices tolerance of others' beliefs, but also supports those religions "so that they do not degenerate." The king must also protect the natural environment that is the home to the country's spirits, a reminder that the king's duties extend beyond the human world. Most of all, he must care for people by instilling in them a sense of morality. The privileging of ordinary people in Mipham's ethics draws heavily from the Mahāyāna tradition, albeit reconceptualized in a political register. The king, in this respect, becomes the equivalent of the bodhisattva, and his subjects stand in the place of "all sentient beings," the object of the bodhisattva's love.

To conclude, a lot is required of the righteous ruler, but that is precisely why he must first engage in a long program of intellectual and moral self-fashioning. Only then will the king be able to rule justly and effectively.

Mipham's system of political ethics is a top-down model akin to Plato's, a trickle-down theory of the just state. Only when the uppermost position in the political hierarchy is occupied by a just and moral sovereign will righteousness spread to the masses. Only when the kingdom is ruled by a righteous king will it attract the favor of the gods and flourish. We could say so much more about the principles of just rule in Mipham's *Treatise*, but perhaps this is enough to orient the reader for what is to come.

The Author

Considering that he was one of Tibet's greatest scholars, we do not have many sources on Mipham's life. As John Pettit notes, "Tibetan scholars of lesser importance have been remembered in reminiscences much more extensive than the small but inspiring biographical sketches of Mipham available at present."[10] Nonetheless, a few short Tibetan biographies do exist, and the most important of these is the *Essential Hagiography* written by Khenpo Kunzang Palden (1862–1943), a direct disciple of Mipham.[11] Other brief biographies have also been written by the most important Nyingma lamas of the twentieth century, including Dilgo Khyentse Rinpoche (1910–1991), Dudjom Rinpoche (1904–1987), and Khenpo Jigmé Phuntsok (1933–2004).[12]

Over the last decade or so, Western scholars have published studies and translations of some of Mipham Rinpoche's most important works. These books contain concise biographies of Mipham's life that draw on these short Tibetan hagiographical works.[13] I recommend these books to readers who

10. John W. Pettit, *Mipham's Beacon of Certainty*, 19.

11. Kun bzang dpal ldan, *'Jam mgon mi pham rin po che'i rnam thar snying po bsdus pa*, in *Mi pham bka' 'bum*, vol. 9, 551–648, which also includes a table of contents of Mipham's works. Several of his biographies have been collected, along with various prayers and praises to Mipham, in *Rje mi pham pa'i bla ma phyogs bsgrigs*. Another short Tibetan biography is found in Bstan 'dzin lung rtogs nyi ma, *Snga 'gyur rdzogs chen chos 'byung chen mo*, 425–39.

12. See also Dil mgo mkhyen rtse bkra shis dpal 'byor, *'Jam mgon bla ma mi pham 'jam dbyangs rnam rgyal rgya mtsho'i rnam thar*, in *Dil mgo mkhyen rtse'i bka' 'bum*, vol. 15, 267–99. Dudjom Rinpoche's biography is found in his magisterial *Rnying ma chos 'byung*, which has been translated by Gyurme Dorje with Matthew Kapstein in *The Nyingma School of Tibetan Buddhism*, vol. 1, 869–80. Khenpo Jigmé Phuntsok's biography of Mipham has apparently been translated by Ann Helm in 2008 as *Miracle Stories of Mipham Rinpoche*, but this work was unavailable to me.

13. See, for instance, E. Gene Smith, *Among Tibetan Texts*, chapter 16; Steven D. Goodman,

wish to gain a more holistic picture of Mipham's life and thought, but for the sake of completeness I will sketch out his biography here.

Mipham was born to an aristocratic family in the kingdom of Dergé in 1846. His family had ties to the Dergé royal court from both his maternal and paternal side. His father, Gönpo Dargye, was a renowned physician, which makes it likely that Mipham received some training in the medical sciences in his youth; he would later write various works on medicine and alchemy. At age twelve Mipham took novice vows and entered Ju Mohor Sang-ngag Chöling, a branch of the great monastery of Zhechen.[14] By all accounts a child prodigy, his intellectual gifts were quickly recognized and it was not long before he was known in the monastery under the moniker "the little monk scholar." Around 1861 Mipham undertook an eighteen-month retreat on Mañjuśrī, the bodhisattva of wisdom, at Junyung Hermitage. He later told his close disciples that from that time on he could understand almost any work on any subject without studying it, simply by receiving a brief explanatory transmission.

Shortly after completing this retreat, Mipham took to the road, fleeing, as did many others, the turmoil of the Nyagrong wars in Kham (see below). Traveling with his uncle, he first went to the nomadic region of Golok and then to Lhasa, where he spent one month studying at the Gelug monastic university of Ganden. Mipham became well versed in Gelug philosophy and continued to take exoteric teachings from Gelug masters even after returning to Kham.

On his return journey from central Tibet, Mipham took the southern route. At Lhodrag Kharchu, a retreat place of the great tantric saint Padmasambhava, he had a spontaneous mystical experience of blissful heat that he attributed to the sanctity of the site. It was during this time, while traveling in southern Tibet, that he met two of his most important teachers: Patrul Rinpoche (1808–1887), the fifth abbot of Dzogchen Monastery, and

---

"Mi-Pham rgya-mtsho: An Account of His Life, the Printing of His Works, and the Structure of His Treatise Entitled *Mkhas-pa'i tshul la 'jug pa'i mgo*," John W. Pettit, *Mipham's Beacon of Certainty*, 19–39, which contains a translation of Khenpo Kunzang Palden's *Essential Hagiography*; Douglas Duckworth, *Mipam on Buddha-Nature*, xx–xvii; Douglas Duckworth, *Jamgön Mipam: His Life and Teachings*; Karma Phuntsok, *Mipham's Dialectics and the Debates on Emptiness*, 13–19; also Douglas Duckworth, "Mipam Gyatso," *Treasury of Lives*, http://treasuryoflives.org/biographies/view/Mipam-Gyatso/4228.

14. See "History of Ju Mohor Monastery," *Amnyi Trulchung Rinpoche*, www.amnyitrulchung.org/monastery/history/.

Jamyang Khyentse Wangpo (1820–1892), one of the greatest scholars of his day who, together with Jamgön Kongtrul (1813–1899) and Chogyur Lingpa (1829–1870), was at the center of an important trans-sectarian religious revival in Kham known as rimé. Mipham's relationship to rimé is complex. On the one hand, he was a student of the "founders" of this tradition. On the other hand, Mipham is known for his attempts to revitalize Nyingma, to create a distinctive identity for the school, and to defend this tradition vis-à-vis other Tibetan schools.[15]

Mipham took Khyentse Rinpoche as his root guru and Khyentse in turn considered Mipham as his heart-son. He gave Mipham many teachings and empowerments and on more than one occasion publicly acknowledged Mipham's extraordinary erudition and high realization, on one occasion even prophesying his future worldwide renown. Mipham's service to Khyentse Rinpoche is often touted as exemplary—for example, he gave away all his belongings to his master on seven different occasions. Of course, Mipham also studied under many other famous Khampa masters, including Khenpo Padma Vajra (1807–1884), the eighth abbot of Dzogchen Monastery; the Sakya lama Jamyang Loter Wangpo (1847–1912), from whom he received teachings on Sakya Paṇḍita's *Treasury of Reasoning*; and the great Jamgön Kongtrul, from whom he received, inter alia, teachings on the "worldly sciences" such as grammar and alchemy.

Once Mipham had returned to Kham, Khyentse Rinpoche commissioned him "to write some textbooks for our [Nyingma] tradition." This was the beginning of a period of intense literary activity for Mipham that focused chiefly on exoteric subjects; many of the textbooks written during these years are used in Nyingma monastic universities to this day. Mipham realized that there was a need to explain the classical Indian texts from the viewpoint of the Nyingma tradition. "Nowadays," he wrote in his *Essential Hagiography*, "the Early Translation [or Nyingma] teaching . . . does little more than imitate other systems, there being few who even wonder what our own philosophical system is." Mipham therefore set out to elaborate the doctrinal foundations of a specifically Nyingma understanding of the great Indian texts. In doing so, he was not reluctant to defend his views against the prevailing opinions of his day, even if it meant critiquing other schools.

15. On the rimé movement, see Sam van Schaik, *Tibet: A History*, 165–69; Ringu Tulku, *The Ri-Me Philosophy of Jamgon Kongtrul the Great*; and especially Alexander P. Gardner, "The Twenty-five Great Sites of Khams," 114f.

Of course, as scholars of other traditions (most notably the Gelug) began to learn of Mipham's criticisms, "polemical responses began to arrive from all directions."[16] Mipham, however, maintained a very open and critical perspective in his debates with rival scholars. While affirming his right to critically examine all views, he was also open to the fallibility of his own position. "If someone who possesses the Dharma eye refutes me in accordance with scripture and reasoning, I should rely upon him as a doctor and would never reply out of anger. Thus, with a noble and honest intention, I have debated upon occasion."[17] True to his word, Mipham often acknowledged the greatness of other scholars. For example, in a competition not of words but of magical powers with the famous Jonang scholar Bamda Gelek (1844–1904), Mipham is said to have praised his rival. "I have met many scholars," he said, "but in this day and age, to meet a scholar of the highest rank is rare. Dzamtangpa Gelek is such a scholar."[18]

Mipham was a true polymath. His collected works—some 320 titles in more than thirty volumes—spans the entire range of Indo-Tibetan learning. It includes classical religious subjects like Madhyamaka philosophy, Tantra, and ritual.[19] As Gene Smith notes, "Mi pham's greatest contributions to the cultural history of Tibet lies in his brilliant and strikingly original commentaries on the important Indic treatises."[20]

But Mipham also had a keen interest in the practical arts—magic, crafts, erotics, alchemy, medicine, divination, and astrology. In these texts he preserved, in quasi-anthropological fashion, many of the local traditions and folk practices of Kham. Mipham was also known for his interest in the literary sciences: grammar, poetics, dramaturgy, and prosody, including the great Tibetan epic of Gesar.[21] Given his insatiable appetite for learning, it

16. The words are found in the *Essential Hagiography*; see Pettit, *Mipham's Beacon of Certainty*, 27.
17. Ibid.
18. See José I. Cabezón, "Bamda Gelek," *Treasury of Lives*, http://treasuryoflives.org/biographies/view/Bamda-Gelek/7272.
19. For a list of a few of his most important ritual and liturgical works, see "Mipham Rinpoche," *Rigpa Wiki*, www.rigpawiki.org/index.php?title=Mipham_Rinpoche.
20. Smith, *Among Tibetan Texts*, 231. Smith goes on to describe Mipham's interest in Tibetan literature, including his important work on the Gesar epic. Some important texts of the Gesar corpus, based on works written by one of Mipham's disciples, have been translated by Robin Kornman, Sangye Khandro, and Lama Chönam in *The Epic of Gesar of Ling*.
21. Western scholars have focused almost exclusively on Mipham's philosophical works (see note 12), but the vast bulk of his writings have yet to be explored. For brief overviews of his *Collected Works*, see Duckworth, *Mipam on Buddha Nature*, xxiv–vi; and Karma

is not surprising that we should find works that belong to the Indian genre of *nītiśāstra* in his collected writings. In addition to the work translated in these pages—which deals specifically with royal ethics and political theory—Mipham also composed a shorter work of the *nīti* genre called *A Treatise on Ethics: A Jewel That Brings Together the Gods and Glory*.[22] However, unlike the work translated in this book, the *Jewel* is not specifically a work on political ethics, but rather a treatise on how to cultivate a moral life.

One might wonder, given his tremendous literary output, whether Mipham had time for anything else but his writings. However, all the biographies agree that Mipham also extensively taught and that he spent a great deal of time in meditation retreat. Although he was neither a recognized incarnation, or trulku, nor a revealer of hidden treasure, or tertön, his saintliness gave rise to a number of miracle stories that have been chronicled in various sources.[23]

In his final days Mipham wrote some verses in which he confessed to having suffered from a debilitating illness for the last seventeen years of his life, a "severe illness of the energy channels" that had made him experience "uninterrupted and intense suffering." Despite this, he states, he chose to remain in the world for the sake of others, but now welcomed death.[24] Mipham passed away in 1912 at his hermitage, located near Dzogchen Monastery, in his home district of Ju. He claimed that he would not take rebirth again in the "impure" states of existence—that is, in the human world. "Now is a critical moment in these final times; the barbarians and so forth are close to destroying the teachings, so there is no point whatsoever in my taking

---

Phuntsok, *Mipham's Dialectics*, 13–19. And for an analysis of one of his more interesting nonphilosophical works, see Bryan J. Cuevas, "The Calf's Nipple" (*Be'u bum*) of Ju Mipam: A Handbook of Tibetan Ritual Magic," in José I. Cabezón, *Tibetan Ritual*, 165–86.

22. *Lugs kyi bstan bcos lha dang dpal 'du ba'i nor bu*, in *Mi pham bka' bum*, vol. 7, 194–212. The colophon states that it was written at Dzongsar, the monastery of Mipham's teacher Jamyang Khyentse Wangpo, but the date of composition is not mentioned. A translation by the Ari Bhöd Translation Committee can be found online, "The Treatise on the Modes of Being: 'The Jewel that Gathers Forth Divinities and Glory,'" *Treasury of Lives*, http://aribhod.org/wp-content/uploads/2014/07/NORBU_CHOS-Web-021115.pdf.

23. See the comments of the *Essential Hagiography* translated in Pettit, *Mipham's Beacon of Certainty*, 33–34, and the work of Khenpo Jigmé Phuntsok translated by Ann Helm, *Miracle Stories of Mipham Rinpoche*.

24. Pettit, *Mipham's Beacon of Certainty*, 36.

rebirth."[25] But as Douglas Duckworth shows, several individuals have since been identified over the last century as Mipham's reincarnations.[26]

The Historical-Political Context

Mipham tells us in the colophon of the *Treatise* that he wrote the work in 1895 in Dergé. This was the largest principality of eastern Tibet with its own king. It ruled a vast area that contained some of Tibet's most important monasteries, including Mipham's own Dzogchen Monastery. The Dergé kingdom's seat of government included the monastery of Lhundrup Teng, renowned for its vast library and printing house. Lhundrup Teng was officially an institution of the Sakya order, but there was a tradition going back to at least the last decade of the eighteenth century of inviting eminent scholars from other schools to the monastery and the royal court. Mipham, we know, was such a visitor, and may have been a court chaplain or royal tutor, *ula* (*dbu bla*), at the time he wrote the *Treatise*.[27]

The last half of the nineteenth century was an extremely tumultuous period in Dergé's history. Lauran Hartley has lucidly documented these events, making it unnecessary to go into detail here.[28] In brief, despite decades of attempts by the Dalai Lama's government in Lhasa and the Qing court in Beijing to bring Dergé under their respective control, the kingdom had remained effectively independent throughout the first half of the nineteenth century. This began to change in 1862 when Dergé's southern neighbor, Nyagrong, attacked and seized the kingdom. Large numbers of refugees from Dergé began to arrive in Central Tibet, and among them was Mipham. The Lhasa government saw Nyagrong's annexation of Dergé as an opportunity to exert its authority and it dispatched an army that defeated Nyagrong and brought the entire region under its control.

Not long after the end of the Nyagrong war, a series of events pitted the Dergé royal family against the chiefs of the different districts of Dergé. Faced with revolt, Chimé Tagpey Dorje (d. 1898), the forty-fifth king of Dergé,

25. Ibid.

26. See Duckworth, "Mipam Gyatso," *Treasury of Lives*.

27. Lauran Hartley notes that Dezhung Rinpoche lists Mipham among the *ula* of Dergé, but we do not know for sure when his tenure of the position began. Lauran R. Hartley, "A Socio-Historical Study of the Kingdom of Sde-dge (Dergé Khams) in the Late Nineteenth Century," 43.

28. Ibid., Part One. The brief account that follows is based principally on this work.

requested Chinese military intervention, but the tribal chiefs united against the king and convinced the Chinese general that Tagpey Dorje was weak and ineffectual and that he needed to go. The Dergé royal family was therefore seized and put under house arrest in Chengdu, the capital of Sichuan, in 1895, the very year that Mipham wrote the *Treatise*. Chimé Tagpey Dorje and his wife died three years later in Chengdu.

The final straw in the fall of the house of Dergé was a struggle for succession between Tagpey Dorje's two sons: the elder Jigmé Dorje Sengé (1877–1926), and the younger Ngawang Jampel Rinchen, the prince who requested Mipham to write the *Treatise*.[29] The king and elder son were pitted against the mother and younger son, with different factions of the Dergé kingdom (and of Lhundrup Teng Monastery itself) taking sides with one or the other faction. The struggle continued for a decade after the death of the king and his wife, leading at times to bloody confrontations between the two sides. It took an invasion by the Chinese warlord Zhao Erfeng in 1908 to bring the struggle to a conclusion. In the end, neither brother was allowed to rule.

Mipham states that he wrote the *Treatise* while lecturing at Lhundrup Teng and that the work had been requested by the "lama-ruler of Dergé" Ngawang Jampel Rinchen.[30] We do not know precisely when Jampel Rinchen was born, but it must have been after 1877, the year of his elder brother's birth. That means that Jampel Rinchen could not have been more than sixteen years old at the time Mipham was requested to write the text. Mipham praises Jampel Rinchen effusively, even identifying him as a bodhisattva:

> He is a son of the Conqueror, a member of the royal line who took birth [in the world] through prayers [equal in extent] to the great sāla tree. From childhood, the nature of his holiness was manifest, without being concealed. He really exerted himself in the way of righteousness. He showed unrelenting effort and zeal for the holy Dharma. His wisdom-eye is supremely broad in

29. Hartley, "A Socio-Historical Study," 50–57, explains some of the issues in the succession struggle, not the least of which was the paternity of the younger son, Jampel Rinchen. Other sources claim, however, that both sons were born of the same parents.

30. I do not know what to make of the fact that Mipham characterizes Jampel Rinchen as the king, for in 1895, the year that Mipham wrote these words, Jampel Rinchen's father, Tagpey Dorje, was, by all accounts, still in power and involved in the aforementioned struggle against the regional Dergé chiefs who were opposing him.

> scope. He has an utterly pure intention to benefit both sentient beings and the teachings without any bias. Having the splendor of oceans of such praiseworthy qualities, the gods who protect virtue enthroned him on the fearless lion throne.

But despite such lavish praise, given Jampel Rinchen's age, the young king—or "young prince" as Mipham calls him elsewhere in the text—was probably just coming into his own. In fact, it is quite possible that the *Treatise* was not requested by Jampel Rinchen at all, but by one of his surrogates, perhaps by his mother, in an attempt to bolster his legitimacy as the future ruler of Dergé.

Because Mipham's work was written in a period of great political turmoil, one might wonder whether the *Treatise* evinces traces of the real-world events unfolding in the Dergé kingdom at the end of the nineteenth century. Lauran Hartley has posed this very question and has concluded—rightly, it seems to me—that the *Treatise* does not reflect historical events on the ground.[31] On the one hand, this is because Mipham chose to compose the work based almost entirely on the model of the classical Indian *nīti* literature. On the other hand, perhaps Mipham realized that the political problems in Dergé, including the struggle for succession, were far from being decided, that it was better to remain aloof from the politics, and that he should follow his own advice in the *Treatise*:

> The lama who serves as tutor
> should . . . be concerned only with dharmic activities,
> and should not intervene in legal or political matters.

The Tibetan Text and the Translation

This translation of Mipham's *Treatise* is based chiefly on the edition of the text found in the Bhutanese edition of *Mipham's Collected Works*, but I have also consulted the Ladakhi edition. The page numbers interspersed into the translation are to the pages of the Bhutanese edition. The publication details of these two works and various other Tibetan editions of the *Treatise* can be found in the bibliography at the end of this book. In my translation

31. Not only is this Hartley's own opinion, but it was also the opinion of three Tibetan informants to whom she posed the question.

I have attempted to capture some of the poetical character of the work by preserving its verse structure and by trying to render each stanza in the same number of lines as in Mipham's text. Breaks between verses in the translation are my own; the Tibetan contains no such divisions.

The notes to the translation are of two kinds. Some are explanatory, clarifying difficult points or explaining references to myths and tales that Mipham simply assumes his reader will know. Other notes are of a more philological nature. Scholars of the *nīti* literature have spent decades trying to unravel the "intertextuality" of these works. A verse from one source will often be found in another—sometimes verbatim, but sometimes with modifications. Occasionally, an author will borrow a metaphor from a verse found in another text and use it to make a quite different point in his own work (Mipham also does this). I have attempted to show some of the connections between the *Treatise* and other *nīti* texts in the notes to the translation, although I readily admit that a lot remains to be done in this regard. Only when all of the extant *nīti* and *subhāṣita* texts preserved in Tibetan have been critically edited and studied will we gain an accurate picture of how all of these works relate to one another. That being said, I hope that my references to similar verses or comparable ideas found in other texts will be interesting to the casual reader and useful to future scholars who may wish to explore the intertextuality of this literature.

I started working on this translation with students during an advanced literary Tibetan class I taught at UC Santa Barbara in 2011. A fellowship from the John Simon Guggenheim Memorial Foundation and a sabbatical leave from UC Santa Barbara during the academic year 2015–2016 allowed me to complete this book; I am grateful to both of these institutions for their generosity. Finally, words of thanks to Joshua Eaton and David Ellerton, who first brought Mipham's text to my attention, to Nikko Odiseos at Shambhala Publications, whose interest in the project, despite many delays, never waned, to Casey Kemp for her invaluable editorial help, and to L. S. Summer for compiling the index.

A Treatise on Ethics for Kings: An Ornament for Rulers

༄༅།རྒྱལ་པོ་ལུགས་ཀྱི་བསྟན་བཅོས་ས་གཞི་སྐྱོང་བའི་རྒྱན་ཞེས་བྱ་བ་བཞུགས་སོ།།

Jamgön Mipham

Homage

Homage to the lama and to the protector Mañjuśrī!

I bow down with reverence to the three jewels:
to our teacher, the supreme king, the true authority;
to his precious teachings, the doorway to liberation;
and to the supreme hosts of āryas, the ornaments of the world, who uphold the teachings.

May the Lion of Sweet Speech, the sun,
protect the lotus patch of beings' intelligence,
clearing away creatures' mental darkness
with the brilliance of his gnosis, as vast as space.

The conquerors and their royal sons, the great noble āryas,
dwell in the world as the protectors of living creatures, fulfilling their various needs. [3]
May these supreme lords of gods and humans
and the hosts of the world's guardian deities bring us good fortune.

The true path of happiness and well-being
depends on the activities of the holy.
Hence, to bring about the two goals
wished for by both rulers and subjects alike,
I will, out of a sense of mercy, explain and make clear the principles of royal ethics
using words that are easy to understand and condensing the essence
of the treatises of the supreme conquerors, their great royal sons,
and the greatest of scholars.

1. Self-Control

A true king is someone who is extremely bright,
who has a stable and unwavering commitment to justice,
who administers the affairs of his retinue and subjects with impartiality and mercy,
and who accumulates vast amounts of spiritual merit. [4]
Such a king ought to be praised
as if he were the sun, Mount Meru, the earth, or the ocean.
He is the source of spiritual nourishment for the members of his retinue.

To educate the ignorant, the king upholds the principles of ethics
using proper laws.
When a ruler is good, living beings will be happy;
when a ruler is evil, the retinue and subjects are bound to suffer.

Therefore, because the king is more powerful
than all the commoners[1] combined,
the greatest results—both beneficial and harmful—
arise from a ruler's actions.

Because they are in the public eye,
the good and bad activities of the king and the aristocracy,
down to the most minute good or evil action,
are commented on and scrutinized by society.

1. I've emended the reading *phal mo che* to *phal po che* (commoners).

Intelligent rulers
have great admiration for the way of righteousness,
just as the sun, possessing a thousand rays of light,
is considered the most beautiful thing in our world.

When commoners act like outcastes,
without respect for the way of holy and righteous people,
this is considered distasteful,
and much more so when the aristocracy acts in this way.

No one would praise individuals
whose behavior has come under the influence
of barbarous, low-class people.
Instead, they are denounced with insults.

Most nobles who have power and wealth
are reckless in their behavior.
They wander about like crazy elephants,
and the members of their retinue do likewise.

Moreover, subjects look upon
the actions of kings and nobles,
whether good or evil,
and they imitate them.[2]

A king who has depleted his wealth [5]
starts to apply the royal laws improperly.
When a ruler delights in sex,
then assemblies of prostitutes have a high status in the court.

2. Cāṇakya, *Rājanītiśāstra*, v. 5.25: "Whether people do actions that are virtuous or nonvirtuous is related to whether the king does good or evil." There is no published edition of Cāṇakya's text; the verse numbers are therefore based on my own informal edition. Compare Mipham's verse also to Mātṛceta, *Kaniṣkalekha*, vv. 39–40, which suggests that subjects imitate their leaders, whether they do good or evil. I have followed Michael Hahn's enumeration of the verses of Mātṛceta's work. See Michael Hahn, *Invitation to Enlightenment*.

If he listens to slander, the court breaks up due to dissension.
If he does not know how to analyze what people tell him, he is deceived by lies.
If he is too open to suggestion, everyone tries to sway him.
If he is susceptible to flattery, they speak deceptively to him.[3]

When dishonest people see an opportunity
to deceive one or another of these types of rulers,
they start thinking about
how best to gain an upper hand.

Because the king is the common source
of the various things that people want,
unless the king reflects carefully,
his kingdom will, in the end, be destroyed.

When individuals have a high status,
the evil members of the retinue flatter them,
pretending that their faults are good qualities,
making it difficult for them to know their own virtues and vices.[4]

Especially in this disputatious, degenerate age,
there are many scoundrels in the retinue.
Seeing faults to be good qualities,
they have huge ambitions and deceive the king.

It is rare to find an advisor who truly has in mind
what is best for the court and the kingdom's districts.
Hence, the king should examine all advice well,
and disregard everything except for what is truthful.[5]

3. Ravigupta, *Lokasaṃvyavahārapravṛtti*, v. 171; Michael Hahn, "Ravigupta and his Nīti Stanzas (II)," 22: "When a king shows predilection for evil persons, neither virtues nor noble people will assume a prominent position [in his presence]. In houses that are full of poisonous snakes lamps will not shine brightly."
4. Cāṇakya, *Rājanītiśāstra*, v. 7.7: "If you do not examine other people's character, then, like the deer who is attracted by the hunter's song (only to be killed), you will be fooled by people's hypocritical words. So inform yourself regarding other people's character."
5. *Prajñāśataka*, v. 21: "A wise person should not trust the sweet words spoken by a crafty

The king is not bereft of wealth;
there is no form of false praise that he does not hear from the retinue.
So he should not be deceived by wealth,
nor delight in false praise and flattery.

A person of noble blood should, in all cases,
engage in such critical reflections: [6]
"The happiness or misery of the living beings
who belong to my retinue depend on me.

"When it is I who must mold them,
unless I first understand
what is right and wrong,
I cannot be a worthy arbiter
of what people should and should not do.

"So I ought to study what has been taught
in the treatises of royal ethics
composed by the supreme conquerors and their sons.
Single-pointedly analyzing the meaning of what I have studied,
once I have found confidence in these truths,
I will be praised as the eye[6] and savior
who protects living beings.

Even if I do not rise to an exalted status,
at least I won't be the equal of the lowest of men."

---

person without first examining them carefully. A peacock has a beautiful cry, but it eats virulent poison as food." The *Prajñāśataka*, or *Hundred Verses on Wisdom*, is attributed to Nāgārjuna, although like many of the *nīti* works that bear his name, this attribution is questionable. There is, to my knowledge, no published edition of the work, and the verse numbers in this book are based on my own informal edition. *Shes rab brgya pa*, Sde dge bstan 'gyur, Toh. no. 4328, Thun mong ba'i lugs kyi bstan bcos *ngo*, fols. 99a–103a. Compare also the *Drop of Nourishment for the People* (*Jantupoṣaṇabiṇḍu*), v. 13: "Do not listen to the sweet words of deceitful people." In this book I have followed the verse enumeration of Stanley Frye, *Nāgārjuna's a Drop of Nourishment for the People*, but because Frye's translation is based on the Mongolian (which is a translation of the Tibetan), I have retranslated the cited verses directly from the Tibetan.

6. The eye is used here as a metaphor for "guide," since it is sight more than other senses that allows us to make our way in the world.

The ruler who understands himself and is self-controlled
has a true purpose in life.[7]

Once the king has obtained good qualities,
he blocks every possibility
of the members of the court
engaging in selfish, evil deeds.

But those who, with pride in their royal status,
and with no commitment to self-cultivation,
control their retinue with violence,
end up being destroyed, even if they are of royal blood.[8]

A king's power
is measured by whether or not his retinue is flourishing.
Therefore, the true king is the one who properly reflects
on how to bring happiness to his subjects.

7. Amoghavarṣa, *Vimalapraśnottara*, v. 41; "What should you be thinking about both day and night? That saṃsāra is hollow; and that one should not lose self-control." For the verse enumeration of Amoghavarṣa's texts, I have followed the edition of Anton Schiefner, *Vimalapraçnottararatnamālā*.

8. Kauṭilya, *Arthaśāstra* (8.2.21–22) considers the question of whether noble birth is more important than effectiveness and strength as a ruler, and concludes that it is since "a natural capacity to rule devolves on one of noble birth" even if he is weak and ineffective. This, claims Kauṭīlya, is due to the fact that the king's royal pedigree inspires love or attachment (*anurāga*) in his subjects which a commoner can never achieve. R. P. Kangle, *The Kauṭilīya Arthaśāstra*, vol. 1: 208 (Sanskrit ed.), vol. 2: 392 (English trans.).

2. The Wise Ruler

So as to understand right and wrong
the best of rulers [7]
will study the various treatises
and rely on learned people.[1]

If they do not read the treatises,
their inferior intellectual understanding
will not be able to really distinguish between what to do and what to avoid.
So they should study the scriptures and their commentaries.[2]

Come time to train in good qualities,
give up your sense of self-importance and rely on a guru.[3]

1. Cāṇakya, *Rājanītiśāstra*, v. 6.1: "Always rely on the learned and avoid the unlearned. Wise persons possess all good qualities. Fools have only faults."
2. Compare these two verses to Cāṇakya, *Rājanītiśāstra*, v. 1.2: "Having studied this treatise, you will perfectly understand the virtues and nonvirtues—what is to be done and avoided—spoken of in the precious explanations on righteousness; you will achieve fame and never encounter poverty."
3. Like Mipham, the *Jantupoṣaṇabinḍu*, v. 20, also stresses the importance of humility as a prerequisite to learning: "Exert yourself in good qualities. What is the point of putting on airs? No one wants to buy a cow that has lost its milk even if you adorn it with a bell." Other works stress the importance of relying on a guru or spiritual master. See, for example, Nāgārjuna, *Ratnāvalī*, vv. 5.91–93, and Amoghavarṣa, *Vimalapraśnottara*, vv. 1, 3, 9: "(1) Lord, what is to be taken up? The meaning-laden words of the guru. . . . (3) Who has the status of guru? Someone who understands things as they are, and who always strives to benefit all sentient beings. . . . (9) What is the worse poison? Deprecating the lama." Non-Buddhist Indian works like the *Arthaśāstra* (1.9.9–10) speak of the king appointing not a guru per se but a "priest" or "chaplain" (*purohita*), and also a "teacher" (*ācārya*) who is learned in the

If you rely on holy people,
Good qualities increase, like a river in spring.[4]

The root of all good qualities,
both visible and invisible, is wisdom.[5]
Without wisdom, you won't be able
to rule your country and entourage simply by means of love.

There is nothing that the wise cannot accomplish,
no matter what they undertake.
When Buddhahood requires wisdom,
what need to say that other lesser goals do as well.

The portal to increasing wisdom is study,
so strive to learn.
What is the point of trivial pursuits
while disregarding learning?

Penetrating intelligence is the great source for those
who desire to understand the Dharma and who want emancipation.
Those who, when presented with fine treatises that increase wisdom,
have no use for them are animals, aren't they?[6]

Vedas and their ancillary sciences, who can decipher signs and omens, is knowledgeable in statecraft, and is able to counteract calamities through the magical arts.

4. Nāgārjuna, *Suhṛllekha*, v. 62: "The Conqueror said that relying on a spiritual master brings about spiritual perfection. Therefore, rely on the holy. Many others have relied on the Conqueror and attained peace." I have used throughout this book the verse enumeration of the *Suhṛllekha* adopted by Geshe Lobsang Tharchin and Artemus B. Engle, tr., *Nāgārjuna's Letter*, which contains a fine translation of the root text as well as the commentary of Rendawa Zhönu Lodrö (1349–1412).

5. These two lines are found verbatim in *Prajñaśataka*, v. 4. See also *Ratnāvalī*, v. 1.5, where Nāgārjuna explains that the essence of all Buddhist practice is faith and wisdom, and that of these two, "wisdom is the chief."

6. Compare to Cāṇakya, *Rājanītiśāstra*, v. 8.17: "Those who do not analyze what is helpful and harmful, who are devoid of intelligence and erudition, who are only concerned with filling their stomachs: how different are their thoughts from those of animals?" In another work attributed to Nāgārjuna, the *Prajñādaṇḍa*, or *Tree of Wisdom*, v. 98, it is people who "do not know ethics or Dharma" that are compared to animals. All references to the *Prajñādaṇḍa* and the enumeration of verses follow the edition by Michael Hahn, which has appeared in three parts between 2009 and 2011: (1) "The Tibetan *Shes rab sdong bu* and its Indian Sources

Someone who only possesses wisdom can defeat
hordes of powerful enemies,
just like the sun, the supreme source of light,
can make the hosts of stars vanish in the sky.[7]

Without wisdom, whatever wealth and possessions you have
just becomes sustenance for your enemy.[8]
Without wisdom, even if you're powerful, you come under the
influence of others, [8]
like an elephant that has been bound into service through the hook.[9]

Whoever wants to be wise
should memorize one verse each day.[10]
The moon waxes to fullness
by increasing in brightness each day.

Untutored persons who sit indolently by
won't have anything good to show even after a hundred years.
If you wish to attain the status of a wise person,
you must be diligent and accept hardships.

There is no learning without diligence,
and without learning,

(I)," covering verses 1–110; (2) "The Tibetan *Shes rab sdong bu* and its Indian Sources (II)," covering verses 111–85; (3) "The Tibetan *Shes rab sdong bu* and its Indian Sources (III)," covering verses 186–260.

7. *Prajñāśataka*, vv. 6–7: "Someone who possesses wisdom alone cannot be harmed by others. . . . When the body is protected by wisdom, what can the hordes of enemies do to you? When you possess an umbrella in your hand, you won't be bothered by a torrent of rain."

8. Those who lack wisdom will eventually be defeated by enemies, and everything that they owned becomes the enemy's property.

9. *Prajñāśataka*, v. 8: "Someone who lacks the radiance of wisdom will never be more than a servant to someone else, like the case of [a working] elephant." Compare also to Sakya Paṇḍita, *Sa skya legs bshad*, v. 204. The verse enumeration of Sakya Paṇḍita's follows John T. Davenport et al., *Ordinary Wisdom*.

10. Compare to Cāṇakya, *Rājanītiśāstra*, v. 8.43: "If you want to develop your intellect, choose a verse—or half a verse, or a single line, or just some words—and study this. Those who do this will not waste their day."

even if you acquire a little wealth
it will be as fruitless as a tree in winter.

But once you have learning,
even if you temporarily fall on hard times,
you will quickly obtain a good outcome,
like a healthy fruit-bearing tree in autumn.

A king is considered special within his own country,
but someone who is learned is also praised in other lands.[11]
Learning, which is of greater worth even than a kingdom,
is something within your own reach.

Some people who have the capacity to learn
not only fail to avail themselves of that opportunity,
they also offend those who are learned.
Oh my! They are destroyed by the power of karma.

A single intelligent person can conquer and strike down
a multitude of individuals
who lack the luster of wisdom,
just as the lion can defeat a herd of elephants.

Someone who is intelligent can enslave
even a powerful opponent.
When Garuḍa fought Viṣṇu, Garuḍa initially won,
but in the end, Viṣṇu made Garuḍa into his mount.[12]

11. Compare to *Prajñādaṇḍa*, vv. 135, 227cd; Vararuci, *Śatagāthā*, v. 8; and Cāṇakya, *Rājanītiśastra* 3.13. I have followed the verse enumeration of Losang Norbu Shastri, *Śatagāthā of Ācārya Vararuci*.
12. The tale of Viṣṇu's battle with Garuḍa is told in the Mahābhārata (*Udyoga Parva* 103.3), and takes place during Garuḍa's quest for the nectar of immortality. To humble the half-man half-bird spirit, Viṣṇu has only to place his arms on his shoulders and Garuḍa is defeated. Viṣṇu later grants Garuḍa the boon of immortality, and Garuḍa in turn agrees to be Viṣṇu's mount (*vahana*). But the version of the story that Mipham has in mind is the one briefly mentioned by Sakya Paṇḍita in his *Sa skya legs bshad*, v. 17, and then explained in its commentaries. See Davenport, *Ordinary Wisdom*, 40–41. In this version of the story, Viṣṇu realizes that he is losing the battle with Garuḍa, and requests a break. He then tells Garuḍa that he is so impressed with his fighting skills that he will grant him a boon. Garuḍa is outraged and

A single, solitary king
who rules over many lands,
can make the entire earth his own
simply by virtue of possessing the luster of wisdom. [9]

Wherever the lamp of wisdom is raised up,
there the darkness of frailties cannot remain.[13]
A wise one who understands the sciences
is an ornament of the world, just like the sun.

All spiritual and temporal goodness
depends on the power of wisdom.
First you must obtain the eye of wisdom,
then you will obtain whatever you desire.

Those who do not understand what ought and ought not to be done
may, through effort, achieve some minor goal,
but even this proves difficult for them;
What need to speak of the difficulties they face in obtaining great goals.

What is impossible for ordinary beings to accomplish
the wise achieve through skillful means.
Pūrṇa could not subjugate the assembly of the Naked Ascetics,
but the wise Mañjuśrī subdued them all.[14]

When one's wisdom really increases,
any deed is easy.

---

replies that lesser beings don't offer boons to greater ones. He then arrogantly offers Viṣṇu a boon, and Viṣṇu asks Garuḍa to become his mount, thereby bringing him under his control.

13. *Prajñāśataka*, v. 9: "When your wisdom-eye is open, it destroys your frailties, just as a lamp destroys the darkness and lights up your path."

14. The tale is found, for example, in the *Ratnakāraṇḍa*, a Mahāyāna sūtra. Many tens of thousands of Naked Ascetics had convened at Vaiśāli, and the monk Pūrṇa, seeing that they were fit for conversion, started to preach to them, but none of the heterodox monks would listen to him. Then Mañjuśrī manifested 500 Naked Ascetics and took his position as their teacher, and through various deceptions managed to convert all of the Naked Ascetics. The point, of course, is that what Pūrṇa was unable to achieve through his limited knowledge and power, the bodhisattva Mañjuśrī could easily achieve because of his greater wisdom and might.

Just one person with sight can travel streets
that a thousand blind people cannot navigate.

Commoners can accomplish great goals
simply by using wise speech.
The king called Mirror Face
brought happiness to others just through words.[15]

For scholars there are never enough fine sayings.
For the holy there are never enough good qualities.
For the ocean there is never enough water.
For the childish there is never enough sense pleasure.

Only the wise, and never fools, can distinguish
between faults and good qualities;
between the right and wrong time to do something;
between what is skillful and what is not. [10]

You can tell the difference between sages and fools
from whether or not they can apply the meaning of the profound
treatises
to the most important activities of life.
Only superficially do sages and fools seem to be similar,
for sages get rid of faults and acquire good qualities,
whereas fools acquire faults and abandon good qualities.[16]
And even when fools deride sages,
sages feel compassion for fools.

No matter how wealthy fools become
their deeds are like the sterile bamboo plant.

15. Although a nāga king by this name (Me long gdong = *Ādarśamukha) is known to Indian Buddhist literature, the reference here is probably to an early Tibetan king by the same name who is said to have proclaimed a set of regulations or laws called the *Sne mo las 'dzin gyi zhal lce*. Reference to this is found in the law code of Karma Tenkyong Wangpo (d. 1642). See *Bod kyi khrims yig chen mo zhal lce bcu drug*, fols. 26b–27b.
16. Compare to Cāṇakya, *Rājanītiśāstra*, v. 6.1cd: "Wise persons possess every good quality; fools have only faults."

No matter how poor sages may become
they flourish like powerful seeds.

Sages who possess good qualities
learn moral lessons even from children.
Fools, who have an inflated sense of themselves,
turn away when sages draws near.

They do not appreciate fine moral sayings.
When they hear profound truths, they pay them no heed.
Instead, they make great effort for things of little significance.
These are the marks of the fool.

They squander whatever beneficial advice they receive.
They consider the unholy to be special;
and they oppose the holy.
These too are the marks of the fool.

When you tell them the truth, they don't believe it.
If someone leads them on wild goose chases, they follow.
Only flattery delights them.
Such are the signs of the ignorant.

Whatever they see they instantly believe it.
Whatever is told to them they consider it true.
They throw themselves into whatever task occurs to them.
These are signs that mark the fool.

They agree to work that they cannot accomplish.
They repeat whatever they hear, without analyzing it.
They preach nonsense about things they don't understand.
These too are indications that someone is a fool.

They claim to have good qualities that are unfamiliar to them.
They harm others with no justification. [11]
They insult others and have a high opinion of themselves.
Such are the frivolous acts of the fool.

Although the signs of foolishness are limitless,
based on these examples,
sages can easily understand the nature of fools.
Know that those who exhibit the opposite of these traits are sages.

You obtain your own happiness
by turning away from conceited fools,
bad kings, bad wives, and bad nations.[17]
Your own joy increases
by relying on disciplined and steadfast sages,
on good kings, good spouses, and good nations.

Therefore, having understood the faults and good qualities
of sages and fools, respectively,
you should seize the good qualities of the sage
by mastering the king's code of conduct.

Study the worldly arts and sciences
and, in particular, the texts of the king's code of conduct,
the treatises on material sciences, on medicine, grammar and logic,
and on the inner spiritual science of Buddhism.
There is no wise noble person
who has not also studied
the numerological sciences like astrology, and poetry and prosody.

Sageliness is the best of the king's ornaments.
In particular, one who studies the scriptures of the Conqueror
and the meaning of their commentaries,
will attain fearless self-confidence
in regard to every form of knowledge.

The king who possesses the highest discernment about such matters
becomes an ornament that is unparalleled on the face of the earth,
even surpassing the sun's extraordinary ability
to destroy all darkness from the face of the earth. [12]

17. Compare to *Prajñādaṇḍa*, v. 3, which also includes "bad friends" in the list.

Such a ruler is infinitely more amazing than the sun
because the ruler's sunlight can dispel
every bit of the inner darkness of beings,
something that the day-maker or sun cannot vanquish.

In the regions below, upon, and above the earth,
the Friend of the Sun,[18] the wise Lord of Men,
shines upon the lotus ponds of the minds of intelligent people,
bringing glory to the three worlds.

18. Ādityabandhu, "Friend of the Sun," is an epithet of Śākyamuni Buddha.

3. The Conduct of Kings

The conduct of rulers
needs to be carefully monitored and restrained.
When it is not monitored, their behavior becomes common;
even the smallest fault can become the cause of infamy.

Rulers should remain hidden in their own homes
as if they were a jewel.
There is an apt saying that goes,
"A king should never be separated from his throne."

When he is not seen, he is valued from afar.
If he is seen or heard from too often, he resembles a commoner.
Others should not have intimate knowledge
of the country and the king.

When the king travels along the thoroughfare,
he should travel with his army, and with the insignia of greatness
such as banners held aloft.
He should never wander around at inappropriate times.

Even if they are not proud, persons of royal blood
should never be separated from the insignia of greatness.
To abandon this greatness and to circulate like a commoner is a sign of
the deterioration of royal power.

Sages act in such a way that, externally, their exalted behavior
is unbearable in its awe, like a fire. [13]

But when approached up close,
they act in a disciplined manner, like a humble lamp.

If he shows great deference to those worthy of respect—
lamas, ascetics, and brahmins—
and respects the elder members of his family,
the royal line itself obtains greatness.

An unworthy man who acts arrogantly,
and a worthy man who loses his self-confidence,
are equally despised.
So behave appropriately as befits your attainments.

When your mind has become self-controlled,[1]
there is no way that you cannot correct
the actions of your body and speech.
Therefore, act in a self-controlled way as befits the occasion.

Someone who lacks self-control early in life
but who later develops it—
as did Nanda, Ajātaśatru, and so forth[2]—
becomes as beautiful as the moon in cloudless sky,

Peoples' status as good or evil can be adduced
based on their attire.

1. The semantic range of the word *bag yod* (*apramāda*)—in this verse translated as "self-control," but elsewhere in this book as "being careful"—is difficult to fully capture in English. It can mean to act with care, concern, and mindfulness—that is, to act with caution, attentiveness, and vigilance—but also to be in control, decent, and ethical. It also has the sense of conscientiousness. Its opposite *bag med* (*pramāda*) refers to carelessness in one's actions, epitomized by the wild and unrestrained behavior of people who are intoxicated or insane. Nāgārjuna, *Suhṛllekha*, v. 13: "Self-control is like the nectar of immortality, and being careless (or out of control) is the realm of death. Therefore, always act politely and with self-control so as to increase your virtuous qualities."

2. Nanda, the Buddha's cousin, is said to have led a life of sexual excess before the Buddha enticed him to the monastic life. Ajātaśatru (r. 492–460 BCE) murdered his father, King Bimbisāra, in order to assume the throne. That latter story is recounted in Tibetan in the *Sūtra of Eliminating Ajātaśatru's Remorse*, Dpe sdur ma ed., 566–700.

So do not violate the customs
of the ancient noble tradition.[3]

Even if you possess all good qualities internally,
if your attire is poor, everyone despises you.
Therefore, dress according to what is fitting for the wealthy
and adopt the proper customs in vestments and ornaments.[4]

When those who lack wealth wear excessive jewelry,
and when the wealthy wear rags,
they become the laughingstock of the world.
So act appropriately as regards attire and ornaments.

A retinue that wears fine clothing and jewelry
reflects the greatness of its leader,
just like a horse bedecked with ornaments
makes his owner more resplendent. [14]

The ability to converse in various tongues
does not impress the barbarians.
They only rejoice when someone
speaks their own barbarian language.

Likewise, small-minded, worldly people
have no understanding of inner good qualities.
So bring joy to the world by following the worldly custom
of donning external finery.

Therefore, even though great beings
are unconcerned about their own wealth,
they don amazing attire
so as to impress the world.

3. The point is to dress appropriately, following the accepted tradition. This is especially important in the case of royalty, who should dress formally in public, donning the vestments that accord with their rank.
4. Compare to Cāṇakya, *Rājanītiśāstra*, v. 7.24: "Even if you are adorned with various good qualities—beauty, high caste, wisdom, a good family lineage, a good education—bad clothes will spoil the looks of a man." Compare also to Sakya Paṇḍita, *Sa skya legs bshad*, v. 217.

The higher the status you bestow on the wise
the better the country's conduct becomes.
When you worship the jewel atop the banner
you are granted everything you could need or want.[5]

But if you place an evil person in a high position,
people's bad behavior worsens.[6]
If you worship a demon as if it were a deity,
malicious black magic increases.

You should not allow within your retinue
individuals whose behavior is evil.
The king gets blamed
for the faults of his evil servants and retinue.

All beings rejoice when they see
that the retinue is good and their behavior is proper.
Therefore, only include in your entourage
those who are morally upright.

If you constantly distract yourself with games,
except at the time of festivals,
your goals deteriorate. When this is so even for commoners,
what need to say that it also applies to royalty.

When your mind is impaired by alcohol, it leads to carelessness,
and that causes proper conduct to deteriorate.
Fools have accustomed themselves to thinking
that throwing their minds into such a dark stupor is happiness.[7] [15]

5. When the wish-granting jewel, placed atop a banner, is worshipped, it brings about all desired things. Likewise, when the wise are properly revered, the good conduct of the subjects increases and the kingdom flourishes.
6. Ravigupta, *Lokasaṃvyavahārapravṛtti*, v. 173. Hahn, "Ravigupta and his Nīti Stanzas (II)," 22: "Even Munis cannot make a wicked person friendly who has been placed in a [high] position."
7. Compare to Sakya Paṇḍita, *Sa skya legs bshad*, v. 265.

When it is improper for the ruler
to wander here and there even during the day,[8]
what need to say that he should avoid
wandering around at night like a ghost.

Study and do your prayers as best you can
on a daily basis and with mindfulness,
and think about what will benefit your subjects.
If you are lazy, all your goals will be thwarted.

If you cultivate sinful friends,
faults increase and goodness is obstructed,
like a tree eaten by termites.
Evil friends are the root of all faults.[9]

Do not engage in frivolous pastimes,
like gawking at large gatherings.[10]
How can the royalty's conduct be considered attractive
when they behave like pieces of cotton wool being blown around by
the wind?[11]

That is why the protector Nāgārjuna has said,
in his *Letter to a Friend*,[12] that there are
six causes that diminish one's reputation:

8. Ibid., v. 221.
9. *Jantupoṣaṣabiṇḍu*, vv. 5, 15: "Do not rely on bad friends. Those who rely on bad friends will be destroyed.... Even when you are friendly with a sinful friend and say various nice things to him, that sinful one is in fact a demon [who will destroy you], like a demoness on an island." The metaphor of the tree eaten by termites is used in a different way in *Prajñāśataka*, v. 45: "It is not a pretty thing when someone speaks friendly words to you while hiding some ill will towards you in his or her heart. [Such a person] is like a rotten tree that has been eaten by termites."
10. Amoghavarṣa, *Vimalapraśnottara*, v. 32: "What is the highest happiness? To not be attached to frivolous distractions."
11. *Jantupoṣaṇabiṇḍu*, v. 76: "You should not speak purposeless babble. You should not attend large gatherings. You should not drink intoxicants such as liquor. You should be as generous as you wish to be."
12. Nāgārjuna, *Suhṛllekha*, v. 33; *Bshes pa'i spring yig*, Sde dge bstan 'gyur, fol. 42a: "Those who gamble, gawk at crowds, are lazy, cultivate sinful friends, drink alcohol, and wander around at night are reborn in the lower realms, and [in this life] they lose their reputation. So

gambling, gawking at crowds,
laziness, cultivating sinful friends,
drinking alcohol, and wandering around at night.
Taking these as illustrations,
abandon all irreligious activity.

Any action, whether proper or improper, will increase
the more you engage in it and habituate yourself to it.
That is why the mind improves
when you correct it with mindfulness and self-control.

Everyone respects
people whose conduct is self-controlled.
But when the reckless see such people,
they grow fearful that they will be outshined.

Desire is the cause of all self-destruction.
The Conqueror has said that it is like the *kimpāka* fruit.[13]
Even if you do not completely overcome attachment to pleasure, [16]
at least do not go overboard in your desires.[14]

In this world, a king who practices the rules of conduct
of a celibate or of a layman
stands out like the moon among the stars,
increasing the happiness of everyone.

If a member of the royalty has forbidden sex—
sex with someone other than his own wives—
he gains a bad reputation in this life,
and falls into the lower realms in the next.[15]

---

abandon these six." The evils of intoxicants and gambling are also mentioned in Nāgārjuna's *Suhṛllekha*, v. 5, and in his *Ratnāvalī*, vv. 2.46–47.

13. The fruit of the *kimpāka* plant (of the genus *Trichosanthes*), a kind of wild cucumber, is said to be pretty but bitter and even poisonous.

14. Nāgārjuna, *Suhṛllekha*, v. 23: "Your desires are the cause of your destruction. The Chief of Conquerors (Buddha) has compared them to the *kimpāka* fruit. So abandon them, for they are chains that bind you to this world, the prison of saṃsāra."

15. Compare to Masūrākṣa, *Nītiśāstra*, v. 4.11: "Others' women are poison. So is a wife who

Once ensnared by the hook of desire,
you come under another's influence, even if you are royalty,
just like an elephant, even though powerful,
is made subservient by being struck with the hook.

If you overly cultivate sense pleasures,
it comes back to consume you like fire does grass.
It ruins your glory and reputation.
Hence, being satisfied is true happiness.

Even if a single individual were to acquire
all of the wealth on the face of the earth,
that person would not be satiated and just crave more.
So cultivate satisfaction in regard to your desires.[16]

Being satisfied is the highest wealth.[17]
Self-evaluation is the greatest act.
Moderation in work results in endurance.
The person with the greatest wish to help others is the supreme
sovereign.

Therefore, adorn your conduct
with an attitude of self-discipline.
Even the Buddha tamed his ordinary disciples
through his behavior.

It is like the case of the lead ox of the pack,
who, though normally confident in his stride,
walks lazily and slowly gives up
simply from seeing the yoke that is about to be put on his neck.

---

has sex with another. People who trust in either of these two are walking toward death's door." I have adopted the enumeration of the Masūrākṣa verses found in Hugh M. Flick, Jr., *Carrying Enemies on Your Shoulders*; but the translations of Masūrākṣa's text is my own.

16. A similar sentiment is found in *Prajñādaṇḍa*, v. 107.

17. Amoghavarṣa, *Vimalapraśnottara*, v. 23: "Who is the poorest person? Someone who is not satisfied."

The person who sits up straight on the cushion without moving,
and with a posture that is comfortable and relaxed, [17]
achieves a stability akin to a mountain of gold:
what an utterly beautiful sight that is.

That ruler is happiest who eats to moderation,
who is not too busy or frenetic,
who gets up early and dons the proper attire,
and only speaks harshly when warranted.

The king should never associate
with hunters, trappers, or prostitutes;
nor should he ever wander
in lonely forests without his retinue.

He should never cross rivers unnecessarily;
nor ride wild horses,
nor be around poisonous snakes, wild animals, and so forth.
If he does so, he may be met with ruin.[18]

Therefore, the body and behavior
of the king and royal court
should be perfectly controlled and upright
as per the standards explained in the scriptures and treatises.

The Lord of the Constellations, the moon,
the sight of which bring the highest joy,
rests in the immortal path of space.
The ruler, the most beautiful object of beings' gaze,
circulates on the face of the earth, and achieves the highest position
amidst the constellations that are the assemblies of people.
Resting within the spacious divine path of the sky of morality,

18. Compare to Cāṇakya, *Rajānītiśāstra*, v. 2.15, and to Masūrākṣa, *Nītiśāstra*, v. 5.9, which advise one not to trust in rivers, men who carry weapons, animals with claws and horns, women, and members of the royal family. Similar very practical counsel is found in Masūrākṣa, *Nītiśāstra* (v. 1.5f), which advises the king not to walk too close to wells or near fires, not to walk close to a bull that is not tethered, not to walk around at night, or without shoes, or without a companion, not to play with snakes, not to climb tresses while drunk, and so forth.

and radiating the beautiful light of righteous conduct,
when the full moon, the ruler,
brings joy to the gods who dwell above the earth,
what need to say that he also gladdens the hearts of the people on
its surface.
Therefore, rulers whose conduct is ethical
increase the good fortune of the country in which they live. [18]

4. Analyzing Your Own and Others' Speech

All the actions to be cultivated and avoided in the world,
are known through language.
So we must now contemplate and mention the faults and benefits
that inhere in the spoken word.[1]

Sometimes goals are not accomplished unless you state them,
but sometimes goals are accomplished without saying anything.[2]
If you do not know when to speak and when to remain silent,
speech becomes frivolous, and many faults ensue.[3]

Speaking the truth is the best of good qualities.
Therefore, royalty should speak truthfully.[4]
Those who speak truthfully ought to be praised.
Liars should be reviled and avoided.

1. On virtuous and nonvirtuous speech, see also Nāgārjuna, *Ratnāvalī*, vv. 2.33–35, 2.41, 5.13–15, 5.94. The *Karṇa Parva*, Book Eight of the Mahābhārata, also contains a long analysis of speech which explains the importance of truth, when it is permissible to lie, how to distinguish truth from falsehood, when to speak, when to keep silent, and so on. See Kisari M. Ganguli, *The Mahābhārata of Krishna-Dwaipayana Vyasa*, vol. 3, 69f.
2. Compare to *Prajñādaṇḍa*, v. 167ab.
3. Compare to Nāgārjuna, *Ratnāvalī*, v. 3.74, where he encourages the king to always speak the truth even if it means his death or the loss of his kingdom. Compare also to Masūrākṣa *Nītiśāstra*, v. 1.3d: "Speak the truth, but you should not talk about all things." See also Sakya Paṇḍita, *Sa skya legs bshad*, v. 228.
4. Amoghavarṣa, *Vimalapraśnottara*, v. 47: "How to win over all sentient beings? By speaking the truth to them and by having patience."

Even though you should not divulge secrets,[5]
there is no fault in doing so for a good reason.
But the speech of ordinary people is not like this;
even their small lies are signs of how vulgar they are.

Wise and honest individuals
delight in honest speech,
but there is little point to explaining something forthrightly
to those who are foolish and dishonest.

Explain things straightforwardly without convoluted explanations
to individuals who are benevolent.[6]
But to those given to judging people on the basis of what they say
do not speak straightforwardly, but rather say only what is appropriate.[7]

When, in casual conversation,
you inopportunely reveal
information about your most important plans,
everyone hears about them, and your goals are thwarted.[8]

When something ought to be utterly secret,
keep it to yourself, and share it with no one else.
Word spreads from one friend to another
until it is finally known throughout the entire kingdom. [19]

Without good reason, you should not share secrets
even with those who have become friends.

5. Masūrākṣa, *Nītiśāstra*, v. 1.10b: "Never reveal anyone's secrets."
6. *Jantupoṣaṇabinḍu*, v. 75: "You should be humble and extremely disciplined, and should speak to everyone straightforwardly. You should be tolerant and abandon pride, and should speak to everyone honestly and with a smile."
7. Compare to Cāṇakya, *Rājanītiśāstra*, v. 7.28: "Do not be too forthright (lit. straight). Look at what happens in the forest. There, the straight trees are cut down, but the crooked ones are left behind." *Jantupoṣaṇabinḍu*, v. 75: "You should be humble and extremely disciplined, and should speak to everyone straightforwardly. You should be tolerant and abandon pride, and should speak to everyone honestly and with a smile."
8. On the need to keep secrets and to keep one's plans and goals hidden, see also Cāṇakya, *Rājanītiśastra*, v. 2.7, and Masūrākṣa, *Nītiśāstra*, v. 1.4b: "The king ought to conceal his fears and plans," and v. 1.11a: "Guard secrets, and do not speak frivolously."

Consider the losses most men have experienced
by telling their secrets to women.[9]

Nor should you tell all even in matters not requiring secrecy;
there is no need to always explain everything.
When the time is right to consult,
set aside any sense of self-importance, and speak forthrightly.

Being praised brings joy to the world.
It brings happiness both to self and others.
So do not belittle the good qualities of others
but rather praise them.[10]

When you praise others,
others will also praise you.
However much you slander others,
to that same extent will they slander you.

Jealous people of little merit
only slander others.
That does not actually harm others,
it only makes those who slander lose their own reputation.

Intelligent people who have merit
speak pleasantly and eloquently
about others' good qualities, even when minimal.
Through that they themselves attain renown.

Even though praise is an ornament in this world,
when offered to the proud fool it is poison.
You should never praise anyone
using deceptive words mixed with lies.

9. An example is mentioned in *Prajñādaṇḍa*, v. 184. The tale has to do with a nāga who divulges a secret to a woman and ends up getting eaten by a garuḍa bird-god as a result. Hahn, "The Tibetan *Shes rab sdong bu* and its Indian Sources (II)," 43.
10. Masūrākṣa, *Nītiśāstra*, v. 2.2: "Do not speak directly about people's faults. It isn't right to hurt someone's feelings. People say that verbally pushing other people's buttons is like using a weapon on them."

There is nothing worse than individuals
who, like two-tongued snakes,
praise people to their face and slander them behind their back.
People who speak honestly are ornaments for the world.[11]

Harsh words counteract others' good opinion of you
regardless of how helpful and charitable you have been. [20]
You can influence the world just by speaking pleasantly,
even without being charitable, helpful, or supportive.

There are different kinds of words:
some are weapons that, without actually striking you, pierce you to the core;
some are medicines that, without ever being drunk, become internally assimilated;
some have the captivating taste of honey without ever being eaten.

Few people have attained the status of enemy or friend
on the basis of actions,
but many have attained it on the basis of their words.
So think about the words you speak.

Everyone belittles
speech that is ill-timed;
but fine words that are appropriate and opportune
benefit both self and other.

How can water enter a small vessel
even when left out in a massive rainstorm?
It is impossible to be of much help to people of lesser intellect
no matter how much you instruct them.

Holy beings with fine minds
are greatly helped through a mere hint.

11. I've emended *rgya na* to *rgyan*.

But even more rare are those who can explain and preach
those helpful words that are like medicine.[12]

You should never listen to, much less speak,
slanderous words meant to divide people.
Should it become necessary to listen to this,
examine it until you reach the truth of the matter.

Too many harsh words creates dissent in the retinue.
Lies lead to the destruction of both self and others.
Frivolous speech causes you to fail in your goals.
So avoid all of these.

Language therefore has many faults and qualities,
such as the ones just outlined.
Having learned to distinguish these,
learn what to say and what not to say.

Large kingdoms
have a variety of people. [21]
It is difficult to control
stupid[13] and evil people just using encouraging words.

But having established a fair system of royal laws,
in which violators are punished
in specific ways according to their acts,
you make this known throughout the kingdom.

If you do not enforce appropriate punishments
against those who utterly refuse to mend their ways,
evil will increase, and the kingdom will be destroyed.[14]
Therefore, firstly, act according to your word [and enforce the laws].

12. Compare to *Prajñādaṇḍa*, v. 76.
13. I've emended *blan* to *glan*.
14. Mipham follows a tradition that is arguably more realistic (and somewhat harsher) as regards legal punishments than, say, Nāgārjuna, who counsels the king to treat criminals compassionately: to forego not only capital punishment but also life imprisonment, to free

Once you know which people
aid and protect the retinue and subjects—
who are concerned with the welfare of the country's outer districts—
you should praise them with helpful words.

But even if civil servants have been appointed to a governorship,
if they are only concerned with their own welfare,
you should issue an edict that they have committed an offense
and must henceforth desist.

To get courtiers who adhere to the Dharma to act lovingly toward
the people,
to treat them as if they were their children,
you must first issue orders gently.
Do not use harsh tactics from the start.

If you do this, most individuals
will likely turn away from the wrong path;
and even those who refuse to reverse their course
will not feel hostility toward the ruler.

Praise the righteous
and show contempt for the accomplishments of the wicked.
Wherever there is a ruler
who distinguishes between good and evil in this way
righteous people will rejoice,
and the wicked will take heed.[15]
If you do the opposite, the wicked will destroy your sovereignty
wherever it exists upon the face of the earth. [22]

Having properly analyzed things, rulers
should not vacillate from the policies they have issued.

---

prisoners on a regular basis, and to treat them humanely even while they are imprisoned. See Nāgārjuna, *Ratnāvalī*, vv. 4.30–37.

15. *Prajñāśataka*, v. 35. "Wherever a king contemplates the good and bad that people are engaged in—that country is said to 'have a king.'"

There is a well-known saying in the world:
"The orders of kings are given but once."

Do not contravene any of the edicts
issued by former Dharma kings.
When righteous royal laws are later changed,
the authority of the king's own word diminishes.

A ruler skilled in rhetoric
enlightens the world
just like the sun,
and accomplishes all necessary goals.

People who lack supernormal powers
can only understand what is good and evil in the world
based on language.
So properly examine rhetoric.

People speak various words
due to their various ideas.
Most of what they say, though well intentioned,
is nonsense due to their lack of mental clarity.

Crafty people resort to deceptive words
to accomplish their selfish goals.
But mostly they just say harmful things to others
motivated by their jealousy and deceit.

Especially in this degenerate age,
baseless lies bring about the ruin of the kingdom.
Therefore, the fact that someone says something
is not a reason to follow it.

But neither should you assume that everything people say is a lie.
Instead contemplate whether something is true or false
until it becomes clear to you.
Once clear, then pursue the appropriate course. [23]

Analyze the reports you receive about the happiness or misery of your subjects,
and come to your own conclusions about their truth or falsity,
without being influenced by how skillfully this is explained,
and paying no heed to the eloquence of the language
used by your administrative staff.
This is how to know what good exists among your subjects, the problems they face,
and the true character of your ministers.
In this way you will yourself become an expert in the law.

Ignorant about what course of action to adopt,
pleas for new information
could give rise to crazy advice.
So best to be aware of your own goals and hold onto them.

When you are trying to apprehend whether something is true,
you should abandon all advice that contradicts your temporary and long-term goals
even when such advice comes from your own lama.
What need to say that you must be careful about the advice you receive from others.[16]

Most of the country's happiness and suffering, and its faults and virtues,
can be gleaned from pointless speech.
Examine and interrogate[17] truthful men;
there is much to be gleaned from meaningless speech.

Therefore, the wise members of the aristocracy
will not, out of a sense of self-importance, disregard
anyone's testimony, regardless of who they are.
It is a quality of the sage to make opportune inquiries.

16. Nāgārjuna, *Suhṛllekha*, v. 30: "Do not commit sins even for the sake of a brahmin, a monk, a god, a visitor, your parents, a son, a queen, or your retinue, for [none of them] will share in the burden of [that sin's] result in hell."
17. I've emended *dri* to *dris*.

Remain neutral, neither asking nor making inquiries
about the various opinions that your family members have about you,
whether they praise you or despise you.
But when something is important, then you should ask.

For the most part, you can know people's inner thoughts
from the words they speak;
From this you will be able to fathom
some of the things that you should and should not do.

Those who themselves are truly skilled in how to speak
and who understand what is proper and improper in the speech of
others [24]
can properly engage in the correct ways of rhetoric
and obtain the fame of the likes of Śrī, the goddess of speech.

Even if you are ugly, you will captivate others' minds.
Even if you have nothing to give away, you will gather many beings
around you.
Even without light, you will clear away inner darkness.
A fine speaker has many kinds of amazing abilities.

In this world, rulers who are experts in speech
are more radiant even than the sun.
Having cleared away the mental darkness of beings,
they cause the great festive lotus garden to bloom.

5. Examining the Members of the Retinue

To safeguard the well-being of his country
the ruler must appoint
those who are righteous
to appropriate positions.

The appointment of exalted people as governors
shows the great love you have for your subjects.
Through such acts your administration of the districts becomes stable.
This is what King Mahāsaṃmata did.[1]

If you place the wicked in high positions,
this brings great harm to your side.
In the end it brings destruction,
as happened with the blue-skinned fox.[2]

1. This is the first human king, whose name means "Elected by the Many," so called because he was chosen by the masses and did not inherit his position from another monarch. Mahāsaṃmata is considered the founder of the Śākya clan, the Buddha's ancestral lineage. He is mentioned in a variety of Pāli and Sanskrit scriptures and post-canonical texts. In one Pāli work, he is equated with Manu, the great systematizer of the Brahmanical legal system. See Stanley J. Tambiah, "King Mahāsammata: The First King in the Buddhist Story of Creation, and His Persisting Relevance," and Robert E. Buswell, Jr., and Donald S. Lopez, Jr., "Mahāsaṃmata," *The Princeton Dictionary of Buddhism*, 507–8.
2. Similar verses are found in the *Prajñādaṇḍa*, v. 45, and in the *Jantupoṣaṇabindu*, v. 41, with the latter probably being the source of Mipham's verse. The story of the blue-skinned fox—or in some version, the blue jackal—is found in the collection of Indian tales called *Pañcatantra*. The jackal wanders into a village and accidentally falls into a vat of blue dye. Returning to the forest, he succeeds in convincing the animals that, because of his unusual color, he is meant to be the king, and he actually rules for some time, but is eventually exposed and killed.

Someone is worthy of being a minister
if he or she is very brave and has a vision of the future,
is skilled in properly analyzing what ought to be done and avoided,
and if he or she has little self-interest and thinks about the people.[3] [25]

The wives of the aristocracy should come from good families.
They should have a sense of propriety motivated by shame and modesty.
They should have an appreciation for the Dharma,
should be agreeable, and possess righteous conduct.

If their conduct is good, if they listen to your orders,
exercise self-control in gossip, have affection for the king,
and speak truthfully, only then should you give
your relatives power in high administrative positions.

3. A brief list of the officials appointed by the king is found in Nāgārjuna, *Ratnāvalī*, vv. 4.22–26. Most of the positions mentioned by Mipham here are also described in the final (seventh) chapter of Masūrākṣa's *Nītiśāstra*, although the descriptions and qualifications of each post as outlined by Masūrākṣa are sometimes different from those we find in Mipham's text. In Masūrākṣa, the king is described (vv. 7.4–5) as "compassionate, having a helping attitude [to his people], someone who hides the faults of his guru/s; once he enters a war, he does not retreat; he is equanimous whether he is experiencing happiness or suffering; his lineage and ethics are impeccable; he is skilled at explaining religion; he is disciplined, pious and alert." A minister (v. 7.6) "speaks clearly, has an excellent intellect, is an expert in the ethical-political treatises, is pious, gentle, but also critical." In subsequent verses Masūrākṣa explains the ideal qualities of princes (*rājaputra*), messengers or emissaries (*dūta*), priests (*purohita*), scribes (*lekhaka*), readers/reciters (*pāṭhaka*), bodyguards (*daṇḍadhāraka*), physicians (*vaidya*), door-keepers or chamberlains (*pratihāra*), the commander of the military (*senādhyakṣa*), cooks (*sūpakāra*), the prime minister (*mantripati*), the queen's guards (*rājñīpāla, antaḥpurarakṣaka*), and protectors (*rakṣa, pālaka*) who are described as entertainers skilled in song and dance. The Sanskrit is my own reconstruction in each case. The qualifications of the members of the royal court are also outlined in Cāṇakya, *Rājanītiśāstra*, chapter 5, which largely overlaps with Masūrākṣa's list but also provides further details on each of the categories. For example, it mentions (v. 5.11) three ranks of servants: lesser, middling, and great. It elaborates on who the guardians of the queens' quarters should be (v. 5.10): "lame men, one-eyed men, *paṇḍakas* [in this context meaning eunuchs], hunchbacks, old men, and those with well-disciplined senses." It also mentions (v. 5.12) those individuals who should *not* be employed in the court: "those who talk too much, who are haughty, lazy, malicious, deceitful, have the attributes of the poor, are unsatisfied, have inauspicious bodily markings, and who eat meat."

Clerks, the "holders of the pen,"
should not be ignorant of the grammatical works.
They should be knowledgeable of the sciences such as poetics,
and skilled in calligraphy.

Kitchen workers, the "holders of the stores,"
should be ethical, and should not be foolish in regard to expenditures.
They should not waste money on purposeless things,
should be capable of managing time, and should be intelligent.

Good judges should be experts in the law,
and should be impartial.
They should be honest and serious about examining the facts.
And they should properly contemplate cause and effect and what ought
to be accepted and rejected.

Appoint to the position of generals
those who have great courage and the capacity to be terrifying,
who know the strategies for subduing others,
and whose minds are stable and do not vacillate.

The most fitting advisors
have keen intellects and pure intentions.
They increase merit and expand good fortune,
and are surrounded by gods and protector deities.

The lama who serves as your tutor
should possess the training[4]; should be learned, inclined toward yogic
practice,
concerned only with dharmic activities,
and should not intervene in legal matters.

In the king's palaces [26]
there should always be experts in the cultural sciences—

4. To "possess the training" (*bslab ldan*) usually refers to monks, those who possess the monastic vows or "rules of training" (*śikṣāpada, bslab pa'i gzhi*).

individuals skilled in astrology or mathematics,
and [physicians] trained in proper medical diagnosis and so forth.

Guards, eunuchs, messengers,
servants, workers, and so forth,
should be appointed according to what has been explained in the texts
regarding their individual job descriptions.

Your villages and cities will be happy
when you appoint as their governors
individuals who are equanimous toward the general populace,
and who do not conflate causes and effects.

When you act in the opposite manner,
and bestow on people various statuses indiscriminately,
their work will bring no fruit,
and will act as the cause for the kingdom's decay.

Therefore, the wise ruler
bestows people their specific rank
according to the degree of their good qualities;
he should not appoint people to official positions haphazardly.

Just as different medicines are prescribed for different illnesses,
you accomplish your aims by bringing together individuals
endowed by nature with certain specific qualities.
It is rare that a single individual will accomplish all your goals.

The nobles of this degenerate age
are individuals who do as they please.
Controlling whatever is done in the court,
they ultimately bring grief to both themselves and others.

Intelligent rulers always assert
their independence.
Even though they are not under other people's control,
they are skilled at pleasing others.

Bodily ornaments and the assembly of servants
should each be placed in their proper place in the palace.
Messengers and construction tools
should be used for the work that befits them.

It is not permissible for just anyone
to be one of the ruler's workers. [27]
Only the ones with good qualities should be appointed,
selecting the gold nuggets from among rocks, as it were.

From many thousands of individuals, only on occasion
will there arise someone who has really great qualities,
and even then ordinary beings will not recognize them
just as a frog in a well has no notion of the vast ocean.[5]

Anyone can tell whether an action or an individual is good or evil
when this is self-evident,
but only a wise person can determine this beforehand,
just as knowing whether a seed is viable.

It is wrong to treat the all-knowing horse[6]
and the best of men as you would common things.
It is inappropriate to grant special status
to evil men in the court and to place images of demonesses on altars.

When intelligent people skilled in the cultural sciences
and individuals who are righteous and have great merit
become the prized ornaments of the land,
this ought to delight the king.
The righteous take pleasure in those who have good qualities.
The evil delight in the company of thieves, cheats, and hunters.

5. Compare to Ravigupta, *Lokasaṃvyavahārapravṛtti*, v. 234; Hahn, "Ravigupta and his Nīti Stanzas (II)," 30. The *Jantupoṣaṇabiṇḍu*, v. 44, uses the same metaphor (actually a turtle caught in a well), but is making a different point—that haughty and proud people have a hard time seeing their own faults and limitations.

6. This is a mythical horse, the *aśvajāneya*, who has the power to travel swiftly and easily over great distances.

The lustful delight in prostitutes.
Misers delight in food and wealth.
Most of the nobles of this degenerate age
have no interest in doing good.

When evildoers are not exterminated,
good people lose heart.
But wherever a good ruler shows affection
for those who do good,
people who side with goodness are inspired,
and even the evil apply themselves to goodness.

Wherever an evil leader
favors evil people,
those who side with evil rejoice,
and even good people apply themselves to evil. [28]

Even when, under the influence of his negative karma,
a king becomes the object of others' pity,
he should still delight in what is just;
what is the point of supporting injustice?

If members of the royal family
engage in inappropriate conduct,
you should not punish them using extreme violence,
but rather show mercy and banish them.

You should not get angry at members of the inner retinue
over trifling matters.
When the king cares for the members of his retinue as if they were his only son,
they will think of him as a father.

You should always affectionately care
for your ministers and workers.
Whether the king is happy or suffers
is in the hands of the entourage.

The king should not stand in the way
of appropriate provisions for his workers;
nor should he impede festivals
that celebrate their accomplishments.[7]

He should not forget their good works,
but rather repay their kindness and praise them.[8]
When the feeling of being loved pervades your entourage,
the members of the entourage come together and accomplish all
your goals.

In like fashion, the members of the entourage should feel affection for
the king
as if he were their only son.
Whatever greatness the entourage attains
is due to the king's own glorious status.

Even when the nobles are out of control,
the entourage protects the king as best they can.
When you suffer from some eye disease,
you should treat it, and not pluck the eye out.

On Ministers

Ministers and judges should render judgments
according to what is right and wrong. [29]
If they look out for their friends and for those who bribe them,
the kingdom will be destroyed.

When there is a minister
who is greedy and disregards the king's outer districts,

7. Cāṇakya, *Rājanītiśāstra*, v. 8.6cd: "The best of people love to praise accomplishments. Being praised for accomplishments is the highest form of wealth."
8. On the importance of repaying the support of loyal ministers, see the edicts of the Tibetan king Tri Desongtsen (d. 814/815) found at the "Temple of the Hat" (Zhwa'i lha khang), in which the emperor rewards the many acts of kindness of his guardian and tutor, the monk Myang Ting nge 'dzin. Hugh E. Richardson, *A Corpus of Early Tibetan Inscriptions*, 43–62.

shouldn't we expect that thieves, hunters, and prostitutes
will also then be influencing the ministries?

A true minister is someone who, with no regard for his own goals,
concentrates and focuses only on the kingdom.
In bringing happiness to the kingdom,
he accomplishes his own goals, but only incidentally.

Even if there is only one such precious minister
whose actions accord with these standards,
because he is of such benefit to the king's districts,
he should be honored throughout the kingdom.

Intimately informed about the faults and good qualities
of the various types of people found within the population,
he knows with certainty what they are doing with their hands
regardless of what they may be saying with their mouths.

Therefore, the king should examine and differentiate
who among the royal workers
is and is not worthy of being a minister.
Having understood that the kingdom deteriorates
when someone acts erratically,
the king bestows power only on those who are good
and avoids empowering the evil.

The King

The greatest type of king
desires what is best for the country and acts accordingly;
he chiefly thinks about righteousness;
he strives for the welfare of the kingdom.
As a result, his kingdom prospers like the waxing moon.

The middling type of king
thinks about how to extend his sphere of influence.

He looks after his own lineage and community well,
and is concerned with the long-term preservation of his empire.[9]

The lowest type of king [30]
does not think about his subjects, but only about money,
and his kingdom is quickly toppled,
like a tree whose roots have decayed.

Evil rulers rejoice
when the royal income is derived
from fines imposed on the people.
How amazing the dishonesty of this degenerate age!

People primarily need Dharma.
Dharma helps us both in this life and in the next.
Next come power and fame,
which bring glory in this life alone.
Some people, however, focus on neither of these;
concerned only with wealth, they break the laws.
Such individuals are not fit to lead living beings
and should not be appointed to important positions.

Therefore, whether you are a king, a minister,
or the head of a city,
you should only accept wealth that is legally permitted
and never give a single thought to ill-gotten wealth.

Among men, a position of greatness is rarely achieved
by buying it with jewels and gold.
Rather, it is the king who is the chief cause
of someone achieving an important position.

9. Note that Mipham does not denigrate this second type, which corresponds to the *vijigīṣu*, the ambitious expansionist king of the Hindu *nīti* tradition. Kāmandaki's *Essence of Ethics* is mostly concerned with advising such a king. See Raja Rajendra Lala Mitra and Sisir Kumar Mitra, *The Nītisāra by Kāmandaki*, 247f.

For the poor, the most important thing is food,
for the wealthy, it is jewels;
for the righteous, it is achievement or rank.
That is why they concern themselves with status,
for they think, "Having obtained a certain status,
how will I be able to help others?"
In this way, they think about giving,
and not about stealing.

When those who have attained a high rank
care for others appropriately,
they naturally achieve food and wealth even without trying.
Even if they become penniless, they still have their rank. [31]
Therefore, those who have a high status
should only think about appropriately benefitting
the king's districts and the kingdom as a whole.

Relatives will not request
a just ruler
to grant them improper favors
that require him to take a side in various intrigues.

If his mother, father, or even his lama
requests something that is inappropriate,
the king politely refuses.
There is never an excuse for acting illegally.

But he will fulfill the wishes
of friends and members of his entourage,
offering whatever help he can,
when this does not transgress the moral and legal norms.

Those who serve as the king's advisors
will not speak to him about their own wishes, nor will they take sides.
Instead, they will accurately inform him about what they have learned,
both the good and the bad—what ought to be accepted and rejected.

The King's Lamas

Those whom the king takes as his lamas
should only be concerned with how to achieve his happiness
in the king's present life, certainly,
but especially in his future ones.

If he does something that contravenes the Dharma,
they exhort him, "That is improper."
To the best of their abilities, they set him on the path
of actions that accord with the Dharma.

A lama will not ask the king for favors
regarding matters that have to do with worldly laws,
except for a few instances such as the reprieve of death sentences and
so forth
which are not in violation of a king's moral code, but are un-dharmic.

Because the lama is exceedingly sacred, [32]
it is improper to violate his advice.
So if the lama asks too much of the king,
he will make life difficult for him.

Therefore, if the lama cares for the king,
and the king cares for the lama,
in this life there will be harmony and good fortune,
and in the next life, happiness.

Anyone to whom the king shows affection
will work exclusively for the welfare
of that same king.
But when someone thinks, "He is affectionate toward me,"
and manipulates the king to some improper end
by making various selfish requests,
the king should dismiss this individual,
for such a person has no sense of shame.

With pure minds resembling fine gold,
the king and his court should analyze the treatises on royal ethics,
the texts that teach the methods of caring for living beings.
In this way, when nobles who possess merit
carefully analyze individuals using the power of their intellect,
the kingdom enjoys the beauty of a retinue that possesses good qualities,
and reaches to amazing heights, like the great sāla tree.

When a fine court truly possesses such purity,
even lowly men will be the equals of the greatest nobles.
When the king is good and the court is also good,
they are able to bear a great and vast land upon their shoulders.

It is difficult for a king to know on his own
the good and bad that people are up to throughout the land.
But if he gathers together a good court,
the maṇḍala of his kingdom becomes virtuous everywhere.
The king properly cares for the retinue, [33]
and the members of the retinue revere the king.
When these factors come together,
the kingdom overflows with happiness and joy.

6. An Explanation of the Chapter on Kingship from the *Satyaka Sūtra*

In the *Sūtra on Skillful Magical Transformations*[1]
King Caṇḍapradyota[2]
asks Satyaka—

1. *Ārya bodhisattva gocara upāya viṣaya vikurvāṇa nirdeśa mahāyāna sūtra.* Satyaka—whose name means "Truthful One" or "Truth Teller"—a bodhisattva manifesting as a non-Buddhist Nigrantha sage, first makes his appearance in the fifth chapter of the sūtra. The work is also known under the shorter title *Satyaka Sūtra* or *Satyakavyākaraṇa Sūtra* in honor of its main character. On the variant names of the sūtra, see Peter Skilling, "A List of Symbols on the Feet and Hands of the Buddha from the *Bodhisatva-gocara-upāya-viṣaya-vikurvāṇa-nirdeśa-nāma-mahāyāna-sūtra*," 47–48. The entire sūtra has been translated into English from the Tibetan by Lozang Jamspal in *The Range of the Bodhisattva: A Mahāyāna Sūtra.* This chapter of Mipham's work summarizes the *Satyaka Sūtra*'s sixth chapter, in which the bodhisattva explains the principles that a king ought to follow when ruling his kingdom. This important material—one of the most extensive treatments of ancient Buddhist political theory—has been discussed in a number of scholarly sources. See, for example, Stephen Jenkins, "Making Merit through Warfare According to the *Ārya-Bodhisattva-gocara-upayaviśaya-vikurvaṇa-nirdeśa Sūtra*," in *Buddhist Warfare*, 59–75; Michael Zimmermann, "A Mahāyānist Criticism of the *Arthaśāstra*"; and Michael Zimmermann, "Only a Fool Becomes a King," in *Buddhism and Violence*, 213–42, and esp. 228–35. See also Samdong Rinpoche, "The Social and Political Strata in Buddhist Thought," 5–7.

2. Caṇḍapradyota (Gtum po rab snang), "Pradyota the Cruel," also known as Mahāsena, was a contemporary of the Buddha and the king of Ujjayinī, the capital of the Avanti kingdom. He is mentioned in a variety of narrative works, both Buddhist and non-Buddhist. In the *Vinaya Kṣudraka Vastu* and *Karma Śataka* he is portrayed—just as he is in the *Satyaka Sūtra*—as cruel and ill-tempered. The *Bṛhatkathā* of Gunāḍhya, a non-Buddhist work, concurs in this assessment of the ruler. According to one of these legends, Pradyota, who was an insomniac, spends part of each night inspecting the sentries to make sure they have not fallen asleep. If they did not respond when he called out to them, he would twice forgive them, but at the third offense he would have them beheaded. See Félix Lacôte, *Essai sur Guṇāḍhya et la Bṛhatkathā*, 236–247.

a bodhisattva, a great being,
who has assumed the form of a heterodox religious leader—
how kings should care for living beings.
He replies that he will clearly explain
the points that address this question.

"Listen with reverence, O ruler.
The term 'living being,'
refers to the five aggregates and this is of two kinds:
(1) the sentient beings who take rebirth in the four ways,[3]
(2) and the universe that is their habitat, constituted by the five elements.
How are they ruled? In two ways, (1) self-rule as the result of their karma,
or (2) rule by a lord of living beings, a king.

"The first, those that need no king—like the beings of Uttarakuru
and those that live at the beginning of the eon[4]—
are never bereft of resources.
They neither harm nor quarrel with one another.
Likewise, the humans of the fortunate eon
honor their parents and practice virtue.
They are happy on their own, as a result of their karma,
without having to designate anyone as king.

"All others except for these two [34]
need a 'lord of beings' or king to rule them.

3. The four types of birth are (1) from a womb, (2) from an egg, (3) from warmth and moisture (the way insects are born), (4) and miraculous birth (the way gods and hell beings are born).

4. Uttarakuru, the northern "continent" of Buddhist cosmology, is a utopia where human beings' needs are always readily met from the environment. Since these beings are happy and self-sufficient and do not need to compete for resources, there is no strife. The beings born at the beginning of a cosmic cycle are reborn in the world magically, like the gods. Initially, their bodies are extremely subtle and radiant; they fly everywhere, and subsist solely on meditation. As they begin to eat, their bodies become coarser; they develop sexual organs, begin to procreate, to accumulate food and land, and eventually to steal from one another. It is only then that they require laws and a king to administer the rules. On these Buddhist cosmogonic myths, see José I. Cabezón, *Sexuality in Classical South Asian Buddhism*, chapter 1.

Rulers are of four types: (1) cakravartins,[5] (2) mahārājas,[6]
(3) governors of districts, and (4) vassal kings."

1. The Cakravartin

"Cakravartins begin coming to the world when the human lifespan is
84,000 years.
Such a ruler has a golden wheel.
He is anointed as king through the collective agreement of all.
He is triumphant over the periphery, the four continents,
and he is righteous because
he follows the ten virtuous actions himself.

"His kingdom contains, besides the Dharma king himself,
(1) the wheel that brings him victory in all directions;
(2) the elephant, his amazing supreme mount;
(3) the queen, his supreme lover;
(4) the jewel, his most radiant possession;
(5) the steward, who is responsible for his supreme resources;
(6) the highest minister, his heroic and wise personal companion;
(7) and the supreme horse that allows him to travel anywhere with ease.
These are the seven precious things he possesses.

5. A cakravartin (Pāli *cakkavatti*) is a universal monarch, literally "wheel turner." Like a Buddha, he possesses a number of unusual signs or markings on his body. Nāgārjuna, *Ratnāvalī*, vv. 2.77–97, explains how practicing various virtues result in the major marks that adorn the body of a cakravartin king: hands and feet marked by wheels, feet that are level, webbed fingers, and so on. A Pāli scripture, the *Lion's Roar of the Wheel Turner* (*Cakkavatti Sīhanāda Sutta*, Digha Nikāya 26, PTS edition 3: 58–79) recounts how seven great *cakkavattis* rule the world in its early, utopian period. After that, the eighth ruler does not follow the tradition and moral code of his predecessors. This begins a process of social decline that culminates in an apocalypse, which in turn leads to the coming of the Buddha Metteyya and the regeneration of the ideal social order. More directly relevant to Mipham's text, Vasubandhu's *Abhidharmakośa* speaks of four kinds of cakravartin kings—the kings who possess (in ascending order) wheels made of iron, bronze, silver, and gold. As explained in appendix 1, only the highest of these, the golden wheel king, conquers all four human continents and only one cakravartin can be present in the world at one time. See Louis de la Vallee Poussin and Gelong Lodrö Sangpo, *Abhidharmakośa-Bhāṣya of Vasubandhu*, vol. 2, 1100–5.
6. "Great kings."

"Every land, wherever it may be,
falls under his dominion.
How? In the absence of any negativity
or opposition on the part of others,
he does not need to resort to violence.

"Violence through weapons and torture
are therefore unknown in his world.
He avoids the three improper actions,[7] and being righteous,
he is impartial and does not show any favoritism.

"The kings and vassal rulers
who reside on the four continents
submit to the cakravartin king with these words,
'Please rule us by accepting
our lands, the wealth they contain,
and the people who fill them.
Please accept us all [35]
as your divine majesty's servants.'

"The cakravartin then consents with these words,
'Rule your subjects according to the Dharma
and never act contrary to it.
Detest unrighteous behavior,
and rule your subjects impartially.
This is how you become my servants.'"

2. Non-Cakravartin Kings and Their Need for Treatises

"All other kings assume their office
either through heredity,

7. Mipham does not specify what the three improper actions are, but the *Satyaka Sūtra* at this point in the text mentions desire, anger, and delusion—the so-called three poisons. However, see the discussion of the three improper actions that follows, where they are characterized differently: attachment to evil, greed, and adopting false religious views and practices.

or else through their merit, by appointment in the country
whose dominion they will control."

[Question:] "How do those kings
rule living beings?"

[Reply:] "All other kings rule living beings
following the treatises, but not cakravartins,
for when a cakravartin appears in the world,
the three improper actions do not exist."

[Question:] "What are the three improper actions?"

[Reply:] "(1) Taking delight in the ten nonvirtues
is considered attachment to evil;
(2) not being satisfied with one's own wealth
is improper action of greed;
(3) and relying on false treatises
is considered the action of surrounding oneself with false religion.

"Because there are no sentient beings
who engage in these three actions at that time,
it is a greatness
of the cakravartin's own Dharma [36]
that no one ever transgresses
the orders and will of the king.
Instead, everyone agrees
to joyfully do the king's bidding.
Hence, they do not need to rely on treatises.

"But once sentient beings start to possess
unrighteous thoughts like desire and so forth,
compassionate and knowledgeable sages think about the king's
intellectual training,
and wishing to be of service to him,
they compose treatises on royal ethics
so that he may know what is moral and immoral."

[Question:] "What are those treatises
that are used to rule sentient beings?"

[Reply:] "They are works that teach
the nature, divisions, and benefits
of not desiring, not being angry, and being undeluded,
which are the three antidotes
to the three improper activities:
desire, hatred, and delusion.
The forces motivating these three antidotes
are self-control and compassion."

[Question:] "What is self-control?"

[Reply:] "The king thinks to himself,
'Wealth is as transient as clouds.
I too will die.'
Being mindful of this truth,
he preaches the faults of desire to others,
and he uses his wealth
with a spirit of renunciation.
This is how a holy sovereign rules with self-control.

"To bear compassion in mind
means not supporting oneself with improperly obtained wealth;
even if properly obtained, one should not use it inopportunely;
even when used opportunely,
one should not use it to harm the poor. [37]

"It means to help others in times of famine,
to stop thieves from robbing,
to help people when they are harming one another,
to give charity to those who are poor and who have no protector,
and to justly punish the wicked
with righteous punishments.
This is how one cares for living beings."[8]

8. Amoghavarṣa, *Vimalapraśnottara*, v. 48: "Who is to be worshipped even more than the

Principles of Legal Punishment

[Question:] "How should one punish the wicked?"

[Reply:] "The ruler's punishments
should be (1) just, (2) fitting, (3) principled,
(4) moderate, and (5) benevolent.

"First, the defendant should be guilty,
and worthy of being punished.
It is utterly wrong
to punish the innocent.

"Second, a fitting punishment
is one in which the severity of the punishment
fits the crime.
When this is not the case, then the punishment is unfitting.

"Third, you should follow accepted principles.
If you act according to your whim,
you violate the rule of law;
this is unprincipled.

"Fourth,[9] if punishments are deserved,
and guilt has been established beyond mere accusation,
even then you should not kill criminals, deprive them of their sense faculties,[10]
or sever their major or minor limbs.

---

gods? Someone devoted to compassion." Compassion is also a major theme in Nāgārjuna's *Ratnāvalī* (vv. 3.16, 3.26, 3.43, 4.30–36, 4.78). In the fifth chapter of the *Ratnāvalī* (vv. 5.36–39) Nāgārjuna adds compassion (*karuṇa*) to the classical "six perfections" (*ṣatpāramitā)* of the Mahāyāna, thereby suggesting that bodhisattvas have seven (not six) virtues to perfect.

9. The text actually reads "third" (*gsum pa*) at this point, but the previous division was the "third" and the next is the "fifth," so I have emended the text to read "fourth" (*bzhi pa*) at this point.

10. This refers, for example, to plucking out the eyes, cutting out the tongue, and so forth—forms of punishment that are mentioned in various Hindu political-legal treatises like Cāṇakya's *Arthaśāstra* and Manu's *Dharmśāstra*.

"Instead, out of compassion,
you should punish them as befits their offense:
putting them in chains; imprisoning them;
beating them; threatening, harassing,
or banishing them; or confiscating their wealth.
Any level of harshness beyond that [38]
is considered excessively cruel.

"Because the king is the protector of living beings,
if he kills criminals,
their[11] minds become infected with anger
and, in all likelihood, they will be reborn in the lower realms.
He will then be connected to them through a "flesh-debt"
that lasts for a long time, over many rebirths.

"When criminals are deprived of their sense faculties and limbs,
this cannot be reversed or remedied;
for this reason, it is said that he should only resort to putting them in chains, beating them, or the like,
which are punishments that can be remedied.

"If criminals are not protected
with a compassionate attitude,
the king will not be able to fulfill
his mission of protecting living beings."[12]

Fifth, [Question:] "But how does one act compassionately
toward those who are wicked?"

[Reply:] "Consider the example of unruly children.
Just as a father, so as to correct his children's faults,
will beat and scold them,
but will not kill them,

11. The text is ambiguous and it could be read as referring to the king himself: "his mind becomes conditioned by anger, and he will, in all likelihood, be reborn in the lower realms."
12. Compare to Nāgārjuna, *Ratnāvalī*, vv. 4.30–37.

likewise, there is no fault if the king, devoid of harmful thoughts,
resorts to harsh methods to subdue the wicked."

Types of Wicked People

"The wicked—those deserving of such punishments—
are of five types:
(1) those who harm the king,
(2) those who harm one another,
(3) those who do not obey the king's orders,
(4) those who pursue wrong livelihoods,
(5) and those who follow wrong ways.[13]
All of these increase unhappiness in the world.

"(1) The first includes those who would kill the king
or steal his consorts, wealth, and so on,
those who insult him, and those who cannot keep confidences. [39]
The punishments for these evildoers,
which should befit their crime,
include reviling them, exposing their faults, confiscating their wealth,
putting them in chains, banishing them, and so forth.
This will make them desist from their evil ways.

"(2) The actions of those who harm one another
should be stopped through punishments
such as public scolding, threats,
harassment, beating, and imprisonment.

"(3) Any resident of the kingdom
who disobeys the king's orders
should be overpowered and controlled;
they should not be allowed to circulate beyond their own district.

13. The Tibetan *log par zhugs pa* translates the Sanskrit terms *mithyāpratipanna*, *vipratipanna*, and *vitathapravṛtta*—which have the sense of doing what is wrong, doing something forbidden, or proceeding along a false path.

"By confining them to their own community and not punishing them any more severely
they come to feel grateful to the king for his kindness,
and out of fear, they obey. Everyone then respects the king
and he obtains both fame and merit.

"(4) Those who engage in unethical livelihoods—
fowlers, butchers, prostitutes, and so on—
who have taken up sinful and unethical family traditions
should be stopped through threats,
by striking fear into their hearts:
'Unless you desist from your actions,
I will punish you in such and such a way.'

"(5) Whoever from within the Buddhist order has wrong views,
or has an immoral form of discipline, or practices debased rituals or wrong livelihood,
should be judged by a saṅgha council
that determines whether to expel the individual.

"But if each faction of the saṅgha adheres to its own position
and is unable to expel the individual, [40]
the king first examines the issues well,
and then supports the side that is most worthy.[14]

"If the monastic discipline and so forth are declining
due to a dispute between two saṅgha factions,
then if the king is a true expert in the Dharma,
he decides the issue himself.

"Otherwise, he calls a council of the mendicants and brahmins who live in that country—
those considered righteous and expert in the Dharma—
and gets them to settle the dispute.
The king then provides the proper support

14. In other words, the king intervenes in disciplining members of the clergy only in cases when the monastic community is split and cannot reach a consensus.

to the side that is considered to be in the right,
and he opposes the party that is in the wrong
by whatever method is fitting—threats, banishment, and the like.

[Question:] "In the righteous king's land one also finds
people who do not show respect for their elderly parents,
who do not give adequate food and money
to their dependents, servants, and so forth,
and who shirk the official work assigned to them.
To which of the five types of wicked people do these individuals belong?"

[Reply:] "Those who are only concerned with their own affairs
and who do not provide adequate support
to those who help them,
are engaged in a form of terribly wrong livelihood.
So they fall under the category of wicked people who engage in wrong livelihood.

"All of the following are also tremendous errors:
to say offensive things
to brahmins and mendicants begging for alms;
to invite them to your house and then refuse them food;
to offer them food contravening their religion; to beat them, and the like;
and to show no respect for those worthy of respect.
Those who engage in these and similar acts
are considered wicked people following wrong ways. [41]

"Those who engage in such improper forms of livelihood
and those who follow wrong and evil spiritual paths,
should be known as falling under
the latter two of the five types of wicked people, respectively.

"The gods withhold timely rains,
and consequently torment people with scarcity and famine,
in any kingdom in which there is a multitude
of people who follow such wrong paths.

"The demigods, from their side,
send down various plagues;
and even when there is no illness, lifespans and wealth diminish.
Therefore, the king stops those false ways and livelihoods so that the kingdom may flourish."

[Question:] "Who punishes a king
when he is wicked
or out of control?"

[Reply:] "The king must subjugate himself.
How so?
When he loses self-control and compassion,
he makes a self-assessment using his wisdom,
thinking about the dangers of a bad reputation and bad future rebirths.

"From time to time, the righteous king
calls upon individuals who, throughout his kingdom,
are considered holy and morally upright—
wise mendicants and brahmins—
and he inquires of these intelligent individuals,
'Which is the virtuous path to take and which is the nonvirtuous one?
What types of actions will lead to goodness?
What types of actions are sinful?'
In this way he makes time to be taught the Dharma.

"From their side, the sages ought to teach the king
the fine ancestral traditions.
And when the time is right, they use sweet words
to point out to the king his faults.
In this way, using both external advisors
as well as the power of his own inner wisdom,
the king subjugates his own wickedness." [42]

Protection of the Environment, of the Innocent, and of Cultural Treasures

"A moral king protects the environment
and the creatures who inhabit it
by allowing them to be as they are:
not burning them, not destroying them, and so forth.

"And even when a king becomes enraged
in regard to those who infuriate him,
it is wrong for him to burn their cities and towns;
to destroy ponds, demolish dwellings, cut down fruit trees,
burn crops, destroy religious images,
or destroy anything that has aesthetic merit—
any site that people appreciate,
or any building or work of art that is well made or well painted.
Instead, he confiscates these things from those who are the object of his indignation
and allows them to be used for the common welfare of other beings.

"There are some people who have committed no fault,
and there are many innocent creatures—
gods and herds of animals—
that belong to their households.

"The king should not show enmity to these,
and should not destroy or lay them to waste.
This is how he protects the creatures
that belong to the broader environment.[15]

15. Mipham is here arguing that in the context of warfare kings ought not kill animals or lay waste to another country's cultural heritage. Mātṛceta, *Kaniṣkalekha*, vv. 64–79, has a much longer (and quite radical) criticism of King Kaniṣka. The king, he states, is allowing harm to come to animals, claiming that his compassion for animals "has been obstructed." The world is a darker place, says Mātṛceta, when some residents of the kingdom (i.e., animals) are not given refuge by the king. He concludes by asking the king to protect the animals in his kingdom, "acting toward them with even greater compassion than he has shown to people." Given the importance of meat-eating to Tibet, it is not surprising that Mipham does not reproduce Mātṛceta's defense of animals and his criticism of King Kaniṣka.

One who rules in this way will truly be engaged
in the welfare of sentient beings."

[Question:] "How should the king
protect the gods that live in his realm?"

[Reply:] "He does so by not spoiling the places where they live,
and by offering ritual cakes to them and so forth.
If he cares for all living creatures likewise,
all wickedness will be vanquished,
people will not engage in moral evil,
and he will increase his stock of merit for the next life." [43]

Taxation

"Because the wealth of a kingdom
is the fruit of people's individual labors,
and because the king is the one who protects it,
it is not the private property of the king or of those individuals.

"When fitting taxes
are not paid to the king,
this does not constitute theft,
but it represents the moral fault of stinginess.

"If the wealthy do not pay
their fair share of taxes,
they may be taken through force.
Taxes are like the wages the king has earned.
Thus the king is not stealing when he collects taxes.

"What if he collects taxes from the poor by force?
One such case is sinful, the other is not.
Gamblers, prostitutes, and so forth
cause wealth to be inappropriately squandered.

"If the king expropriates their wealth so as to stop them, he accomplishes two goals,[16]
and it is said to involve no sin on the king's part.
But if he taxes people whose possessions have been destroyed by fire or the like,
or whose wealth is exhausted,
he is not showing care for sentient beings who have no means at their disposal
and can do nothing about their situation; so this is a sin."

The Ten Qualities of Dharma Kings[17]

[Question:] "When does such a self-controlled and compassionate king
become a righteous Dharma king
who has gathered together all the conditions
and has perfected them in their totality?"

[Reply:] "He becomes a perfected and righteous Dharma king
by fulfilling ten conditions:
(1) having the excellence of being appointed by heaven,
(2) having a disciplined retinue, (3) having the highest wisdom,
(4) possessing perseverance, (5) having faith in the Dharma, (6) being skilled,
(7) being gentle, (8) having appropriate worldly comportment,
(9) having forbearance in the face of troubles, and
(10) upholding the Dharma flawlessly. [44]

(1) "'The excellence of being appointed by heaven'[18]
refers to the fact that due to the power of his merit
his ministers and subjects suffer no illnesses,
encounter few problems, and possess happiness and wealth.

16. The two goals are his own goal and the goal of the others who inhabit his kingdom.
17. Mipham identifies these—like the *Satyaka Sūtra* itself does—as the conditions that someone must fulfill to become a perfected Dharma king. But in the descriptions that follow, they appear to sometimes be types of kings.
18. This idea is reminiscent of the notion of the Chinese *tien ming*, "the mandate of heaven," which is so important to Confucian thought. But in the lines that follow, the *Satyaka Sūtra* glosses this in a way that makes no appeal to any metaphysical notion of heaven or God.

(2) "The king who possesses a wholesome and pure retinue
is happy and free from troubles;
he who does not deviate from the way of kings,
is rightly called 'a king with a suitable retinue.'

(3) "The 'king who has excellent wisdom'
does not depend on others
and knows every skillful method
for righteously ruling living beings.

(4) "The 'king who has proper perseverance'
in regard to everything he does
lives happily without being bothered by enemies,
and his treasuries increase and become abundant.

(5) "The 'king who has faith in the Dharma'
is relentless in his pursuit of merit
and in subduing the wicked.
So he only acts according to the Dharma.

(6) "The 'king who is skilled in his focus'
does not procrastinate in any action.
Commencing an action at the perfect time,
his wishes are quickly fulfilled.

(7) "The 'king whose character
is unwaveringly gentle'
is trusted by everyone in the country,
and he unites everyone.

(8) "The 'king who has practical knowledge and proper comportment
in worldly affairs'
knows the difference between what is allowable and what is not.
He is someone who always permits
the accumulation of wealth.

(9) "The 'king who forbears in the face of troubles' [45]
has a perfect capacity to accomplish

any of the deeds of a king,
and never fears suffering.

(10) "A king 'upholds the Dharma flawlessly'
when he himself follows the path
that leads to special spiritual accomplishments,
and when he is not bereft of a spiritual teacher."

Rules of War

[Question:] "When war breaks out
inside the kingdom
of a perfect righteous king,
how does he behave?"

[Reply:] "He uses three types of strategies
during three times: beginning, middle, and end.
Through these he protects his kingdom
without compromising dharmic principles.

"What are the three types of strategies?
Initially, he tries to avoid war and maintain the peace
by approaching allies who are
friendly to himself or to his ministers.[19]
Or else he uses various strategies—
positive enticements, threats, and so forth.
But if he is unable to initially achieve peace in this way,
then in the middle period, the dharmic king
sets his mind on three thoughts.
Only when it is unavoidable, will he wage war.

"He prepares in the middle period by first
setting his mind on protecting living creatures, thinking,
'I, a righteous king, am committed

19. It may not be altogether clear how forming alliances would deter war, but the *Satyaka Sūtra* explains that if the king can show that he has amassed a force that is far more powerful than the enemy's, this might cause the enemy to back down or surrender.

to avoiding the destruction of living creatures.
Is there no option but to destroy them?'

"Second, he sets his mind on how to achieve
victory over his opponents, the enemies.
And third, he sets his mind
on protecting the life of individuals.

If war is inevitable,
he orders his fourfold garrison of troops [46]
to prepare for battle.

"In the final period, he will arrange his troops in such a way
that the regiments of inferior warriors
are placed first.
The average ones are arranged behind these,
and the cavalry is sent in last,
behind these first two.

"The king, accompanied by the regiment
of the most heroic soldiers,
remains at the rear of all the troops.
This permits him to be a source of inspiration;
it allows the infantry to protect him,
and makes it easy for the army to traverse through enemy lines.
If the army is skillfully arranged in this manner,
the troops will fear the king.

"Remembering his kindness, and wishing to repay it,
they will not be able to do anything that is displeasing to him.
Because of the great majesty of the troops who are in the rear,
the troops attack the opposing forces with all their might
and never retreat.
When there is proper leadership and skill,
the gods lend their support and the battle is won.

"The king who properly arranges his troops
using the strategies just mentioned

may kill or wound his opponents,
but this constitutes only a minor moral fault,
and there is no certainty that he will have to experience karmic
retribution for it.
Why is this so? It is because
the motivating force behind his action
was unwavering compassion.

"Because he performs this action—
risking his wealth and even his very person—
to protect living creatures,
and for the sake of his children, wives, and lineage,
such an action makes his merit grow infinitely." [47]

Attitude Toward the Enemy

[Question:] "Now we know how a righteous king should act
when a righteous kingdom, against its will,
becomes embroiled in war.
But what kind of attitude does that dharmic king maintain
while all this is transpiring?"

[Reply:] "This is explained in eight parts.
(1) First, he has the attitude that all beings
comprising the class of living creatures, are his sons.
Just as a father corrects a son,
the king subjugates the wicked
without losing his compassion for them.

(2) "He has the attitude that the wicked are ill.
With this thought firmly in his mind,
he acts to rid them of their faults
without getting angry at the harm they do.[20]

20. There is an alternative reading here, but it requires that the text be emended to read *snod* (vessel) instead of *gnod* (harm). Read in this way, the lines imply that the king works to eliminate the illness/fault that wicked people experience without getting angry at the vessel, the people themselves—a variation on the theme of "hate the sin but not the sinner."

(3) "Generating an attitude of compassion
for suffering sentient beings,
he tries, as best he can, to eliminate their problems
and to accomplish their welfare.

(4) "He feels joy for those sentient beings
who possess happiness and wealth,
and he will rejoice in these
without any stinginess and jealousy.

(5) "He has the attitude, 'Even though these enemies are harming me,
the most direct cause of this is their anger,
which they are powerless to control.'
And he remains close to them while working to eliminate this cause.

(6) "He conceives of himself as protecting friends and relatives:
'Just as, up to now, I have been steadfast
in my love and friendship for those close to me,
let me now show this friendliness to everyone.'

(7) "He sets his mind firmly on the thought
that pleasure is like medicine.
He does not engage in sexual misconduct,
and instead promotes appropriate forms of dispassion. [48]

(8) "He has the attitude that he has no self.
He strives to understand the meaning of the Dharma,
relies on Dharma preachers, and is persistent
in properly practicing the Dharma.

"When a righteous king
has these eight attitudes,
his treasury greatly increases
just from others' gifts.

"This does not in the least compare
to what other non-dharmic kings achieve

who employ all manner
of deceit.

"When he possesses these eight attitudes,
the gods cause the rains to fall in a timely fashion,
harvests are good, there are no famines,
and wealth will never be exhausted.
No one will experience the fear and sorrow
of ferocious wild animals or the like.

"The enemies who would harm that king
will, naturally and with little difficulty,
be destroyed through their own evil doings,
and having been eradicated, no enemies will arise again.

"The king who protects living beings
righteously in just this way
will be hailed as gentle while he's alive.
Without committing any harmful acts,
when his body finally gives out, he will be reborn
in the higher realms, among the gods,
experiencing one happiness after another.
This is how rulers ought to practice."

7. The Theory of Ethical Kingship according to the *Smṛtyupasthāna Sūtra*

According to the *Smṛtyupasthāna Sūtra*,[1]
a most intelligent bodhisattva made a prayer
to take rebirth in heaven so as to dispel
the gods' lack of self-control.

Suparvan,[2] the king of the geese,
during a past life when he was a human king,
studied a Dharma discourse under Buddha Śikhin[3]
called "How a King Practices the Dharma."
He then taught this to the king of the Aviha gods.[4]

1. *Ārya Saddharma Smṛtyupasthāna Sūtra*. This sūtra includes the following passage (Lha sa ed., vol. 70, fols. 400b–441a): "Due to the power of his prayer and of his wish to benefit the gods, he . . . arrived before the sovereign of the Aviha gods. 'I am going to preach the holy Dharma in a way that is relevant to you. This I do for the sake of the welfare and happiness of the gods and of your majesty—to avert your falling into error due to lack of self-control. . . . Listen, Lord of Aviha! When I was a man—in fact, a king—the Blessed One, Śikhin, told me that I should listen, bear in mind, and teach the Dharma discourse of the sūtra called *A Teaching on How a King Practices the Dharma*. . . . Any king that rules over living beings with the thirty-five principles [explained in that scripture] will achieve great wealth and great power and will never be defeated by the armies of his foes; and once he dies, he will be reborn in a higher realm, a happy realm, as the sovereign of the Aviha gods.'" The bodhisattva then lists the thirty-five practices and explains each of them individually. I have translated a portion of this section of the sūtra in appendix 2.
2. Suparvan is my reconstruction of an uncertain Sanskrit equivalent; the Tibetan is *dus bzang*.
3. Śikhin (Gtsug gtor can) is the second of the six buddhas who came to the world prior to Śākyamuni.
4. The Aviha ('Thab bral) god realm is the third of the so-called desire god realms, the lowest of the three types of god realms.

I have condensed these fine instructions,
arranged them logically and systematically,[5]
and will now explain them using clear words,
so listen, O rulers!

Kings who wish to increase their good qualities
both in this life and in the next
ought to practice this Dharma
which has thirty-five parts.

(1) Because wisdom is the foundation of the accumulations
in both this life and in the next,
meditation on the light of true wisdom
is the first thing a king should practice.

(2) The second mental quality
is proper reflection
on the things that are truly meaningful
in this life and the next.

(3) The third is to worship the spiritual master.
When he properly relies on spiritual friends
who are well-behaved and experts on the meaning of the truth,
he will obtain excellence. [50]

(4) Fourth, it is necessary to avoid
sinful friends—evil people
who espouse the doctrines
of nihilism, wrong behavior, and evil views.

(5) The fifth is to abandon
the tremendously false view
that denies karma and its effects,
which is the source of all faults.

5. As mentioned in the Introduction, Mipham changes the order of the thirty-five topics in the presentation that follows. A comparison of the order of the topics in Mipham's text vis-a-vis the sūtra is found in appendix 3.

(6) All inner and outer created phenomena
arise in dependence on causes and conditions.
The sixth is therefore to possess right knowledge
of the correct and incorrect workings of cause and effect.

(7) The seventh is to have an understanding
of the qualities of people—an understanding that does not confuse
the traits of the righteous, who possess good qualities,
and their opposites.[6]

(8) The eighth quality of the ruler is this:
He does not accept as true
everything that people with varying agendas have to say,
accepting only what is suitable and meaningful.

(9) A king is victorious over all lands
when he possesses steadfast friends
who are righteous, helpful, and trustworthy.
This is the ninth quality.

(10) The tenth is the opposite: a king achieves happiness
when he constantly avoids friends
who are untrustworthy, deceitful,
unstable, and unhelpful.

(11) The eleventh—called "purifying one's own people"[7]—
refers to the purity of mind of both himself and his entourage,
achieved by properly paying attention both to this life and the next,
ensuring that actions are consistent with the Dharma.

(12) By engaging in charity, speaking sweetly,
and doing good deeds, all directions will be filled

6. Compare to Mātṛceta, *Kaniṣkalekha*, v. 19: "Always understand each person's special qualities. Your success depends on such knowledge."
7. There is an alternative understanding of the phrase *rang gi skye bo*, on which see appendix 2, n. 1.

with accounts of his great fame.
This is the twelfth. [51]

(13) All goals—both those of this life and the perennial spiritual ones—
are obtained by eliminating laziness,
which is the greatest enemy to increasing good qualities.
This is the thirteenth quality.

(14) No matter what goal one wishes to accomplish,
if one focuses on it without letting too much time elapse,
one will fulfill all of one's aims.
This is the fourteenth good quality.

(15) Excessive craving for food and drink
makes the body and mind unfit.
Abandoning such craving and eating in moderation
is the fifteenth practice.[8]

(16) Having freed oneself from the stain of sleep,
which causes carelessness and the deterioration of goals,
the mind becomes clear and one completes one's work.[9]
This is the sixteenth good quality of a ruler.

(17) The seventeenth quality of rulers
is that they are not controlled by women,
for women are unstable, deceitful, jealous,
and a source of many faults.

(18) The eighteenth supreme quality of a king
is that he has proper self-control that prevents ensnarement

8. Cāṇakya, *Rājanītiśāstra*, v. 3.24: "A king who is attached to food and drink . . . is like a snake."
9. Seeing sleep as a "stain" and as something to be transcended is a common theme in Indian religious literature. For example, Amoghavarṣa, *Vimalapraśnottara*, vv. 28–29, states: "Who does not sleep? The person who remains alert and who understands the specifics of objects. Who sleeps? The individual who is very deluded."

by the five sense objects,
which deceive the childish.[10]

(19) If he controls the rage and excitement
that arise from hatred and desire, respectively,
the king obtains the supreme quality of self-discipline,
which is the nineteenth.

(20) The twentieth quality for which kings are renowned
is said to be their patience.
Having overcome anger,
they avoid anything that harms another.

(21) The twenty-first moral quality of kings
is that they satisfy everyone's minds
by speaking sweet and pleasant words
that are agreeable to everyone.[11] [52]

(22) The twenty-second good quality
is the supreme good quality of always speaking truthfully.
This is what makes someone trustworthy
in the world together with its gods.

(23) "To be impartial"
means to be evenhanded and nonpartisan,
treating all regions of the country as would a parent.
This is the twenty-third good quality.

(24) Because his mind is stable, he does not capriciously increase or
decrease
people's wealth or landholdings.
This perpetual consistency
is the twenty-fourth good quality.

10. A similar point is made in *Arthaśāstra* (1.6.2), where the antidote to controlling the senses is identified as "training in the sciences" (*vidyāvinaya*).
11. Amoghavarṣa, *Vimalapraśnottara*, v. 35: "Who is a tongueless mute person? Someone who does not know how to speak sweetly."

(25) The twenty-fifth of the king's qualities
is that he does not impose even the smallest tax or levy
beyond what is appropriate.
This is called "enjoying a fixed salary."

(26) When those who are wicked, difficult to subdue, and badly behaved
are allowed to live in the country, problems increase.
He gets rid of them and brings happiness to the land.
This is the twenty-sixth of the king's qualities.

(27) Whatever his parents and others have given
in the form of endowments or offerings, he leaves as is,
and even supplements it a bit.
This is the twenty-seventh good quality.[12]

(28) By exerting himself in acts of charity—
giving material goods and protection from fear—
he brings the land completely under his control.
This is the twenty-eighth of the king's qualities.[13]

(29) He makes offerings to the highest things in the world, the three jewels,
and also makes extensive offerings to others.[14]

12. Nāgārjuna, *Ratnāvalī*, v. 4.18 makes a similar point. The king does not renege on the financial commitments—promises of patronage, endowments, land grants, etc.—made by his royal predecessors, and instead shows his support for these past decisions by making additional contributions himself, even if only nominal ones. See also number 24 in this list. Several Indian Buddhist sources show an anxiety about the ruler's possible expropriation of religious goods and land, and for good reason. The *Arthaśāstra* (5.2.37–38) describes methods that kings can use to steal from temples (at least from temples that do not belong to "brahmins learned in the Vedas").
13. Amoghavarṣa, *Vimalapraśnottara*, v. 37: "What becomes precious? Engaging in charity at the right time."
14. In the *Smṛtyupasthāna Sūtra*, the practice is called "worshipping the gods (*lha*)" and the three jewels (*dkon mchog dkor 'phrog*) are not explicitly mentioned. The emphasis on the worship of the three jewels therefore represents a reinterpretation of this passage on Mipham's part.

This causes wise and meritorious individuals to flourish like the
waxing moon.
It is the twenty-ninth quality. [53]

(30) He strives to enlist as the supporters of virtue,
the good gods whose status is the result of good karma.
By worshipping them, good fortune and happiness abound.
This is the thirtieth good quality.

(31) He makes his sons and daughters happy
through the great love he shows for them,
encouraging them to follow the good path.
This type of quality that he cultivates is the thirty-first.

(32) Contemplating how to bring happiness to his subjects,
he rules the land and safeguards the happiness of his retinue and
subjects
using whatever beneficial methods are appropriate to bringing
them relief.
This is the thirty-second.[15]

(33) He protects those living beings who follow the Dharma,
and he leads those who do not to the Dharma.
The dharmic king shines in the world like the sun.
This is the thirty-third.

(34) He himself practices the ten virtues,
and encourages others to do so.
This brings happiness to the king and his retinue
both in this world and in the hereafter. This is the thirty-fourth.

(35) He causes the true holy Dharma
to be properly taught at specific times,[16]

15. This must correspond to item no. 32 in the *Smṛtyupasthāna*. In the sūtra, however, the emphasis is on proper distribution of resources to serfs. See appendix 3.
16. Alternatively, the Tibetan can be read as meaning that it is the king *himself* who teaches.

making him a supporter of the Dharma who benefits others.
This is the thirty-fifth good quality.

By possessing each of these good qualities,
he acquires many good qualities in this life:
fame, wealth, and so forth.
In the next life, he will go to the god realms.

Within the present life, the righteous king
experiences the highest happiness of any living being.
And from this life of happiness
he travels to the true happiness of nirvāṇa. [54]

The extensive praises
of these individual good qualities
are found in that very sūtra.
Intelligent people should therefore examine that work.

8. The *Suvarṇaprabhāsottama*'s "Treatise on Ethics for Kings"

The *Ārya Suvarṇaprabhāsottama*[1]
contains a treatise on ethics for kings
called "The Commitments of the Lords of the Gods."
I will explain its main points clearly.

Long ago, a group of the lords of the gods
asked Mahā Brahmā this question:
"Some human kings
are called 'gods' and 'sons of gods.'[2]
How is it that the gods became human rulers?"

The lord of the Brahmā world
addressed the group of world protectors in this way:

1. The Sanskrit text of this scripture—the *Sūtra of Golden Light*—was edited by Johannes Nobel in *Suvarṇabhāsottamasūtra = Das Goldglanz-Sūtra*. There are three versions of the sūtra in the Tibetan canon: (1) Lha sa bka 'gyur no. 513, rgyud *da*, fols. 1b–215b (translated from the Chinese); (2) Lha sa ed., fols. 215b–405b (translated from the Sanskrit); and (3) Lha sa ed., fols. 405b–507a (translated from the Sanskrit). Mipham's discussion is based on the two versions translated from the Sanskrit, specifically the twentieth chapter of the second version (fols. 361a–66b), and the twelfth chapter of the third version (fols. 463a–68a). That chapter of the sūtra bears the title "The Treatise on Kingship called 'The Commitments of the Lords of the Gods'" (*Devendrasamayarājaśāstra*). The sūtra has been translated many times from different classical Buddhist languages into different European and modern Asian languages. See, for example, Ronald E. Emmerick, *The Sūtra of Golden Light*.
2. Pankaj Mohan, "Kingship," 425, speculates that the notion of a king as the "son of god" probably stems from the fact that the *Suvarṇabhāsottama* was written during the period of the Kushan kings, who thought of themselves as sons of god (*devaputra*).

"The hosts of world protectors,
the Lord of the Gods, and so forth,
so as to destroy unrighteousness
and to protect the kingdom through righteousness,
bless the rulers of men
and proclaim their fame in the god realms
calling those kings 'gods'
as well as 'sons of gods.'

"They were appointed as kings
to reveal to people
the results of the good and evil deeds
performed in this life.

"When a king
does not stop sinners [55]
and people engaged in evil
by imposing fitting punishments,
unrighteousness will spread widely
throughout that king's realm.
Deception and quarrels will increase.
People, together with the gods, will be disturbed.

"When the main responsibility
of the one who is appointed king by the gods
is to stop the flourishing of sinners—
when they shirk that responsibility and cast it aside—
the gods cause horrible disasters:
untimely wind and rain,
wars with opponents, manifold illnesses,
inauspicious astrological events, and so forth.

"Flowers, harvests, and fruits do not ripen.
Much fear and suffering arises:
plundering by brigands, hail, famine,
and various forms of untimely death.
Priests, teachers, and retinues
will turn to unrighteous activities.

"In such times even the king
will worship the unrighteous
and will punish the righteous.
When the righteous are punished,
the waters, stars, and wind become disturbed.
And when unrighteous people are honored,
the essence of the holy Dharma, the luster of sentient beings,
and the vital essence of the earth are destroyed.

"Crops and fruits lose their nutritional potency,
and food ceases to satisfy.
Sentient beings become ugly, degenerate, and unhappy.
They become utterly joyless and anxious, [56]
and are disturbed by hundreds of mental afflictions.
Moreover, even that unrighteous king
loses all of his beauty,
and experiences various forms of suffering.

"When the appointed king is a wastrel,
discussions take place in the god realms:
'This is an unrighteous king.' Because he obstructs rebirths among
the gods
and increases rebirths into the states of woe,
the gods stop supporting the goals
toward which that king is working.

"There will be misfortune
not only in the realms of the demigods,
but even in the realm of the fathers, the kings of the gods.
Even the highest gods worry;
they abandon that evil king
and his kingdom quickly collapses.

"However, when a king destroys unrighteousness
and rules his kingdom righteously—
ruling even the people
of other vassal states impartially—

the fame of that righteous king
pervades the three worlds.

"Indra, the lord of the gods,
who resides in the realm of the Thirty-Three,[3] rejoices and thinks,
'In Jambudvipa, my son,
a righteous king
rules his kingdom righteously,
bringing joy to everyone on the face of the earth,
and replenishing the god realms.'[4]

"In this way, Indra, the lord of the gods, and his retinue,
rejoice in the righteous king
and always protect him as if he were their son. [57]
Many exceedingly wonderful things occur in that kingdom,
which are the opposite of the problems mentioned earlier:
the stars are always auspicious;
the winds and rains come at the right time, and so forth.

"Therefore, even at the cost of his life, the king
will never abandon
the jewel of the Dharma,
the source of happiness in the world.
He will rule the kingdom righteously,
relying on his righteous qualities;
he always abandons unrighteousness,
and he teaches the Dharma.

"He will incite sentient beings to do good,
and turn them away from doing evil.

3. The heaven called "Realm of the Thirty-Three" is the first or lowest of the desire god realms, and is ruled by the god Indra. It is so called because there are thirty-three chief gods there: eight gods of wealth (*nor lha*), ten wrathful gods (*drag po*), the twelve *ādityās* or sun gods (*nyi ma*), who represent the twelve months of the year, the twin sons of the goddess Aśvinī (*tha skar gyi bu*), and Indra.
4. Because people practice virtue under a righteous king, they are reborn into the god realms. The assumption is that the gods appoint a king, in part, to make righteousness flourish on earth so as to replenish the god realms with new gods.

When he disciplines incorrigible evildoers
with suitable punishments,
the king achieves fame,
the splendor of the kingdom increases,
and living beings will be happy."

Bear the meaning of these words in mind.

The Lord Buddha taught
that before, a long time ago,
a king named Balendraketu
had a son named Ruciraketu,
who received this treatise from his father, who said,
"By properly relying on this work,
while I served as king for 20,000 years,
never once did I commit
an unrighteous deed."
Let contemporary kings
also think about these words of our teacher. [58]

9. On Constancy and Perseverance

Just as the great ocean is unchanging,
neither increasing nor decreasing,
likewise, good rulers are constant,
never wavering from righteousness.

Both the Ancient and New Schools[1] maintain
that one ought to chiefly uphold one thing:
the ancestral tradition.
To do otherwise increases unhappiness.

So long as the lineages of those who hold
ministerial and other such positions
are properly maintained,
the ancient system will not deteriorate, which is a beautiful thing.

The system of religious patronage and political governance
should be preserved just as it was in the ancient tradition.
When a few improper actions, not previously known, begin to
  proliferate
this is a sign of impending destruction.[2]

1. This refers to (1) the Nyingma or Ancient School of Tibetan Buddhism, Mipham's own school, which chiefly follows the earlier translations (*snga 'gyur*) of the Indian texts, and to (2) the Sarma or New Schools (Sakya, Kagyu, Gelug, etc.), which follow the later translations (*phyi 'gyur*).
2. Mātṛceta, *Kaniṣkalekha*, vv. 42–43, also suggests that the king ought to follow the ancient royal traditions (*gna' yi rgyal po'i spyod pa*), but not without first critically examining them, "taking up whatever is good and putting that into practice, but . . . abandoning whatever is inappropriate, including faulty laws."

No one considers pleasing
transgressions of their own traditions.
In particular, a king's most important quality
is not to transgress righteousness.[3]

But among the people of this degenerate age
the different standards for behaviors—
pleasant and unpleasant, arrogant and humble, gentle and harsh—
are manifold and change on a daily basis.

When it is initially easy to befriend someone,
but, as the relationship develops,
the friend causes you grief for no reason,
then consider this person to be untrustworthy and of bad character.

When it is initially difficult to get to know someone,
but the relationship becomes stable and indestructible
the more you cultivate the friendship, [59]
such a person is called a resolute friend.

Evil people's moods swing back and forth like the arms of a scale.
Sometimes an insignificant thing makes them elated and conceited;
at other times, something trivial makes them disturbed and
discouraged.
That is just what ordinary people are like.[4]

The emotions that people feel
when they hear ancient folk tales
and the deeds, both good and evil, of their heroes
show people to be as silly as monkeys.

3. In this verse Mipham is playing off of two senses of the word *lugs*: (1) what is righteous or ethical, and (2) a system or tradition.
4. Compare to Vararuci, *Śatagāthā*, v. 53. On the importance of repaying other people's kindness, see also the *Nāgarājabherī Gāthā*, vv. 26–27, Lha sa ed., fols. 314a–20b. There is no critical edition of this work and so the verse enumeration is my own.

Most praise and blame, and most sweet and harsh words
will fade away like echoes,
but stupid people argue to the point of exhaustion over such words,
like dogs who bark when startled by a noise.

Because happiness and suffering are uncertain,
the things that appear to us in saṃsāra are like a dream.
Don't be arrogant when things go your way.
Don't be discouraged when they don't.[5]

People who forget the kindness of others
are the lowest of human beings.
Those who appreciate and repay others' kindness
are considered glorious lords among people.[6]

It is true that one should keep track of
even the smallest favors received,
but a king will not get easily exhilarated over trivial favors
that are like the water that accumulates in a hoofprint.[7]

Evil people vacillate every which way,
like gourds floating on the ocean.
The greatest being in this world
is a ruler who is as immovable as Mount Meru.

Like an elder witnessing the spectacle
of children playing games,
you should get neither angry nor elated
at the actions of silly people.

5. Compare to Nāgārjuna, *Ratnāvalī*, v. 3.73, and to Ravigupta, *Lokasaṃvyavahārapravṛtti*, v. 147ab.
6. *Jantupoṣaṇabindu*, v. 27: "The ocean, Mount Meru, the continents, and all of the lands of the earth are not such a personal burden (to have to carry). An unrepaid favor in the world is a truly great personal burden." Compare also to Sakya Paṇḍita, *Sa skya legs bshad*, v. 276.
7. By comparison to the water in the ocean, the amount of water that accumulates in a hoofprint is insignificant. Likewise, although the king never forgets small favors, he does not marvel at them since the scope of his activity and his perspective is vast.

When honorable people make a promise,
they do not go back on their word even in trivial matters. [60]
How then could they renege on an oath
in a matter of great importance?[8]

People do not venerate
anyone whose speech and actions are haphazard.
But it is difficult for anyone to go against
the words of someone who speaks meaningfully.

When someone's commitments are as stable as mountains,
all his aims are accomplished.
When someone threatens an individual who has such confidence,
even the gods fear the repercussions.[9]

People whose minds are unstable
accomplish nothing—either spiritually or materially.
Their deeds are many, but their achievements are few.
They make big promises, but their legacy is small.

People who are steadfast
accomplish whatever they set their minds on
by exerting themselves over long periods of time,
just as the ocean fills up one drop at a time.[10]

A few good qualities sometimes rub off
on someone with an unstable mind,
but these qualities do not last long and quickly disappear,
like the scent of camphor on stone.

8. Compare to *Prajñādaṇḍa*, v. 11; and to Vararuci, *Śatagāthā*, v. 93. In these texts the wise are said to make few promises, but once made, they are as stable as something etched in stone.
9. Compare to *Prajñādaṇḍa*, v. 96.
10. Mātṛceta, *Kaniṣkalekha*, vv. 14–15. "When you listen to holy beings from time to time, collecting a little bit from them on each occasion, it is certain that before long you will have a lot to show for it. Is there any vessel that would not be filled when a continuous stream of waterdrops falls into it without interruption?"

Do not follow everything told to you
by people with varying opinions.
Instead, first analyze their claims well,
and then do not deviate from those that are worthy.

A weak mind that is like a bubble of water
accomplishes nothing in either the spiritual or temporal spheres.
All proper goals are easily accomplished
with indestructible, diamond-like fortitude.

Just as Meru, king of mountains, surrounded by a diamond fence,
stands immovable at the center of the earth,
likewise, the earthly ruler, steadfast and resolute in righteousness,
surpasses everyone on the face of the earth. [61]

He is not moved by the waves of evil friends.
He is not swayed by the winds of sudden conceptual thoughts.
Enjoying a state of permanent stability, the Lord of Mountains
outshines even the highest peaks of suspended thought.[11]

Those who are steadfast
have great fortitude and indefatigable perseverance.
Hence, no matter what actions they undertake,
discouraging thoughts never occur to them.[12]

When you do not give up on a project,
you eventually accomplish the highest aims.
Even though it is difficult to budge a boulder,
you can get it to the peak of the mountain a bit at a time.[13]

11. The Tibetan for "suspended thought" reads *sems med*, literally, no-mind. The reference may be to certain high meditation states in which ordinary consciousness (*'du shes*) temporarily ceases. People who cultivate such *samādhis* are said to be reborn into a distinctive god realm called the *asamjñisamāpatti*.
12. Compare to Vararuci, *Śatagāthā*, v. 17ab.
13. Pushing a boulder to the top of a mountain is a common metaphor in various Sanskrit verses (e.g., *Prajñādaṇḍa*, v. 68), but Mipham's use of the metaphor here is distinctive as far as I can tell.

When fools agree to some course of action,
at first they keep their focus, but in the end they lose it.
When sages commit to some plan,
they may be initially casual, but in the end they are focused.

It is difficult to get holy beings to initially agree to do something,
but once they have agreed,
their resolve is as firm as a drawing etched on stone.
They will not go back on their word even if it means their death.[14]

For someone who possesses great perseverance,
even a mountaintop does not seem high,
and even the bottom of the ocean does not seem deep.
Even the gods fear
those who possess this kind of fortitude;
what need to say that human beings should be in awe of them.
This is like the case of the sea captain Great Charity
who scooped out the water of the ocean.[15]

Possessing pure perseverance
you should rely on a spiritual master
and train in many kinds of textual traditions.
By studying these, you accomplish the eye of wisdom, [62]
and then, as fearless as a lion,
you should apply this knowledge to the work you do—

14. *Prajñādaṇḍa*, v. 11.

15. The story of Great Charity (Sbyin pa chen po, *Mahādāna) is found in various collections, including the *Sūtra of the Wise Man and the Fool.* See Stanley Frye, *The Sūtra of the Wise and the Foolish*, chapter 31. It is the tale of a prince who feels compelled to give away as much of his father's wealth as possible. Coming close to depleting the royal treasury, he stops and decides to set sail in search of the wish-granting jewel, a source of infinite wealth. Although finding many other jewels and wealth, he never gives up on his original goal—fending off the attacks of venomous snakes, deadly insects, and so forth until finding not one but several different wish-granting jewels. On his return voyage home, the nāga spirits living in the ocean steal the wish-granting jewels. Great Charity then makes a vow to empty the ocean one scoop of water at a time until he retrieves the jewels. "There is nothing one cannot do if one truly wishes to. . . . My mind knows no fatigue; it never wearies." The worldly gods are so impressed with Great Charity's perseverance that in the end they come to his aid and he recovers the jewels.

to work that is worthy and fitting,
and especially to the most important of tasks.[16]

Those who rely on inferior people as guides will decline.
Those who rely on their equals remain as they are.
Those who rely on the best of people will achieve holiness.
Therefore, rely on someone superior to you.

It is rare for someone to possess all good qualities,
but it is also rare for someone to have no good qualities.
Relying on someone who possesses a preponderance of good qualities,
forget their faults and emulate their good qualities.[17]
You are empowered even if you are touched on the head
with a ritual vase that is only half filled with water.[18]

It is very difficult to respect
a common person who has little learning and great pride.
Evil people act wholesomely
so long as they are poor and humble,
but as soon as they obtain riches and honor
their true nature comes out.

The best of people are those who, though young, admire the
 peacefulness of elders;
who, when they become scholars, are not proud of their knowledge;
who, despite their great charisma, are patient and gentle;
who, though having attained the heights, are devoid of arrogance.[19]

16. Mātṛceta, *Kaniṣkalekha*, v. 17: "For your own sake, cultivate relationships with good people who can help you to strive in virtue—people who are wise, compassionate, grateful to others, and not stingy in giving Dharma."
17. Compare to Sakya Paṇḍita, *Sa skya legs bshad*, v. 212.
18. The first of the tantric empowerment rituals is the vase empowerment (*bum dbang*), which is achieved when the master touches the vase to the top of the adept's head. Mipham is making the point that to obtain this empowerment, the vase does not have to be filled to the brim. Likewise, to become a wise person, one does not need a perfect teacher, a master who is perfected in all forms of learning and who possesses all good qualities.
19. The verse is essentially identical to *Prajñādaṇḍa*, v. 91.

Who will not obtain exalted status
when they associate with the very powerful?
People wear the thread of the flower garland around their heads
(because it still contains the smell of the flowers).[20]

When you associate with the holy, however,
it is your mind that comes to possess good qualities.[21]
When a stone is placed next to the *kaustubha* jewel,[22]
it is transformed into gold.

Of what use is a garland of flowers to a donkey? [63]
Of what use is delicious food to a pig?
What good is light to the blind or music to the deaf?
Of what use is the Dharma to idiots?[23]

If you do not pay homage to masters,
even if they have taught you only a single verse,
it is said that you will have to pass through a hundred rebirths as a dog,
only to then be reborn in other states of woe.[24]

20. Identical lines are found in *Prajñādaṇḍa*, v. 94, and in Vararuci, *Śatagāthā*, v. 83. Mipham, however, reworks the sense of the verse by adding another one (the next verse). The meaning then becomes that befriending or associating with the powerful gets you some worldly benefit, but this is limited (the thread of the garland). On the other hand, befriending the holy, as the next verse implies, brings much greater benefit, since it has the power to transform the mind.
21. Cāṇakya, *Rājanītiśāstra*, v. 1.6: "When you associate with the holy, converse with the wise, and befriend people who are not greedy, you will have no regrets." See also Cāṇakya, *Rājanītiśāstra*, v. 8.10.
22. This is the name of a famous magical jewel that emerged during the churning of the ocean, one of the most famous Indian cosmogonic myths. The jewel is said to be worn by Viṣṇu on his chest. Mipham implies that, like the philosopher's stone, it has the ability to turn ordinary rocks into gold.
23. An identical verse is found in *Prajñādaṇḍa*, v. 219, and in Vararuci, *Śatagāthā*, v. 43. Compare also to Sakya Paṇḍita, *Sa skya legs bshad*, v. 244.
24. Almost identical lines are found in *Prajñādaṇḍa*, v. 235; and in Cāṇakya, *Rājanītiśāstra*, v. 8.54. In the latter, the consequence of not paying homage to the teacher is different, however: "He will be reborn one hundred times as a crow, and then be reborn as a butcher." Compare also to *Prajñādaṇḍa*, vv. 186, 236: "If a master teaches a student only a single verse, there is not enough wealth on the face of the earth for [the student] to repay him." This latter verse is also found verbatim in Cāṇakya, *Rājanītiśāstra*, v. 8.53. See also Nāgārjuna, *Ratnāvalī*, v. 3.36.

The mind should be trained while one is still young.
The cow should be nourished during winter.
The fields should be sown when they are moist and warm.
These three are the conditions that ensure a good result.[25]

The ant hill, honey,
the waxing moon, the trained mind,
the wealth of the king, and the wealth of the beggar
all increase in small increments.[26]

What is the point of advertising your worth
when you are still striving to achieve good qualities?
To feign greatness while devoid of good qualities
is but to bring disgrace upon yourself.[27]

How can good qualities and vast objectives be achieved
by someone who is distracted by trivial forms of happiness?
Hence, while you are studying, train in good qualities,
ignoring all sufferings that you may be experiencing.

The cultural sciences[28] and the treatises of the holy
cannot be understood without studying them.
Study opens the fine eye of intelligence,
allowing you to see everything that is to be accepted and rejected.

Knowledge that does not rely
on a truly wise teacher

25. The verse is almost identical to Vararuci, *Śatagāthā*, v. 1, and to *Jantupoṣaṣabinḍu*, v. 19. The latter reads: "Study the sciences in your youth. Those who want yogurt (or milk) start (feeding the cow) in winter. Plant the seed when it is warm. These three bring about their effects quickly."

26. The verse is identical to *Prajñādaṇḍa*, v. 29; to Cāṇakya, *Rājanītiśāstra*, v. 6.3; and to Vararuci, *Śatagāthā*, v. 37.

27. Compare to Sakya Paṇḍita, *Sa skya legs bshad*, vv. 206, 266.

28. There are many enumerations of the classical cultural sciences (*vidyāsthāna*, *rig gnas*), but a standard ten-member list includes five major sciences—grammar, medicine, arts and crafts, logic, the "inner" science of Buddhist spirituality—and five minor ones that include poetry, etymology, metrics, drama, and astrology.

is as unreliable
as the son of a prostitute.[29]

But those who rely on wise and holy individuals
and on an exalted and worthy lineage [64]
are held in high esteem by others
simply because of the source of their knowledge.

When you have properly completed your studies,
you shine like the sun even if you know but a single text.
Those who pride themselves on having memorized many texts
but are filled with doubts about all of them are like the less
luminous stars.

Single-pointedly analyze the meaning of what you study
using the path of reasoning.
Unless you find certainty born of critical analysis,
you are mostly just repeating what you hear and read, like a parrot.

If you do not investigate what is right and wrong,
and do not strive to learn and to make merit,
how different are you from an animal
who spends its time filling its belly and having sex?[30]

Make an effort even if you have grown old and decrepit,
and cultivate the wisdom born from study and thinking.
When your consciousness has been infused with such learning in the
present life
you will become a sage in another life.[31]

29. The verse is similar to Cāṇakya, *Rājanītiśāstra*, v. 8.55, which, however, uses a different metaphor: "Knowledge that comes from studying books, and not from studying under a guru, is said to be as ugly in society as a pregnant prostitute."
30. The verse is very similar to Vararuci, *Śatagāthā*, v. 51. Compare also to *Jantupoṣaṇabinḍu*, v. 17: "Therefore exert yourself in learning even at the risk to your life. Someone who does not train in good qualities is like a dumb animal."
31. The verse is very similar to Vararuci, *Śatagāthā*, v. 2; and to *Prajñādaṇḍa*, v. 133.

Knowledge that just stays in books,
Tantra that has not been accomplished,
and belongings that have not been stored away:
it is difficult for these things to be available to you when you
need them.[32]

The ruler ought to dedicate himself in a timely manner to two things:
preparations for this life and the next,
and meeting all of the needs of his subjects.
He ought not to procrastinate due to laziness.

It is difficult to accomplish even small goals
if you are devoid of perseverance.
But when you possess perseverance,
it's as if all good qualities are already in your hand.

You are your own protector. [65]
Who else can protect you?[33]
Therefore, those who know what is good for them
strive hard to achieve good qualities.

If you want to make your enemy unhappy,
cultivate your own good qualities.
An angry mind and harsh words
do not vanquish others; they only hurt you.[34]

32. Compare to *Prajñādaṇḍa*, v. 164, where the point is to denigrate "knowledge stored in a book" and "money requested from others," neither of which are available when you need them. See also Sakya Paṇḍita, *Sa skya legs bshad*, v. 242.

33. The first two lines of this verse are found throughout the twenty-third chapter of the *Udānavarga*, the chapter on "Self." *Udānavarga*, Lha sa ed., fols. 351b–352b; and for the Sanskrit, see "Udānavarga Home Page," *Ancient Buddhist Texts*. www.ancient-buddhist-texts.net/Buddhist-Texts/S1-Udanavarga/23-Atma.htm.

34. Compare to *Nāgarājabherī Gāthā*, v. 25, Lha sa ed., fol. 315b: "If a wise person wishes to make his enemies unhappy, he eliminates the faults from his own mind; that is what will harm that [enemy]." *Prajñāśataka*, v. 88: "Any wise person in this world who wishes to make his enemies' heart ache will always accumulate more personal good qualities." *Jantupoṣaṇabinḍu*, v. 28: "If an intelligent person wishes to upset his enemies, he is gentle—not speaking harshly to them, and using only sweet words. This is what really harms them." Compare also to Vararuci, *Śatagāthā*, v. 30, and to *Prajñādaṇḍa*, v. 36.

When superior people find they are in trouble and declining,[35]
their courage and intelligence especially increases.
When a place is overcome by heavy darkness,
that is when you especially need to light lamps.

Hating something does not destroy[36] it,
and liking something does not assist you in obtaining it.
What then is the point of hating or liking something
when doing so cannot destroy or safeguard it?

People who do not repay a favor
and who do not avenge a harm
are despised by everyone,
like a useless cairn along the road.[37]

Wise people, the best of beings,
repay even the smallest kindness in great measure.
They are not perturbed, remaining unmoved like the earth,
even when others cause them great harm.
And vice versa for those who have not attained such a saintly state.

Everyone holds rulers in high regard[38]
when they understand what is beneficial and harmful
and have the power to destroy and protect.
But in some places people may bestow political power on someone
because they admire his ability to decapitate people,
thinking that there is little point to calling someone "ruler"
if he does not have great power.

Even if others dare you to do something,
you should resist it if it's something you can't do.

35. I've emended *nyam* to *nyams*.
36. I've emended *'jigs med* to *'jig med*.
37. A *tho yor* or "cairn" is a heap of stones usually found on mountain paths to help guide people along the way, but sometimes people pile up stones for no apparent reason, and these types of cairns are functionally useless.
38. I've emended *de srid* to *sde srid*.

Who would jump into a fire simply because others say,
"Wow! That would be fantastic!"[39] [66]

But when you see that you do have the skill to do something,
and can accomplish the goal no matter how difficult,
then you shouldn't stop yourself, even if others try to block you.

You should accomplish even minor tasks
with a great deal of caution,
as carefully as experts collect gems
from the heads of poisonous snakes.[40]
Never undertake anything frivolously.

Sane people should not engage
in the dangerous deeds
that self-destructive people undertake,
like having sex with a leper woman.[41]

People who eat proper foods
never suffer from food-born illness.
Likewise, those who examine a situation
rarely encounter problems in their work.

Those who are attached to small goals
do not attain the highest happiness.
So expand your perspective as much as you can
and set your sites on the very best quality.

As regards attainments, you can even achieve godhood.
As regards conquest, you can even level mountains.

39. The four lines of this verse are identical to *Prajñāśataka*, v. 57.
40. The metaphor of the jewel on the head of the snake is also found in *Prajñāśataka*, v. 13, and in Cāṇakya, *Rājanītiśāstra*, v. 5.16, but those verses are otherwise quite different. For example, the Cāṇakya verse reads: "Even if they are endowed with the ornament of knowledge, bad people ought to be avoided. Even if snakes are ornamented with a jewel, they're really dangerous, aren't they?"
41. I've emended *mdze can mer* to *mdze can mar*.

Hence, you should constantly strive for your goals
without ever feeling discouraged.

There is nothing that doesn't get easier
the more you accustom yourself to it.
Geese and vultures
are accustomed to enjoying charnel grounds.

Powerful lions who always eat flesh and blood
have sex only once a year.
Donkeys who will stoop to eat the dust
have constant, casual sex.[42]

The dispassionate have become weary of desire through training.
Beings follow their minds, [67]
and their minds follow what they have accustomed themselves to.
That is why controlling your own mind is the highest spiritual
accomplishment.

Living creatures are driven by their karma.
They mostly have no freedom.
But karma is created by the mind,
so be diligent about taming your mind.

In this entire world there is no distinguishing
between happiness and suffering.[43]
Whether you accomplish a worldly or a supramundane goal
depends wholly on you.

Hence, lion-like individuals
are those who give rise to this thought:
"I will bring about my goals on my own
without depending on others."

42. Compare to Vararuci, *Śatagāthā*, v. 40.
43. I take Mipham to be saying that even the greatest forms of worldly happiness have some degree of suffering associated with them, if only because they eventually end.

When wind stokes a fire,
it can burn down a dense forest.
Likewise, those who exert themselves in acquiring the right methods
will emerge victorious over whatever obstacles they face.[44]

They will ascend to heaven on the ladder of virtue
and will make their own a great ocean of glory and wealth.
To invite a universal assembly as your guests requires that you persevere
as if this goal is already in the palm of your hand.

44. Exertion (*utthita*) is also praised in a variety of Brahmanical sources as an essential quality of a king. See, e.g., *Arthaśāstra* (1.19.1).

10. The Disciplined Ruler

Those good rulers who, while possessing abundant glory and wealth,
are also exceedingly disciplined [68]
are like the moon shining in a cloudless sky,
surrounded by a garland of stars.

People with inferior qualities have great pride.
Those with the best qualities are devoid of arrogance.
An ear of corn without kernels thinks it's perfect from its height,
while fine ripened rice remains low to the ground and humble.[1]

It is ugly to praise yourself,
even if you are the god Indra.[2]
So be steady like the ocean
without spewing out tidbits of nonsense.[3]

There is no fault like pride.
It is the special enemy of the learned.
It strikes down those who are poised for greatness.
It prevents you from seeing your own faults.

1. On the evils of pride, see also *Nāgarājabherī Gāthā*, vv. 28–30, Lha sa ed., fol. 316a. The comparison of the humble person to ripened rice is also found in Vararuci, *Śatagāthā*, v. 94, and in *Prajñādaṇḍa*, v. 44.
2. The first two lines of this verse are almost identical to *Prajñādaṇḍa*, v. 156cd. Compare also to Nāgārjuna, *Ratnāvalī*, v. 3.68, and to *Jantupoṣaṇabiṇḍu*, v. 4: "One ought not to praise oneself. Whoever praises himself or herself is considered small-minded and weak in wisdom."
3. Compare to Vararuci, *Śatagāthā*, v. 21.

People dislike the proud from the moment they see them.
Others compete with them for their fame.
The demon of pride possesses the proud,
beckoning them to a banquet of insults.

Other demons can be tamed through spells,
but when you speak nicely to the proud,
it is like offering milk to snakes:
it just doesn't pacify them.[4]

You can't get rid of the naturally foul smell of garlic
even by using unguents like sandalwood, musk, and camphor.
It is difficult for the proud to abandon their naturally bad character
even if they have trained in many holy texts.[5]

Pride is like an ornament to those individuals
who have reached the loftiest of heights, like the peak of Mount Meru;
who know how to speak elegantly; who trust in what is right;
and who have self-confidence in decrying injustice. [69]

To exhibit self-confidence only when happy and wealthy;
not to listen even when things are explained; to denigrate everyone;
to lose courage when a dangerous situation arises:
these are the signs of the vulgar.

To beg from others and hope for delicious meals,
to live on alms and yet be arrogant,
and to be ignorant of the treatises and yet want to debate:
these are the three causes of laughter in the world.[6]

4. *Prajñaśataka*, v. 91: "When you pour out some milk for a snake, it only makes its poison stronger. Giving advice to evil people only makes them angrier and not more peaceful." Compare also to *Prajñādaṇḍa*, v. 239; to *Jantupoṣaṇabinḍu*, v. 6; and to Sakya Paṇḍita, *Sa skya legs bshad*, v. 177.

5. The verse is more or less the same as *Prajñādaṇḍa*, v. 176, and as Vararuci, *Śatagāthā*, v. 54. It is also found in some of the stray verses of Ravigupta in the anthologies of classical poetry; see Hahn, "Ravigupta and his Nīti Stanzas (II)," 37.

6. The verse is identical to *Prajñādaṇḍa*, v. 40; Vararuci, *Śatagāthā*, v. 69; and Sakya Paṇḍita, *Sa skya legs bshad*, v. 259.

Riches and respect make fools proud
and hide their faults.
Praise destroys the vulgar man
just as pregnancy does a female mule.[7]

The higher an achievement holy beings attain,
the more disciplined they become and the more they strive to
help others.
Their fame spreads in all directions
simply through word of mouth.

The sweet fragrance of flowers only travels in the direction of the wind,
but the sweet news of exalted beings' fame spreads in all directions.
Even if they are disciplined and try to hide their good qualities,[8]
word of their virtue spreads from one person to another, bringing them
satisfaction.

Due to the meagerness of their good qualities, of their lineage, body,
learning, and so forth,
ignorant people, puffed up with pride,
and as arrogant as frogs in a well,[9]
have a special dislike of holy beings.

Still, this does not impede the good qualities of the holy;
instead, it causes the egotists' good qualities—both present and
future—to become depleted.
It is like those who hold a torch upside down
and in the process burn their own hands.[10] [70]

7. Most mules—both male and female—are infertile, but pregnancy, though extremely rare, is possible. Indian oral lore has it that female mules who get pregnant will almost certainly die. Masūrākṣa, *Nītiśāstra*, v. 6.12, and Cāṇakya, *Rājanītiśāstra*, v. 3.15 both use this example to make another point: "Someone who reconciles with an individual who used to be an enemy is flirting with death like a pregnant female mule."
8. The idea of hiding one's own good qualities is found in a number of sources, including Cāṇakya, *Rājanītiśāstra*, v. 7.6cd: "Hide your own good qualities like a turtle hides its limbs."
9. Frogs who live in a well believe they know the whole world (including the ocean), when in fact they only know what is found within the confines of the well.
10. Similar analogies are found in a variety of sources including a verse autobiography by

It is a huge mistake for those who have elevated to higher and
higher levels
the good qualities of their lineage, body, wealth, learning, and so forth,
to compete with small-minded people who have only an average
lineage, and so on,
and to act proudly in front of them.

When the proud are not putting others down,
their qualities, although small, can appear to be great.
But when their words are infused with the poison of pride,
their wealth and learning seem small, no matter how great they may be.

Those blinded by desire cannot see sin.
Those who are blind from birth cannot see forms.
Those who are arrogant cannot see their own faults.[11]
Those who believe in the self cannot see reality.[12]

What intelligent people respect,
lesser beings despise.
The stūpas worshipped by sages
are used as perches by crows.[13]

Just like shit thrown into the sky
falls back onto your own head,
when you rely on a disreputable and proud person
it rebounds on you in the form of disaster.

But just by associating
with a sagely, upright, and disciplined person,

Könchog Jigmé Wangpo: "Those who hold the torch of slander upside down will burn the limbs of their virtues." *Rgyal sras rgya mtsho 'jug ngogs*, Asian Classics ed., fol. 4a.

11. Cāṇakya, *Rājanītiśāstra*, v. 6.22: "Bad people think that even the smallest thing is someone else's fault. They do not see themselves as having even the slightest fault."

12. *Prajñādaṇḍa*, v. 62. On the doctrine of no-self, see also Nāgārjuna, *Ratnāvalī*, vv. 1.27–37, 1.80–83, and *Suhṛllekha*, vv. 48–50.

13. An almost identical verse is found in *Prajñādaṇḍa*, v. 153, and in Vararuci, *Śatagāthā* v. 91. See also Ravigupta, *Lokasaṃvyavahārapravṛtti*, v. 153; Hahn, "Ravigupta and his Nīti Stanzas (II)," 20.

your good qualities, glory, and fame increase,
as if you had acquired a crown made out of jewels.

Just as a host of elemental spirits protect you
when you keep the name of the Lord of Secrets in your heart,
those who have a relationship with sagely beings of high lineage
are also worshipped.

Of what use is pride to great beings? [71]
When they lack pride, they are all the more beautiful.
Of what benefit is pride to the lowly?
When they have pride, they are all the more despised.

Befriending foolish people who possess the three faults—
pride, jealousy, and dishonesty—
just increases their evil.
Keeping them at a distance, you obtain happiness.

It's easy when good people become your enemies:
when you reconcile, they help you.
But evil people, who are more malicious than a poisonous snake,
should never be befriended.

When you befriend them, they get angry.
When you help them, they think you're up to no good.
When you speak truthfully, they rise up against you.
Evil beings cannot be cured.

Knowing this, no sage
will attempt to entice them through his sweetness.
Instead, like the forceful methods needed to cure a phlegm illness,
the skillful person will treat them aggressively.[14]

14. See *Prajñādaṇḍa*, v. 87, where the analogy to the phlegm disease functions in precisely the opposite manner, for the aggressive treatment of phlegm is said to cause it to increase. However, a later *Prajñādaṇḍa* verse (v. 245) more closely resembles Mipham's here: "Ema! Evil people and phlegm disease both have the same nature. Treating them mildly makes them worse, while treating them aggressively pacifies them." See also Hahn, "The Tibetan *Shes rab sdong bu* and its Indian Sources (III)," 339–40.

Most honest people are defeated.
Most sweet people are despised.
How can it be fitting for sweet and honest people
to have relationships with evil fools?

Evil men, gold, drums,
unruly horses, and haughty women:
When you beat these five, they become workable.
It is a mistake to treat them sweetly.[15]

There are no lotuses on the faces of the righteous.
Horns do not grow from the heads of the unrighteous.
It is through the quality of his behavior
that the nature of a prostitute's son is known.[16]

Noble people do not [always] engage in charity,
and the proud do not [always] steal others' wealth. [72]
It is on account of their specific faults and qualities
that people should be liked or disliked.[17]

When you associate with people who are humble and noble,
this will bring you happiness and your friendship will be stable.
Reliable people bring you happiness
akin to relaxing under the deep shade of a fine, fruit-laden tree.

15. The verse is very similar to *Prajñādaṇḍa*, v. 246, and to Vararuci, *Śatagāthā*, v. 58. Both the *Prajñādaṇḍa* and *Śatagāthā* verses contain one category not mentioned in Mipham: "disrespectful servants." The *Śatagāthā* does not mention the drum; and instead of Mipham's "haughty women," the *Śatagāthā* reads "bad wives." The verse is understandably disturbing to modern sensibilities, but we must remember that corporal punishment of children, servants, and wives was encouraged (or at least condoned) in European and American culture until modern times.
16. The source of the verse is almost certainly *Prajñādaṇḍa*, v. 177. But the equivalent verse in the *Śatagāthā* (v. 60) seems to make the opposite point: that a person's body bears telltale signs of a person's character. "A noble son has a face like a lotus. Poisoned leaves grow from the brain of a prostitute's son."
17. Mipham seems to be saying that we should not be too swift to judge others by their occasional actions, but rather by their overall character. Compare this also to Ravigupta, *Lokasaṃvyavahārapravṛtti*, v. 169; Hahn, "Ravigupta and his Nīti Stanzas (II)," 22.

Those who have great pride and are undisciplined
can be of no help to you even if they are born into an exalted family,
just as the shade of a small passing cloud is of no benefit to those
seeking refuge from the sun.
Therefore, you should rely on rulers who are noble and not haughty.

They may not be the moon, but when people are humble and
disciplined, they make everyone in the three worlds rejoice.
They may not be a pool of ambrosia, but when the holy are befriended,
they serve as a source of real happiness.
Even when congregations of happy people gather together by virtue of
their common view, this does not make a society a divine pleasure
grove.
It may not be an exalted divine palace, but this work contains the
method to open the hundred doors to goodness and the happiness of
both this life and the next.

11. Balance and Impartiality

The great rulers of men
contemplate all the people of their empire
with a balanced, impartial mind that sees them all as one,
as if they were contemplating a vast world from high above.[1]

Partiality and bias are ugly
even in regards to sailors on the same boat; [73]
what need to say that this is true of the one who, in his present life,
has become the captain of the multitude of beings.[2]

All of the people who are your subjects
are equal in relying on you as their chief.
Imagine the disappointment, therefore,
when there is unequal treatment of those who should be cared for
equally.

You must show affection for those who possess good qualities
and you must vanquish evil people,

1. Mipham calls this chapter *mnyam pa*. But as will become evident throughout the chapter, that word has two different senses: equality and balance. I have tried to capture this dual meaning by rendering it with two words in the chapter's title. Mipham plays off of the ambivalence. Hence, the king should treat everyone equally, but he should also cultivate the personal quality of inner balance.

2. Many sources consider impartiality to be an important attribute of the king. For example, Masūrākṣa, *Nītiśāstra*, v. 2.1cd, states: "When you are impartial toward all, like the earth is, everyone rejoices." See also Ravigupta, *Lokasaṃvyavahārapravṛtti*, v. 226; Hahn, "Ravigupta and his Nīti Stanzas (II)," 29: "Nowhere do excessive partiality or hatred amount to anything good."

showing them the consequences of their own actions.
These do not count as being biased.

How can there be any redistribution of resources
when people have individual karmic fates?
But if you are biased in regard to taxation, laws, and the protection of people,
this constitutes inequality.[3]

The king must, to the best of his ability,
protect all his jurisdictions
from enemies, dangers, and poverty.
If he fails to protect just one region, then he is not king.

Through what means should he protect them?
He protects the powerless and those who don't know how to achieve their own welfare
through a legal system:
"Do this. Don't violate that law."

Whoever violates the law
should receive the same punishment.[4]
No violator should be treated more leniently than anyone else.
When you act in this way, there is equality under the law.

Once the laws are being applied equally,
you must cultivate the happiness of living creatures.

3. People's past karma, Mipham implies, causes basic inequalities in the world. There is nothing the king can do about this. But this does not give the king license to be biased as regards the areas that are under his control: taxation, justice, and governance.

4. This is in contradistinction to other South Asian legal traditions that see legal punishment (*daṇḍa*) as dependent on a person's class, social standing, or caste. See, for example, the Mahābhārata (*Śāntiparva*, chapter 15, v. 9), which explains that brahmins should be punished with words (*vacidaṇḍa*, i.e., censure); kṣatriyas (members of the warrior caste) by confiscating their property (*bhujārpaṇa*) except for what is necessary to survive; vaiśyas (merchants) by imposing fines and forfeiture of possessions (*dānadaṇḍa*); for śudras there is little or no punishment (*nirdaṇḍa*) since śudras have no wealth to speak of and are already engaged in menial work for the upper classes. Pratap Chandra Roy, *The Mahabharata of Krishna-Dwipayana Vyasa*, vol. 8, 26.

With a sense of kindness, kings collect, at the proper time,
taxes consisting of a sixth part.[5]

The kings of this degenerate age
do not properly care for living beings.
They act like shameless household servants
in their practice of tax collection.[6] [74]

Shameless servants constantly collect for their own use
whatever food and drink they see.
When they see hard work ahead, they quickly flee.
They want wages without doing any work.

What is the just way of collecting taxes?
They should be collected impartially from everyone,[7]
based on a sliding scale that depends on people's wealth.
When taxes are collected inequitably, how can there be equality?

You should collect what is owed in taxes and services from all your subjects
taking into account the region, the time, and people's wealth.
You should not cause harm to farms or estates,
nor torment those who are unable to pay.

5. A fixed tax of one-sixth of the harvest is known to the ancient Indian law codes. The *Arthaśāstra* (2.15.3) also mentions a one-sixth share, but Rangarajan suggests that agricultural taxes were much higher and depended on a variety of factors such as who provided the seed, water, and so forth. See L. N. Rangarajan, *The Arthashatra*, 229. The Mahābhārata also speaks of a tax of one-sixth (*Śāntiparva*, chapter 71; Roy, *The Mahābhārata*, vol. 8, 164). In Tibet, the one-sixth tax is found in the law codes of Tai Situ Jangchub Gyaltsen (1302–1364 or 1371), which replaced the old Mongol law codes when Situ assumed power in the mid-fourteenth century. See David Snellgrove and Hugh Richardson, *A Cultural History of Tibet*, 153. Taxes on agricultural produce was of course only one of the sources of revenue in ancient South Asian polities. There were also taxes on other products (such as textiles, alcohol, forest products, etc.), and on recreational services (such as prostitution, entertainment, and gambling). There were also sales taxes. Levies and legal fines were also important sources of revenue. See Rangarajan, *The Arthashastra*, chapter 5, section ii.
6. Nāgārjuna, *Ratnāvalī*, vv. 3.52–53, encourages reducing the tax rate and reducing tolls.
7. Again, this is in contradistinction to some Hindu law codes that claim that brahmins are exempt from taxes. See Mahābhārata, *Śāntiparva*, chapter 71; Roy, *The Mahābhārata*, vol. 8, 165.

A herdsman plucks flowers, leaving their roots intact.
Likewise, it is wrong to damage the root of a person's livelihood.[8]
If the root deteriorates,
from whom will the king henceforth take his taxes?

The wealth that your subjects achieve
through the work of their own hands is not extensive.
Only rarely is the annual food, drink, and clothing they obtain
enough to lead a worry free life.

Even if you only collect small amounts of taxes
from many cities, the combined revenue is substantial.
Therefore, the king should collect his taxes in small quantities,
with a sense of pity for his people.

It is fitting that everyone pitch in proportionately to ensure the king's welfare
through the taxes they pay, the work they do, and so forth.
When wealth and poverty are equalized through taxation,
all the subjects will be happy.

Some people enjoy freedom no matter what they do.
Others constantly suffer from being dependent on others.
But living creatures never have peace of mind
in kingdoms in which there is too much inequality. [75]

It is improper for subjects to compete
in their service to holy objects of veneration,

8. For instance, the king should not confiscate a farmer's fields as tax. The Mahābhārata (*Śāntiparva*, chapter 71) uses a vivid metaphor: "Someone who wants milk never obtains it by cutting off the cow's udders." A king, the text continues, should be like a flower farmer and not like a coal miner—that is, he should not seize from people any wealth or property that is non-renewable, and that leaves them destitute." The flower cutter and coal miner analogies are also found in Vararuci, *Śatagāthā*, v. 36, and in *Prajñādaṇḍa*, v. 8. Cāṇakya, *Rājanītiśāstra*, v. 4.3 and 4.7 has a longer treatment of this topic and uses other examples as well: "Use the kingdom as you would [a hive filled with] honey—without killing the bees. The king governs his land as if he were milking a cow."

and in their expressions of gratitude to those worthy of offerings,
but it's fine if they do this in a balanced way that accords with their status.

Because of people's karma,
even the Buddha could not guarantee
equal amounts of happiness and suffering to everyone.
What need to say that other kings are incapable of achieving this.

Nonetheless, when kings,
guided by the principles of parity and equality,
act in a balanced and unbiased way
everyone—both high and low—will heed their commands.

Because a king is the common sovereign of everyone,
his deeds should not be biased,
he should not speak in a partisan manner,
nor should his practice of generosity be partisan.

Chiefly upholding his own religion,
if, no matter what he does to benefit the teachings,
other religious systems condemn him,
this is not the fault of the king, but of his subjects.

If, however, he cherishes his own religious system,
and he persecutes other religions,
whatever condemnation occurs
is not the fault of the subjects, but of the king.

Therefore, the king properly protects
any ancient religious systems, each with its own traditions,
that may exist within his kingdom,
from the non-Buddhist heterodox religions on up.[9]

9. Nāgārjuna, *Ratnāvalī*, v. 3.37, advises the king not to respect, revere, or pay homage to non-Buddhist religions. So too does the *Smṛtyupasthāna*. See appendix 2, numbers 9 and 23.

Neither creating a pastiche out of them,
nor inciting mutual conflict,
he cares for them individually so that they do not degenerate.
This is the way of caring for living beings. [76]

Except for certain special instances,[10]
he should neither encourage nor hinder
the unnecessary and nonsensical partisan chatter that may flare up
among different sects, groups, and ranks of people.

When, without bias,
he makes occasional gifts to these religious groups,
the people can rejoice and say,
"This ruler is truly impartial."[11]

When you are not extravagant
in your attire, behavior, and so forth,
and remain continuously balanced,
you are following the way of noble people.

When praised, you should not be proud.
When criticized, you should not get discouraged.
The king who is always balanced
is brilliant.

With a broad vision that looks toward the future,
the king cares even for enemies as if they were his sons,
and eventually he brings those enemies under his control.
This is the quality of magnanimity.

10. Mipham does not specify what these instances are, but texts like the *Smṛtyupasthāna Sūtra* suggest that the reference might be to nihilists—people who deny karma, past and future lives, etc. (see appendix 2). But Mipham may instead (or also) have certain practices, like animal sacrifice, in mind here.

11. This portion of Mipham's text might be read as a reference to the trans-sectarian tradition known as rimé (see the introduction), but it can also be read as a general defense of religious nonpartisanship, and of the king's duty to maintain an impartial stance in regard to the religions that flourish in his kingdom.

When his intelligence becomes as wide as the ocean,
childish beings cannot fully grasp his accomplishments.
These foolish people then babble nonsense about him.
How odd the behavior of unstable people!

Because a king's goals and attainments are great,
he should not focus on minor matters.
No matter how much he spends on bringing other lands under his
control,
he does not become poor.

It is difficult for small-minded people to fathom
those whose minds are expansive and all-encompassing.
For a short-sighted[12] individual,
today is more important than tomorrow.

Like a fly caught in a spiderweb,
fools become attached to the details,
and cannot give counsel concerning great goals.
They constantly discourage themselves. [77]

Wealth attracts more wealth,
and one accomplishment brings about another.
That is why sages do not become at all discouraged
when they see the great goals that lie ahead.

First, examine a situation well and dispel doubt.
In between, be fearless about whatever you have undertaken.
In the end, sages are always happy and have no regrets
regardless of the good or bad that might have ensued.

No matter what action they engage in,
it is rare for fools to lack fear, regret, or doubt.
For the most part, the actions of sages
lack these three, and so they are happy.

12. I've emended *zung* to *thung*.

It is difficult to accomplish a great deed
in a short time and with little means;
but there is nothing that cannot be accomplished
when you work at it for a long time with great means.

For the righteous, accomplishments are the main thing.
They understand in great detail the methods needed
to increase their good qualities, learning,
glory, and power.

For the sake of the things they hope to accomplish,
they will give up food, wealth, and riches as if these were hay.
Ignoring whatever is unpleasant,
they will even hire out their bodies like slaves.[13]

People who are concerned only with accumulating wealth
may give away food, but they always protect their wealth.
Vulgar people take the opposite approach:
they are obsessed with contemplating food.

They obsess about it at the time of the harvest;
and when they need it, they get upset at having to use it.
One accumulates wealth so as to use it;
to accumulate it and not to spend it is a cause of suffering.[14]

Deeds are like specks of dust: no matter how "fine" they are,
a vision that is as broad as the earth is better. [78]
Good and evil are like rainbows: no matter how "clear" they are,
a courageous mind as expansive as space is best.[15]

13. There is an old Buddhist tale in which a destitute couple sell themselves into slavery in order to raise money to make offerings to the monastic community, thinking that this is the only way for them to escape poverty in the next life. In the end they are ransomed by a prince who is amazed at their piety. See Édouard Huber, *Sūtrālaṃkāra*, 429–33.
14. Compare to Vararuci, *Śatagāthā*, v. 46, where the point is that one should take care of one's body and forget about riches.
15. Mipham means that actions—whether good or evil—are always secondary to one's mental attitude, which should be expansive and broad in scope.

When your eating habits and other behavior are balanced,
your health is balanced and you live happily and disease-free.
When you treat living beings in a balanced way,
you gather around you impartial people and are praised.

When you contemplate the equality of happiness and suffering,
you always avoid pain and live happily.[16]
When you generate a balanced mind that is not attached to extremes,
you possess right view, and rest in the truth of reality.

When a man is impartial and balanced, he is a sovereign lord.
Whoever has this quality is fit to be king.
Bias acts[17] and deeds that are imbalanced
lead to breaking the law and cause many problems.

A king who is as balanced as the earth
becomes a support for the masses of beings in the world.
His good qualities are varied and vast,
and he is the source of many fine and extensive results.

16. Mipham likely means that the experience of ordinary worldly joys and suffering is part of the nature of human beings as karmically conditioned beings. Understanding this, it does not make sense to be overly perturbed by suffering, nor overly elated by worldly joys. But in a more transcendental sense—and as he states in the next two lines—both happiness and suffering emerge from the same fundamental ground of reality. When this more exalted form of "sameness" or "equality" is seen, one comes into contact with the nature of reality itself.
17. I've emended *bshes ngor* to *gzhan ngor*.

12. Compassion

Compassionate rulers
love their subjects as they would an only child.
They care for their followers
even at the cost of their own wealth and life.

Cattle sometimes harm you, but unless you affectionately care for them,
it is you who suffer, isn't it?
In the same way, you should care for your entourage,
understanding that it is in your own self-interest. [79]

The fullness of a tree's foliage
is a sign of the greatness of a tree.
The excellence of a king's retinue
is a sign of the greatness of a king's power.

The title "king"
is bestowed on someone by his subjects.
Who would call someone "king"
just because of someone's family line?

Nobles during this degenerate age
regard their subjects as fodder.
The offspring of scorpions
see their mother as food, and eat her.

The righteous kings of old
cared for their subjects

even at the cost of their own lives.
Just see what a difference there is in their attitude.

Who would not go for refuge to those
who set aside their own interests and work for the welfare of others?
The fruit-laden tree and the pleasing stream
are meeting points for all beings.

Who would consider as a refuge
those who emphasize their own interests and abandon others?[1]
What intelligent person would rely on
a fruitless tree and a polluted stream?

When you rely on supreme persons
who resemble the fine vase and the wish-fulfilling jewel,
you obtain glory and fame,
as well as happiness and excellence.

Who would rely on an evil ruler,
who, when served, brings his retinue
under the influence of faults like anger or craving,
like the toxic hala tree or a poisoned pool? [80]

Therefore, good rulers, worthwhile ones,
are those who spend both day and night thinking,
"May whoever relies on me
be free from suffering and become happy."

And even from the viewpoint of your own self-interest,
what kingly deed is more important
to accomplishing your own goals
than caring for your retinue?

1. This might well be a jibe at Brahmanical works like Masūrākṣa's *Nītiśāstra*, which states (v. 4.1): "Work for your own welfare (or material gain); do not think about the welfare of others in the same way. . . . Do not worry about others' goals; strive to bring about your own plans."

Birds do not gather
at fruitless trees and at dry lakes.
Likewise, everyone avoids
places where royal power has deteriorated.

When your kingdom is happy, it attracts even the gods.
When it is unpleasant, even your sons will flee.
The king should fill all his provinces
with prosperity as extensive as the sea.

Once he is rich in retinue and wealthy,
what power will the king not possess?
When he is wealthy, everyone is his friend.
When he falls on hard times, everyone is his enemy.[2]

The king ought to think,
"Who in this land, except for me,
can protect the most poor and powerless,
those who suffer and who have no refuge?"

Because even truly evil people
are deluded due to their faults,
the king should not be offended
and think, "They are despising me."

"Rather, he should think, because they are deluded, they even hurt their own parents
and harm the three jewels.
How can I not feel compassion
for those who show disregard for my happiness?[3]

2. Cāṇakya, *Rājanītiśāstra*, v. 2.8b–d: "When you are wealthy, everyone is your friend. When you lose your wealth and became homeless, even your family considers you an enemy." Compare also to Masūrākṣa, *Nītiśāstra*, v. 6.18: "When you lose your wealth, friends, children, wives, relatives, and even your beloved friends abandon you. When you become wealthy again, they get close once again. That is why wealth is the true friend of the world."

3. I've emended *bad ba* to *bde ba*.

"When the blind jump off a cliff [81]
they are not despising the cliff.
When people despise me due to their own karma,
they have no choice in the matter, and are just experiencing suffering."

Having generated compassion
for evil people in this way,
he threatens and banishes those whom he cannot restrain
just as a father corrects his son.

To be without your lover, to be despised by your own relatives,
to be heavily in debt, to have to rely on the wicked,
and to be abandoned by friends when they see that you are poor:
these five, although they are not fire, burn your body.[4]

People who lack compassion for the elderly, for children, for the sick,
for the downtrodden, for those who have lost their livelihood, for
    the weak,
for those who have been abandoned by the king, and for those who
    have no refuge:
these compassionless people are inhuman.[5]

Hoping, "If only I had a protector,"
the humble, crying and choked with tears,
beseech the ruler to meet their just goals.
How can you possibly bear forsaking them?

Because there are many extremely humble people
who are incapable of asking the ruler for anything,
the sagely ruler will, from time to time,
contemplate and investigate the happiness and suffering of his subjects.

4. *Prajñādaṇḍa*, v. 58, and Cāṇakya, *Rājanītiśastra*, v. 2.14.
5. The verse is found verbatim in the *Nāgarājabherī Gāthā*, v. 31, Lha sa ed., fol. 316a, and in the *Jantupoṣaṇabinḍu*, v. 34. It is also virtually identical to Cāṇakya, *Rājanītiśāstra*, v. 8.9, and to Nāgārjuna, *Ratnāvalī*, v. 4.20.

To be content with one's own happiness is vulgar.
To think about the other who is in distress is rare.
The good sovereign is the one who has the intellectual skills
to contemplate and understand others' needs.

Then think, "But when I analyze this in every possible way,
I don't see anything more dear to me than my own self.
However, every other person also holds him- or herself dear, [82]
so I will not let my personal pleasures impede others' happiness.[6]

"All beings are utterly the same
in wanting happiness and not wanting suffering,
and since, by comparison to me, other beings are destitute,
I will generate compassion for them.

"Having become the protector of those beings,
they put their hopes in me and will look to me.
It is very easy for me to give up my life for them,
but I should not make them do the same for me."

Is there anyone more shameless in the eyes of those who have a
conscience
than someone who does not provide refuge for those who lack it,
who does not, to the best of his abilities, comfort others,
or who takes the wealth of his subjects without thinking about them?

When you rely on those with good qualities,
you are never abandoned by them, even at the cost of their lives,
just like the lion Noble Limbs did
to protect the baby monkeys.[7]

6. This verse and the two that follow are based—with some modifications to fit the king's context—on Śāntideva's teachings of the "equality and exchange of self and other" found in the *Bodhicāryāvatara's* ninth chapter, vv. 179–98. See Vesna A. Wallace and B. Alan Wallace, *A Guide to the Bodhisattva Way of Life*, 99–110. But see also Nāgārjuna, *Ratnāvalī*, vv. 3.56–57, which also suggest the exchange of self and other.
7. This is the story of a lion king, Noble Limbs (Seng ge ma smad), one of the Buddha's past incarnations, who was so compassionate that "he never ate the flesh of other animals . . . living instead on roots, leaves, flowers, and fruits." Two female monkeys, who live in his kingdom

No matter how much you try to help the wicked,
when the conditions are right, they go astray.[8]
The evil man showed the *ruru* deer to others
even though he had helped him to safely cross the river.[9]

When those who are members of your own party[10]
have turned to evil, regardless of what this may be,
since it is clear that it is you who are in charge,
you must strive to correct them without any misgivings about being criticized.

---

each gives birth at the same time to a baby (past incarnations of Rāhula and Ānanda). On their way to present their babies to the lion king, Razor, king of the vultures, snatches the baby monkeys away. As he is flying off, the lion king warns the vulture that he has seen what he has done and orders him to give the babies back. The vulture at first refuses, "Since I live in the sky, what can you do to me?" The lion then offers to kill himself and give the vulture his own body in exchange for the two baby monkeys. The vulture is so astonished at the lion's commitment to his subjects that he returns the monkeys unharmed and asks the lion king to live a long life and continue his practice of the Dharma. The tale is found in a number of Sanskrit and Tibetan sources. See, for instance, 'Jam dbyangs blo gter bang po, *Ston mchog thams cad mkhyen pa thub pa'i dbang po'i skyes rabs*, no. 98, 247–48.

8. Ravigupta, *Lokasaṃvyavahārapravṛtti*, v. 161ab.

9. The *ruru* deer, a past incarnation of the Buddha, had a resplendent golden body with spots the color of gems. So as not to tempt hunters, he lived deep in the forest away from human beings. But one day he heard the cries of a man being swept away by a river. Overcome by pity, he came out of hiding and saved the man, warmed him with his own body, and showed him the way out of the forest. The man was extremely grateful and asked the deer how he could repay him. The deer asked only that the man keep his whereabouts secret: "My beautiful body makes me too desirable a prey." The man promised that he would keep it secret. Shortly thereafter, a king offered a huge reward to anyone who showed him the fabled deer's whereabouts. The man vacillated between his desire for riches and his virtuous commitment, but in the end greed got the better of him and he led the king to the deer. The story does not end happily for the man, as might be expected. As he lifts his arm to point the deer out to the king, it falls off, and when the king learns that the man had betrayed the deer, the deer has to save him again—this time from the king's arrow—by asking the sovereign to forgive him. In the end, the deer returns to the palace with the king, where he is honored and asked to teach the Dharma. The tale is found in several Indian and Tibetan collections. The present synopsis is based on Āryaśūra's *Jātakamāla* (no. 26). See Justin Meiland, *Garland of the Buddha's Past Lives*, vol. 2, 173–201. See also the Pāli *Jātaka* (no. 482). Ravigupta's *Lokasaṃvyavahārapravṛtti*, v. 217 also makes a brief reference to the tale.

10. The expression *rang gi ris nas 'das* (or *ma 'das*) is not altogether clear. I have translated "someone who is not (or who is) a member of your own party," and I suspect that "your own party" refers to the ruler's own inner circle, family, or clan.

How do you punish those who harm you
when they are not members of your own party?
If they act with contempt toward you, you reciprocate,
and if they get angry at you, you should act wrathfully toward them.

When people are bitten by a snake,
fearing that the potent venom will spread, [83]
they will even cut off
their very own fingers.

Likewise, those who persist in their evil ways
regardless of your attempts
to reform them through just punishments
bring suffering to the kingdom,
and so should be banished.[11]

When people from your own kingdom
commit a crime,
they should be justly punished,
but since you are in charge, you should do so compassionately.

Even a compassionless and vicious mother
will cause her own son to run away;
what need to say that this need for compassion applies to courtiers.
When the retinue declines, so too does the king.

You should, to the best of your abilities,
protect the visitors and the poor masses
that reside within your kingdom.
It is wrong to completely ignore them.

11. Mātṛceta, *Kaniṣkalekha*, v. 18: "You should not allow these people to stay within your kingdom: fools, misers, the greedy, the ungrateful, flatterers, and really cruel people." Later in the text (v. 30), Mātṛceta states that the king should not punish anyone at all—a rather idealistic stance—and suggests (vv. 31–32) that the worst punishment should be banishment, and this in cases where people foment disputes or strife, look down upon the poor, do not admire ethical people, and cause problems for ascetics and vow-holders. Nāgārjuna, *Ratnāvalī*, v. 4.37, also prohibits the killing and torture of murderers, and advises the king to instead banish them.

Accomplishing the welfare of others is praised
as the way to accomplish one's own self-interest.
People who help others
may not be kings, but are like kings.

When the evil kings of this disputatious age
see the excellence of the court
they experience mental torment.
This is an error, like the signs that predict death.[12]
Loving and holy people
are happy and rejoice
even in the excellence of other kingdoms.
This causes their own excellence to increase.

Having understood the nature of things,
rulers whose love extends
even to their enemies
will bring every country under their control.[13] [84]

The king who, with an abiding love in his heart,
is charitable, speaks affectionately,
and works for the welfare of others
will be famous throughout the three worlds.[14]

Whoever rests in the glorious state of love
makes the gods rejoice through the power of his merit.

12. The Indian and Tibetan Buddhist traditions elaborate lists of signs that are supposed to signal death. Mipham perhaps means that these signs of death (*'chi ltas*) are not always accurate—that one can err if one thinks of these signs as certain—just as a king errs if he sees the excellence of the court as a sign that his reign will soon end. But why would a king think this in the first place? Two possible reasons come to mind: (1) When the court has reached its highpoint, there is only one way for it to change, in a downward direction—in other words, that the court's zenith augurs its decline; and (2) a perfect court may have been seen as a threat by weak kings, since it implies that there are many other qualified people in the wings ready to take the king's place.
13. *Prajñāśataka*, v. 29: "A wise person must always act amicably even toward his enemies. A vine wraps itself in a friendly way around the tree until it reaches its tip."
14. Cāṇakya, *Rājanītiśāstra*, v. 8.16: "Those who do not think about helping others while they're walking, sitting, or lying awake, are like animals."

The demigods then also protect him.
What need to say that human societies will as well.

In kingdoms where the ruler has compassion,
many kinds of wealth increase like the waters [of rivers] in spring.
They are not challenged by opposing armies,
and because the society is joyful, everyone is relaxed.

When a loving king, like the waxing moon,
shines as the splendor of the merit of living beings,
all the regions of the kingdom will possess a protector,
and are therefore known as lands not bereft of kingship.

13. How the Ruler Protects Himself

When the compassionate ruler
has become stable, gentle, and balanced,
he contemplates the various methods
for properly ruling his subjects.

What makes people happy is a means of livelihood.[1]
What stops the spread of unhappiness is the law.
He therefore protects living beings through these two:
livelihoods that lead to worldly happiness, and the actions of the law.

Rulers who wish to protect their own state
must first protect themselves. [85]
How can those who are incapable of protecting themselves
protect others?

First you ought to exert yourself
in the long-term stability and sustainability
of your life and body, by stabilizing
the four-fold foundation of happiness.[2]

1. I've emended *'tsho chis* to *'tsho tshis*.
2. The Tibetan text reads *sde bzhi rtsa bar gyur pa*. This refers to what other sources call the four-fold good (*phun tshogs sde bzhi* or *phun sum tshogs pa bzhi*): Dharma, wealth, liberation, and pleasure, in other words, the Buddhist equivalent of the so-called four ends of man (*puruṣārtha*) that are important to the Hindu tradition: pleasure (*kāma*), wealth (*artha*), righteousness or duty (*dharma*), and liberation (*mokṣa*). Mipham elaborates on these with a distinctively Buddhist twist in his *Entrance to Being Wise* (*Mkhas 'jug*), stating that they refer to (1) the Dharma or the spread of Dharma, which brings about higher future births and the highest good, the peace of nirvāṇa, (2) worldly goals, like a home, friends, fame, wealth, and so forth, (3) the enjoyment of pleasure/happiness, which is the result of the first two goals, and (4) the highest goal, the attainment of nirvāṇa. Nāgārjuna's *Ratnāvalī* (v. 2.39)

You properly protect your body
through effective rituals
like the practices of making precious medicines and spells,
or the yoga of the wind-energies.

Merit makes this even easier.
When you have merit, your wishes are fulfilled.
So strive to acquire merit.
Emancipation depends on the power of merit.[3]

Through the power of merit
you effortlessly achieve all possible glory—
glorious intelligence, deeds, home, friends, wealth, and the like—
just as the gods and nāgas do using their jewels.[4]

You should protect your mental qualities
through mindfulness, vigilance, and attentiveness.
Apply yourself with perseverance
to the methods that make these increase.

Receive from a spiritual master the reading transmissions
of scriptures of the Tathāgata:
the *Sūtra of Golden Light*,[5] the *Extensive Play*,[6] the *Ratnaketu Dhāraṇī*,[7]

---

also mentions what it calls the "four-fold good" (*caturbhadra, bzang po bzhi*)—truth (*satya*), giving (*tyāga*), tranquility (*śama*), and wisdom (*prajñā*)—considering these something that an ideal ruler possesses. See also *Prajñāśataka*, v. 5: "The great source of *dharma*, *artha*, *kāma*, and *mokṣa* is knowledge. So devotedly acquire the great mother, wisdom."

3. Amoghavarṣa, *Vimalapraśnottara*, v. 39, also suggests that one should strive for three things: "Training your own mind well; properly using medicine [to preserve bodily health]; and acts of charity [to acquire merit]."

4. Mipham is suggesting an analogy between the magical jewels nāgas and gods use to achieve wealth, and so forth, and the merit that human beings use to achieve the same ends.

5. This is the *Suvarṇaprabhāsa*, which was the subject of chapter eight of Mipham's work.

6. The *Lalitavistara* (Lha sa ed., fols. 1b–352a) is arguably the most important biography of the Buddha in the Tibetan tradition, where it enjoys canonical status. Western scholars date it to around the fourth century. The work ends with the Buddha's enlightenment and his preaching of the first sermon to his five former companions. It has been translated in Gwendolyn Bays, *The Voice of the Buddha, the Beauty of Compassion*.

7. This refers to the *Mahāsannipāta Ratnaketu Dhāraṇī* (Lha sa ed., fols. 289b–432a). In that

the *Ten Wheels Kṣitigarbha Sūtra*,[8] the *Root Tantra of Mañjuśrī*,[9] and
so forth.
Worship these texts and show them great respect,
and then read them and contemplate their meaning from time to time.
The members of the royalty who do this increase their merit.

Those who have faith in Tantra should enter
into the many maṇḍalas of the Secret Mantra tradition. [86]
When you receive empowerment and guard the commitments,
your lifespan, merit, and fame will increase.

Your qualities will be pure
to the extent that you do not overly pursue desires.
How can hedonists
be considered respectable?

If you have no sense of shame,
you become the talk of the town, and evil rumors spread.
Therefore, you should protect your good qualities
by having a sense of shame and propriety.

---

work, an ancient king called Lotus Face (Utpala'i gdong) travels to receive teachings from a former buddha. These teachings are arranged in two groups of threes: (1) to achieve "peaceful intelligence" he must practice compassion, strive to pacify beings' suffering, and understand emptiness; (2) to be protected from demons, he must not get angry and not pick quarrels with any being, must give charity to all beings equally, and must see all phenomena as being like space (fols. 312a–b). The work then goes on to teach the *Ratnaketu Dhāraṇī*, a kind of spell, which, among other things, is supposed to transform women into men!

8. This refers to the *Daśacakrakṣitigarbha*, which will be discussed later in Mipham's work. The sūtra was translated into Tibetan from the Chinese. See Hajime Nakamura, *Indian Buddhism*, 217, which discusses different views concerning the origins of the sūtra. Samdong Rinpoche has briefly discussed the theory of state and administration found in the sūtra—the so-called wheels related to the election of the ruler, his qualifications, the various posts and titles in his administration, and so forth. See Samdong Rinpoche, "The Social and Political Strata in Buddhist Thought."

9. This refers to the *Mañjuśrīmūlatantra* (Lha sa ed., fols. 53b–448b). Western scholars date it to about the seventh century. One of the chapters of the work (the *Rājavyākaraṇa*) contains a history of the Indian kings written in the form of prophecies. See K. P. Jayaswal, *An Imperial History of India in a Sanskrit Text.*

A sūtra tells us about a person with this quality:
while this individual's house was burning,
out of a sense of shame, that person took the time to cover his body.
Even though he died, he was reborn in the heaven of Brahmā.

When a mere sense of shame
can bring about such a great result,
what need is there to say that a sense of shame and propriety
should be maintained at all times?

Shameless people are ugly
no matter how much they adorn themselves.
People of great distinction feel that they need
shame and propriety above all else.

When the powerful lack a sense of shame,
who will tame the shameless?
Who can put out a fire that is burning on water, or assuage the fear that people have
of an evil king who is supposed to be their protector?[10]

The shameless lose their status
by virtue of their great disgrace.
But even then, they do not understand their own nature
and consider themselves great. What self-deception!

Those who are tormented by desire lose all sense of propriety and shame.
Those who are tormented by hunger lose their strength and radiance.
Those who are tormented by illness lose sleep and happiness.
Therefore, practice self-control in your pursuit of pleasure.[11] [87]

10. Compare to *Prajñādaṇḍa*, v. 79, and to Sakya Paṇḍita, *Sa skya legs bshad*, v. 262. Since the king has absolute power, no one can "tame" or control him. He must therefore control himself by leading an ethical life.

11. The first three lines of the verse are identical to Vararuci, *Śatagāthā*, v. 48, but the last line reads, "When you get tired on the road, you lose fear and perseverance." Compare also to Cāṇakya, *Rājanītiśāstra*, v. 8.35: "Those who are suffering financially have no friends or relatives. Those who are tormented by lust are fearless and have no sense of shame. Those

There is no swamp like desire,
no injury like anger.
no trap like delusion,
no cascade like craving.

There is no human defilement like attachment,
and nothing that harms others more than jealousy.
There is no form of intimacy like begging,
and no jewel like generosity.[12]

There is no eye like wisdom;[13]
no mentor like studying,
and no ornament like learning.[14]
So protect yourself by contemplating such faults and qualities.

The backbone of worldly ethics is honesty.
Most of the actions of upright people
are not veiled in the mud[15] of crookedness,
but rather shine forth like pure gold.
Though people may think, "Food and wealth require trickery,"
how awful when this attitude slips out in actual words.
Making a living by deceiving those who trust you
is like not making a living at all.

It's impossible for there to be no cause and effect.
It's impossible for the gods' eyesight to be obstructed.[16]
Deceitful people experience problems and criticisms
both in this life and the next.

---

who suffer from hunger have no strength or luster. Those who are tormented by illness get no sleep and have no happiness."

12. The verse is almost identical to Vararuci, *Śatagāthā*, v. 25, where only the metaphor in the last line differs: "There is no friend closer to you in the world than generosity." Compare this also to *Prajñādaṇḍa*, v. 103, where the last two lines read: "You have no greater friend than a beggar. No closer relation than generosity."

13. Compare to *Prajñādaṇḍa*, v. 104a, and to Vararuci, *Śatagāthā*, v. 95a.

14. Compare to Vararuci, *Śatagāthā*, v. 26c.

15. I've emended *rdzabs* to *rdzab*.

16. Mipham means that evil people may fool other human beings, but they cannot fool either karma or the gods who keep track of everything that people do.

Those who, taking karma and the gods' eyes as their witnesses,
have purified their own minds
are as beautiful as the full moon,
clearly shining over the world of gods and men.

When you resist evil actions,
even Indra can't reproach you.[17]
It's the one who does no evil
who is fit to tame evildoers. [88]

Evil people who forsake goodness and take up evil ways
are like sieves who lose everything.[18]
Those who avoid evil and accomplish the good
are like magnets and nobles who attract others.

If you are always wise about your own aims
and always engage in virtuous deeds,
you are like the shining light of a precious lamp
that cannot be extinguished even by a hurricane.

Even when they're silent and offer you no clues,
you can know others' thoughts from their expressions.
The wise are those who know when the time is ripe
to accomplish their goals without missing their chance.

The sage knows the range of experiences of the wise,
so difficult for ordinary people to understand.
But someone is not a sage simply because he accidentally accomplishes
a goal.
By sheer chance a termite can leave a letter shape on wood.[19]

You do not know who is capable
of really helping or injuring you,

17. Compare to Sakya Paṇḍita, *Sa skya legs bshad*, v. 284.
18. I've emended *chu tshag* to *chu tshags*.
19. Compare to Ravigupta, *Lokasaṃvyavahārapravṛtti*, v. 70; Hahn, "Ravigupta and his Nīti Stanzas (I)," 344.

so be helpful to everyone without looking down upon anyone,
and you will flourish.

The wise engage in charity for the sake of the future.
Fools give when they see that it leads to short-term gain.
Although these are both acts of charity,
they differ in the degree of joy they bring to others.

The wise focus on what is really beneficial to them;
fools only take into account what wealth and prestige they acquire.
The best man analyzes the overall condition of the districts;
the worst man analyzes the quantity of the food supply.

Good friends take care of their companions even when they're in
  trouble;
bad friends take care of their companions only when they're wealthy.
Although they are both ways of caring for people,
from the perspective of the wise, they are very different.[20]

The good man fights for external victory;
the bad man fights for internal victory.
Although both are forms of fighting, [89]
from the viewpoint of opponents, they are quite different.

Fools initially strive for happy results;
the wise initially strive for the causes of that happiness.
Although they are both forms of striving,
from the viewpoint of the knowledgeable, they are quite different.

You will know good and evil people from the differences in their
  actions—
whether they resemble those just mentioned or not.
It is better to have a single learned friend
than it is to have one thousand unlearned ones.

20. Vararuci, *Śatagāthā*, v. 27d.

Having just a single enemy feels like it's too many.
Having one hundred friends feels like it's too few.
Therefore, multiply your friends
and consider no one a foe.

When you care for them, even your enemies become friends.
When you oppress them, even your sons become enemies.
Whether someone is a friend or enemy
depends chiefly on your own actions.[21]

When even brutes can be tamed through sweetness,
what need to say that so too can those who are sweet.
Even enemies find it hard to conquer
someone who is sweet but who, at the right time, is sharp.

Everyone praises someone who has the strength
to act peacefully or wrathfully as appropriate to the situation—
to be gentle with those who despise them, even if they're enemies;
to be harsh with those who run away, even if they're friends.[22]

While always living
an honest and faultless life,
if someone else acts violently toward you for no reason,
do not back off, but rather stand firm.

If they have good qualities, befriend them, even if they're enemies.
If they are evil and unruly, abandon them, even if they're friends.[23]
When they are in between, treat them with neutrality.
Those who know this will always be happy. [90]

Before acting, contemplate,
"Later on, such and such may happen."

21. Cāṇakya, *Rājanītiśāstra*, v. 7.1: "No one is anyone's friend or enemy [by their own nature]. Whether someone is a friend or enemy depends on your own abilities."
22. Compare to *Prajñādaṇḍa*, v. 12.
23. Compare to Sakya Paṇḍita, *Sa skya legs bshad*, v. 210.

Your actions should have an eye to possible consequences.
You should not regret any of your actions after the fact.

Deeds done at just the right time
will be accomplished without any difficulty.
Deeds performed too late or too soon
are, for the most part, difficult to accomplish.

No one can turn away
from the laws of the king in this life
and from the fruits of their karma in the next.
Hence, if you pretend that these are not real, you have admitted defeat.

Although our eyes can see people,
we need a mirror to see ourselves.
Unless you turn your mind within,
it is difficult to see your own faults.[24]

Fools think that all of their happiness and suffering
is caused by external conditions;
their thoughts of attachment and aversion always run here and there
with the goal of avoiding or acquiring various things.

The wise realize that all happiness and suffering
depend on themselves.
Turning their minds within,
they introspect and control themselves.

People who have critical acumen improve
no matter what good or evil they experience.
Uncritical fools gain nothing from witnessing
hundreds of different forms of happiness and suffering.

Like a multifaceted jewel,
the sage exhibits actions that are in perfect harmony

24. Compare to Sakya Paṇḍita, *Sa skya legs bshad*, v. 193. Cāṇakya, *Rājanītiśāstra*, v. 7.6ab: "Others are not privy to your own faults, so you need to be aware of them yourself."

with social position, time, and the interlocutor.
Does the foolish rock ever change its hues?[25]

Even when you are very powerful and wealthy,
you should not oppress others who don't deserve it.
The ruler who knows when the time is ripe to conquer [91]
is the ruler who always emerges victorious.

Who would not make way for the dance of the seven-tongued one[26]
who has been summoned as a guest by the host of forest creatures?
Possessing the drum roar of the clouds of timely rains, the beautiful one,
garlanded by clouds and lightning, brings joy to everyone.

No matter how much they gain and conquer, foolish kings use it up,
burning through it in a fire of insatiable craving.
Even when their gains increase and they triumph over others,
the wise remain as cool as clouds due to their self-control.

To double-cross a villain,
and to make an enemy of a tantric priest
are actions that even kings must avoid.
Not to do so leads to ruin.

Old grudges, lingering debts, and a burning fire:
dispose of these while they are still small.[27]

25. The metaphor is comparing the sage to a magical and versatile jewel that changes according to the situation, and the fool to an inert rock that always remains the same regardless of the circumstance.
26. In classical Indian lore, the seven-tongued one (*saptajihva*) refers to Agni, the god of fire, who possesses seven tongues of fire. He is the brother of Indra, the god of thunder, but in this context, I believe "seven-tongued one" refers to thunder itself. The association of Agni with thunder is not unknown to the Vedas (*Ṛg Veda*, hymn 79): "With drops that bless and seem to smile he comes; the water falls, the clouds utter their thunder." In any case, the verse appears to be a praise of the ruler who acts in a timely fashion, likening him to the god responsible for bringing timely rains.
27. Masūrākṣa, *Nītiśāstra*, v. 3.3: "Loans, the embers of a fire, and lingering enemies will come back to haunt you again and again. So don't let these things linger." Compare also to *Prajñādaṇḍa*, v. 59.

If you delay, they get out of hand,
like a bird who has escaped the net.

The more you are honored and heralded,
the more self-controlled you should be.
The more you are insulted and harmed,
the more aggressive you should be.

People who get angry when you praise them and who calm down when you insult them
would kill the gods if they could, but unable to, settle for worshipping demons.[28]
What wise person could be fond of an evil man
who flees from a fight and torments someone who concedes defeat?[29]

People who sit sipping water even though their enemies are bullying them
and who act violently against the members of their retinue even when they're being helpful
are acting contrary to the way they should.
Even helpful friends turn their backs on them.

Even when he's rich, a wise ruler loves the masses [92]
and he cares for his opponents even when they're weak.

28. The reference appears to be to bullies. Some people respond negatively when you are nice to them, and only back off from their aggression when you assert yourself and put them in their place. On the surface, they appear to have a high opinion of themselves (they would kill the gods if they could); but deep down they suffer from a certain insecurity (they settle for worshipping lowly demons).
29. One can't help but think that Mipham is here responding to the very harsh advice found in texts like Masūrākṣa's that suggest that enemies should be exterminated, even if they ask for mercy; Masūrākṣa, *Nītiśāstra*, vv. 3.1–2: "Until the right time arrives, you should carry the enemies on your shoulders. But when the time is right, you should conquer them like a pot being smashed on a stone. Even if they cry out for mercy like weaklings, you should not give in to the enemy. You should not have pity on them, but destroy them for all the past harm they have done."

This is the most beautiful and worthy thing imaginable, and one can never get enough
of seeing the best qualities of the joint system coming together in this way.[30]

Captivating the minds of others with his gentleness—
acting charitably, peacefully, speaking sweetly, and so forth to all his friends—
a wise man's deeds effortlessly cause his strength to increase
and he reaches the zenith of good qualities.

Without hostility, how can one control just through peaceful means
the enemies of karma, those incorrigibly evil men
who would overthrow the kingdom and so forth?
That is why it is absolutely necessary to generate wrathful self-confidence.

The more you befriend them, the more they help you.
The more you consider them an enemy, the more they harm you.
That is what constitutes friends and enemies;
but nowadays, in this degenerate age, it is rare to find pure examples of either.[31]

Having a good reputation is the root of being human.
Of what use is wealth to someone who is despised?[32]
Those who are counted as neither true enemies nor true friends
may be called "human," but they are actually lower than animals.

30. The "joint system" refers to the combined system of religious and temporal rule. When a ruler, no matter how wealthy he is, has love for the common people, and cares for his opponents even when they're weak, he incorporates the qualities of religion (love and compassion) into his system of governance (temporal rule).

31. Both this verse and the next point nostalgically to an age when people were either pure friends (to be loved) or pure enemies (to be heroically conquered). The implication is that in the present degenerate age everyone is a bit of both, making it difficult to know how precisely to act toward people.

32. The first two lines of this verse are identical to *Prajñādaṇḍa*, v. 20ab. The basic idea is that having a good reputation (not being despised) is more important to living a meaningful human life than having wealth.

They say that the king, irrigation channels,
vines, women, and the blind
go wherever crafty people lead them.
That is why you should not depend on others.[33]

Although dishonest people may show you respect,
they do so out of necessity and not because they like you.
You should not trust anyone without examining them
and becoming convinced of their sincerity.

Some people judge others
by comparing them to themselves.
Some will not trust even a holy being simply because
they've been taken advantage of by an evil one.[34]

Wise men who engage in analysis, [93]
are like swans who suck the milk out of water;
they fathom the meaning of right and wrong
and will not be confused about what needs to be done.[35]

Dishonest people act politely and speak sweetly.
When, without proper forethought,

33. The verse is very similar to *Prajñādaṇḍa*, v. 63. Mipham's wording of the last line is, however, different. The *Prajñādaṇḍa* version reads: "They are dependent on others who guide them."

34. It is of course silly to judge someone else using oneself as a standard. Vararuci (*Śatagāthā*, vv. 88–89) gives the example of an ascetic who manages to achieve a minor power (seeing a hungry ghost) and is, by virtue of that, judged to be great. By the standards of the world, the ability to see a ghost may be special, but in actuality it is something quite trivial. The last two lines suggest that one should not generalize from one person to others. For example, it is silly to consider everyone (including holy beings) evil simply because you've been "burned" in the past by someone who is evil. Compare the verse also to Ravigupta, *Lokasaṃvyavahārapravṛtti*, v. 234; Hahn, "Ravigupta and his Nīti Stanzas (II)," 30: "Those who cannot behold good fortune do not believe in the virtues of the great although they exist." See also *Prajñādaṇḍa*, v. 180.

35. Compare to Ravigupta, *Lokasaṃvyavahārapravṛtti*, v. 5; Hahn, "Ravigupta and his Nīti Stanzas (I)," 335.

you reestablish relations with old adversaries and you trust them,
you are destroyed, as in the case of the crows who burned the
owls' nests.[36]

Like the parasites that live on the body of lions,
great beings experience many problems from their own ranks;
some of these even surpass the problems caused by enemies.
Therefore, keep an eye on the retinue and on those within your
own ranks.[37]

Someone who, though belonging to your own ranks,
is your equal in wealth, your equal in power, who knows your situation,
and who make great efforts
will destroy you unless you are cautious.[38]

36. Similar verses are found in *Prajñādaṇḍa*, v. 97; Cāṇakya, *Rājanītiśāstra*, v. 7.26; and Sakya Paṇḍita, *Sa skya legs bshad*, vv. 279, 340. The *Prajñādaṇḍa* version makes a reference to the same story of the owl and the crows. The Cāṇakya verse uses a different image: "Having reconciled with enemies and then feeling relaxed and sleeping happily is like sleeping on the very top of a tree, where you can awaken and fall." The story Mipham refers to is found in a number of Indian sources, including Viṣṇu Śarma's *Pañcatantra*. A slightly different version is also found in the Buddhist *Avadānas*. In the *Pañcatantra* version, the owl king and crow king are—as they are in many such takes—sworn enemies. The owl king spends the night picking off sleeping crows from the tree in which they sleep. Because the crow population is declining, they decide to shift to another site, but they also hatch a plan to defeat the owls for good. A crow minister pretends to have a falling out with his king. The owl king learns of this from an owl spy, and when the crow minister approaches him, offering to betray his king and divulge the location of the crows, he takes him in and gives him a nest outside the owl's cave. During the day, while the owls are asleep, the crow brings small bits of wood and piles them in the owls' nests. When all is ready, he gets his fellow crows to each bring a burning twig and sets fire to the owls' nests, burning them alive while they sleep. The moral of the story: "Trust not a former enemy who comes professing amity." See Viṣṇu Śarma, *The Pañćatantra*, Book 3. And Maurice Bloomfield, "The Fable of the Crow and the Palm-Tree: A Psychic Motif in Hindu Fiction," 6. See also Sakya Paṇḍita, *Sa skya legs bshad*, v. 279.

37. Compare to Sakya Paṇḍita, *Sa skya legs bshad*, vv. 209, 261.

38. The verse is very similar to *Prajñādaṇḍa*, v. 78, however in its last line, the *Prajñādaṇḍa* advises the king to kill such an individual, or else be killed by him. Mipham changes this, and advises the king simply to be cautious. Masūrākṣa, *Nītiśāstra*, v. 5.1. suggests that the person being spoken of here is a minister. "The minister who has an excellent mind, who can fearlessly maneuver through all the treatises, who has a large treasury and is powerful should hide himself lest he be killed." Masūrākṣa (*Nītiśāstra*, v. 6.16) also suggests that an individual who is the king's "equal in wealth, power, understanding and perseverance may overthrow the king," and like the *Prajñādaṇḍa*, Masūrākṣa advises the king to "kill him, or he will kill you."

When they do not see some benefit, even your friends turn against you.
Even opponents will befriend you if they see some benefit in it.
Unless they see the benefits, people won't take
the medicines needed to cure the body's ailments.

You can know the degree of a person's good qualities
from one important pair of facts:
that they repay acts of kindness, and that their plans
are not ill-informed about what is beneficial and harmful.

Even if they worship you,
what wise ruler would be impressed by those despicable people
who abandon their friends when they're down,
and who honor an enemy just because he's wealthy.

Even when they live far away, nice people seem close to you.
Even when they live close by, disagreeable people seem distant.[39]
A fine necklace burns the body[40]
of someone who has had a goiter surgically removed.[41]

Even when the holy and the unholy intermix,
they are never confused. [94]
Two holy beings are amicable even when they live far away,
just like the powerful though distant sun feels close to the lotus patch.
When sunlight meets the eyes,
those with sight can see forms.
Likewise, when one wise person meets another,
an opening for a conversation is seen in just a single word.[42]

39. Very similar lines are found in *Prajñādaṇḍa*, v. 191; Cāṇakya, *Rājanītiśāstra*, v. 8.37; and Vararuci, *Śatagāthā*, v. 23.
40. I've emended *srel bar byed* to *sreg bar byed*.
41. The meaning of the lines is unclear, and the translation is tentative. I take Mipham to be saying that whereas someone can normally tolerate the weight of a fine ornament or necklace (i.e., can tolerate a disagreeable person) for the sake of appearances, this is not the case when one is in a weakened state—after neck surgery.
42. Compare to Sakya Paṇḍita, *Sa skya legs bshad*, v. 15.

It is difficult for fools to distinguish
what their mind was doing
when they were experiencing something beneficial or harmful.
The whole process is just a shot in the dark to them.

The wise are aware of this in the three times:
they do not forget what they did in the past to help or harm them;
they know what they are striving for and what is worth pursuing in
the present;
they are careful as regards their future goals.

In a group of hundreds and thousands of people
there are but a handful of extraordinary, precious human beings
who have a broad outlook, high aspirations,
clear minds, and are aware of all their actions.[43]

A person with strength of mind is as difficult to find
as a particular atom within the earth, or as a drop within the ocean.
But the sage knows who is superior, middling, and inferior
just as a great nāga knows the location of each jewel within the sea.

A bad person is like a pond:
his depth changes by the day or month.
But learned ones are like the ocean: no matter how long you rely
on them,
their depth just increases, with no apparent limit.[44]

43. A variety of *nīti* verses speak to the rarity of virtuous, forthright people. Consider, for example, *Jantupoṣaṇabiṇḍu*, v. 16: "Rich people are found even among the barbarians. Heroes exist even among animals. But those whose speech accords with reality are exceedingly rare in this world." *Prajñādaṇḍa*, v. 132: "A hero will be born in every hundred people; a scholar in every thousand; a wise person in every hundred thousand; a donor [is even more rare] and may or may not arise [amidst those]." Ravigupta, *Lokasaṃvyavahārapravṛtti*, v. 171. Hahn, "Ravigupta and his Nīti Stanzas (II)," 21: "Among the countless number of living beings, those who possess virtues are hard to find." Cāṇakya, *Rājanītiśāstra*, v. 8.29: "Not all mountain people have wealth. Most sea creatures have no pearls. Not all forests have sandalwood trees. Exalted persons are not found everywhere."

44. Ravigupta, *Lokasaṃvyavahārapravṛtti*, v. 170. Hahn, "Ravigupta and his Nīti Stanzas (II)," 22: "He who is utterly shallow becomes [as useless] as an old well because he is [so] limited in depth. Although fathomless, the ocean is extremely wide because it is great by nature."

Sages can distinguish—
but fools don't know the difference—
between harsh words spoken to help someone
and the smiling face of a hypocrite.

Just as the "chal" sound agitates the rabbits,[45]
fools scurry after the famous. [95]
But the wise decide on who to trust by making inquiries and
  distinguishing between people,
just as goldsmiths examine gold by burning, cutting, and rubbing it.[46]

Someone may be helpful and pleasant in the short term,
but harmful in the long run.
Someone may be harmful and unpleasant in the short term,
but once befriended, is helpful.

Hence, you should not cultivate
friends or adversaries just for the moment.
Instant friendships are nice,
but long-term ones are much more dependable.

If really wise people who are diligent and strong
even inspire awe in the gods, how much more so in the masses.
Even the gods delight in someone who is a good friend—
who has a good heart, is resolute, and does not pick fights.

45. I've emended *bkrog* to *bkrug* or to *'drogs*. Compare to Sakya Paṇḍita, *Sa skya legs bshad*, v. 117. The "chal" sound is the splashing sound a tree makes when it falls into water; this startled the rabbit and made it scamper. The rabbit's fear then spreads to other animals in the forest who all start running in a panic until the lion finally sets them at ease. Likewise, rumors that someone is famous agitates fools.

46. In the famous parable of the goldsmith, the Buddha exhorts his disciples not to accept his words simply because he spoke them, but to instead examine them as a goldsmith examines gold he is going to buy—burning, cutting, rubbing, and (in some versions) beating it. Cāṇakya, *Rajanītiśastra*, v. 5.2, suggests four ways of testing a person, comparable to the four ways of testing gold, namely, regarding his level of renunciation, conduct, qualities or learning, and actions. Masūrākṣa, *Nītiśāstra*, v. 4.21, also uses the gold analogy, and suggests that the four ways of examining a person is in regard to their learning, ethics, lineage, and compassion.

When skillful and wise people who have good friends undertake a
venture
at just the right time, then—like a fire stoked by wind—
their plans take off and it's as if they already had within their hands
the goal that was already in their minds: the full extent of the glory that
exists in the universe.[47]

When love is too strong,
it ends up causing hostility.[48]
When guile is too strong,
it ends up destroying you. There are many such cases.

When you know what food and medicine to take
in their proper proportions, for their proper purposes,
and you also know when to take them,
you will not suffer from major physical problems.

If you want a lasting friendship with a man,
do not do these three things:
gamble, have business dealings with him,
and speak in private with his wife.[49]

A sage knows the good qualities of a sage
just as a hero is known by others on the battlefield.[50]
The fool sees sages and dullards,
as well as stones and gems, as the same. [96]

47. This is a difficult verse to render into good English because of the different analogies and metaphors that it employs, but the point is quite simple. When someone has the necessary internal qualities, the right support from friends, and additionally sets a plan into motion at the right time, there is nothing that can stop it, like a fire stoked by wind.
48. Compare to Sakya Paṇḍita, *Sa skya legs bshad*, v. 222.
49. The verse is almost identical to *Prajñādaṇḍa*, v. 193. My translation varies slightly from Hahn's version. In the Sanskrit version of this verse, found in a number of other sources, the last of the three is "to stare secretly at [another's] wife" (*parokṣe dāradarśanam*). The verse is also almost identical to Cāṇakya, *Rājanītiśāstra*, v. 7.3.
50. Compare to *Prajñādaṇḍa*, v. 151. Hahn, "The Tibetan *Shes rab sdong bu* and its Indian Sources (II)," 24: "The reputation of a wise person spreads among people who are themselves wise, just as jewels are known to jewelers, and heroes [are known] in face of battle."

Even when they are sitting in the presence
of holy people who possess good qualities,
ministers do not notice those qualities,
just as owls do not see even when the sun is shining.

Wise men know from afar
the good qualities that people possess.
They deduce these from their words and actions
just as fire can be inferred from smoke.

Heroism is known from a man's conduct in battle.
A wife's true nature becomes evident when your wealth is exhausted.
You know with certainty who your friends are,
if they help you when you're in trouble.[51]

Engaging in business that brings no profit, acting violently against those who have retinues,
begging while putting on airs, wanting sexual pleasures without having wealth,[52]
and using coarse words with a young woman:
people engage in these five mistaken activities.[53]

Those who undertake something that is beyond their abilities;
who antagonize crowds; who oppose the powerful;

51. The verse is very similar to Cāṇakya, *Rājanītiśāstra*, v. 2.9, which, however, adds another line: "You know a true host if he receives you as a guest during a famine." See also v. 2.10c in that same work: "Women abandon men when they have no wealth."

52. In ancient India it was presumed that most young men who went in search of sexual pleasures would have to pay for sex. They therefore had to have some wealth at their disposal. Ancient sources also tell us about fathers who complained that their sons were using up all their wealth on prostitutes. See Cabezón, *Sexuality*.

53. The verse resembles *Prajñādaṇḍa*, v. 47, which has been corrected by Hahn on the basis of the Sanskrit; see his "The *Prajñādaṇḍa* and its Indian Sources (I)," 35–36. Compare also to Sakya Paṇḍita, *Sa skya legs bshad*, v. 259. I have translated the verse following Mipham's version. To take just one example of the differences, if one were to follow the Sanskrit, the third line should be rendered, "a beautiful woman speaking coarsely." See also Cāṇakya, *Rājanītiśāstra*, v. 8.7.

and who trust women:[54] these four types of people are called
"those who live on the edge."[55]

Misunderstanding your level of knowledge is poison.
It is poison for an elderly person to have sex with a young one.
Remaining passive in the face of illness is poison.
It is poison for a poor person to enjoy sleeping too much.[56]

Eating unripe or forbidden foods;
having sex, lying down, or sleeping during the day;
and having sex with older women:
these activities rob men of their bodily energy and not doing these make men strong.[57]

Examine your acts and behavior,
as well as your food, home, servants, and so forth,
and then completely turn away
from whatever is not conducive to your well-being. [97]

54. Masūrākṣa, *Nītiśāstra*, v. 1.9a also advises, "do not trust women"—one of many instances of misogyny that we find throughout this literature.

55. Compare to *Prajñādaṇḍa*, v. 21. Mipham has clearly emended what he sees to be an error in the *Prajñādaṇḍa*. The last line in Mipham's verse literally reads, "they are living close to the Lord of Death," but I have rendered it rather freely. Compare also to *Nāgarājabherī Gāthā*, v. 29, Lha sa ed., fol. 316a; to *Jantupoṣaṇabinḍu*, v. 32; and to Sakya Paṇḍita, *Sa skya legs bshad*, v. 258.

56. Compare to *Prajñādaṇḍa*, v. 10. It is noteworthy that the first line of the *Prajñādaṇḍa* verse reads "Misunderstanding magical spells (*rig sngags*) is poison," and that Mipham's version of the verse is closer to the Sanskrit *duradhītā viṣaṃ*: "inadequate learning is poison." Compare also to Cāṇakya, *Rājanītiśāstra*, v. 7.14: "Loans are the poison for poor people. A young woman is poison for an old man. Knowledge is poison for an evil-minded person. Eating indigestible food is poison."

57. Compare to Vararuci, *Śatagāthā*, vv. 62–63; and to Cāṇakya, *Rājanītiśāstra*, v. 7.16–17. In the *Prajñādaṇḍa* verse (see the previous note), the foods are specified as "newly brewed beer" (*chang gsar*), "new yogurt" (*zho ni gzhun nu*), and "dried meat" (*sha skam*). It is not surprising that Mipham would not have reproduced this list of forbidden foods, since things like beer and dried meat were staples of the Tibetan diet. The Cāṇakya version of the verse (7.17) reads: "Dried meat; old women; new beer; yogurt that has just set; sex while being ill; and sleeping during the day: these six quickly rob you of your life force."

Those who perfect the ability to read external signs as well as people's inner motivations
and who become skilled at determining which places, friends, time, and so on
are most advantageous and auspicious
will achieve their desired goals.

Don't be too loving, even with your friends.
Don't be too oppressive, even with your enemies.
The royal laws should be
neither too loose nor too strict.

Be nice to your sons until they are five years old.
From then until age ten, beat them as if they were enemies.
When they turn sixteen,
treat them as if they were friends. So say the texts.[58]

Treat the retinue kindly, threatening them only occasionally.
Threaten your enemies, treating them kindly occasionally.
Women are subdued through love and care.
Servants and slaves are governed by putting them to work and through money.

Do not preoccupy yourself with small goals.
Do not give up on your important aims.
Do not obsess over minor tasks.
Concentrate closely on your most important goals.

Others don't steal from you,
so don't covet others' wealth and homes.
Don't plunder an opponent's kingdom
without proper cause such as being attacked.

58. With the exception of the last phrase ("so say the texts"), the verse is identical to Cāṇakya, *Rājanītiśāstra*, v. 8.45. The previous verse in Cāṇakya's text, which Mipham does not quote, states: "Faults arise from being nice, and good qualities come from beatings. Therefore, beat your sons and disciples, and do not treat them nicely."

Those who covet others' wealth
will not fulfill their hopes and dreams of acquiring that wealth.
The horrible retribution of this karma
simply hastens their own destruction.[59]

Therefore, rulers who, even when they're powerful,
do not torment enemies,
bring stability to their kingdoms and unite all their lands
through the power of their merit.

In this degenerate age, it is difficult to achieve
wealth, reputation, fame, and so forth in tandem. [98]
That is why you ought to amass as much merit as you can
and be skillful in your methods.

Anything undertaken using method and wisdom
will be achieved, even if it's difficult,
just as poison can be transformed into nectar
using ritual methods like mantras, and so forth.

Sharp and quick methods that are immoral
only allow you to succeed in the short term.
But even though, in this degenerate age, you may be proclaimed "a great man" using such methods,
your fame will not extend very far, like the boundaries of a little pond.

Those committed to acting ethically
may have nothing to show for their efforts in the short term,
but eventually their glory and wealth become as expansive and stable
as the great treasury of waters we call the ocean.

The timely and merely verbal interventions of sages
are superior to the plans that fools work so hard to concoct.
Even when the deeds of skillful people are small,
they yield great results.

59. Compare to *Prajñādaṇḍa*, v. 211, and to Vararuci, *Śatagāthā*, v. 24.

The good qualities of those who are unskillful
are never widely known and, in fact, are disparaged as flaws.
When you are skillful, even your faults
become like strengths and achieve wide renown.[60]

It is like this example:
the fruit of the banyan and seed of the mustard plant
are about the same size when they fall to the ground,
but as they steadily grow, the trees are far from the same.

Many people belong to your ranks,
but those who possess good qualities
will improve month to month and year to year
until they finally surpass all the others.

Therefore, those who know what is good for them
do not waste their days.[61]
Instead, they engage in recitations, accumulate merit, [99]
train, and strive for the goals they wish to accomplish.

Those who wish to bring an end to their sins have faith in the Tathāgata.
Those who wish to use up their merit give rise to evil thoughts.
Those who wish to bring an end to their family lineage produce stupid and dumb offspring.
Those who wish to exhaust their misfortune will want to accumulate merit.[62]

60. A similar idea—that the faults of virtuous people become virtues, and good deeds of the wicked become evil—is found to Ravigupta; Hahn, "Ravigupta and his Nīti Stanzas (II)," 37.
61. Compare also to Masūrākṣa, *Nītiśāstra*, v. 4.5: "Do not waste your day; engage in charity and recitations." Cāṇakya, *Rājanītiśāstra*, v. 6.5: "Whether you are living in the forest or in a house, do not waste your day, but instead engage in charity that will benefit others and in reading for your own edification."
62. The first three lines of the verse are essentially identical to *Prajñādaṇḍa*, v. 61. The last line in the *Prajñādaṇḍa* version reads, "Those who wish to use up the grain [in their stomach?] ought to increase their digestive heat."

When the snake of evil words, which emerges out of the pit of evil
people,
bites holy beings, they should drink
the supreme medicines of wisdom and patience,
the antidotes that counteract that poison.

Lofty and inspired people
have two great sources of joy in this life:
to be as excellent as they wish to be,
and to get rid of mundane distractions.[63]

There are two destinations for the holy,
just as there are for buds of flowers:
to be venerated for their excellence in the world at large,
and to retire into the forest.[64]

Forest dwellers turn their back on glory.
They see striving for this as useless.
For the holy who live as beggars,
there is no greater joy than the forest.

Sages who are not recluses should live in places
where their good qualities are known and praised.
They should not live among lowlifes,
like jewels in a nest of vipers.

A swan is not beautiful when it's in a murder of crows.
A fine stallion does not shine when it's in a herd of donkeys.
A lion is not majestic when it's in a skulk of foxes.
How can a sage be resplendent within a group of fools?[65] [100]

63. Compare to *Prajñādaṇḍa*, v. 24. In the *Prajñādaṇḍa*, however, the two goals are getting rid of all distractions and being extremely wealthy. It is clear that Mipham has changed the latter.

64. The verse is almost identical to Cāṇakya, *Rājanītiśāstra*, v. 3.9; to Vararuci, *Śatagāthā*, v. 16; and to *Prajñādaṇḍa*, v. 26. A similar verse is also attributed to Ravigupta in one of the classical collections of poetry; see Hahn, "Ravigupta and his Nīti Stanzas (II)," 35.

65. The verse is identical to *Prajñādaṇḍa*, v. 152. Compare also to Cāṇakya, *Rājanītiśāstra*, v. 8.63, and to Vararuci, *Śatagāthā*, v. 80.

A fool avoids other sources of clean water,
and drinks from the salty one just because, "This is my spring."
Why be attached to bad retinues and homes
when there are other suitable lands?[66]

Living in a joyful and agreeable place is happiness.
Associating with relaxed and trustworthy friends is happiness.
Accumulating merit and relying on the holy is happiness.
Being independent and possessing the wealth of satisfaction is happiness.

When they are children, their parents take charge.
In their youth, their friends take control.
When they have grown old, they are under the power of their children.
Fools are never independent.[67]

Not being independent, they do not obtain good qualities
and are unable to take care of themselves.
Therefore, always maintain your independence,
and strive to be self-sufficient.

66. Compare to *Nāgarājabherī Gāthā*, v. 33, Lha sa ed., fols. 316a–b: "Those who are being despised in their own country may be better off residing in other peoples' lands. That place where one is not despised by other men is one's own country, and those people are one's own people." See also Cāṇakya, *Rājanītiśāstra*, vv. 1.12, 2.5a, 2.23: "The place where you are nurtured is your country. . . . Abandon a country that does not nurture you. . . . You should not live in any country where you are not respected, not nurtured, where you have no relatives." Masūrākṣa, *Nītiśāstra*, v. 1.10a, states: "Abandon a country in which you have no protection." Compare also to *Prajñādaṇḍa*, v. 23, where the point is that those who have the opportunity to travel do themselves a disservice if, out of attachment to their own country, they choose not to do so.

67. The verse is almost identical to Vararuci, *Śatagāthā*, v. 86. It is also found in several collections of elegant verses or *subhāṣitas*. In some of these other works, men are said to be under the control not of friends, but of women (*strī*) or of wives (*dhayitā*). As various scholars have noted, the corresponding verse in Cāṇakya and in Manu's *Dharmaśāstra* claims that it is women (not fools) who are always controlled by others (specifically, by men) at different stages of their life. Cāṇakya, *Rājanītiśāstra*, v. 8.33, reads: "In her youth she is protected by her father. In her adulthood she is protected by her husband. In her old age she is protected by her sons. A woman is never independent."

Every form of independence is happiness.
Every form of dependence on others is suffering.[68]
There is no greater joy than becoming independent
and then striving for good qualities.

One day of health
devoted to associating with the holy
and free of people's insults
is better than one hundred years of the opposite.[69]

These are the signs of greatness in saints:
giving without hope of reward;[70]
helping those who aren't their friends;
and teaching the Dharma without concern for remuneration.

As long as the full moon of the body—the moon at its most beautiful
point—
is not found by Great Rāhu, the Lord of Death,[71] [101]
so long should you be careful
and properly protect your qualities and lineage.[72]

Time is short, and there are many things to know.
We don't know how long our lives will last.

68. These two lines are identical to Cāṇakya, *Rājanītiśāstra*, v. 6.23ab. Compare also to Sakya Paṇḍita, *Sa skya legs bshad*, v. 216; and to Amoghavarṣa, *Vimalapraśnottara*, v. 31: "What is like hell? To be under someone else's control."
69. With one exception, the verse is identical to *Prajñādaṇḍa*, v. 43. In the *Prajñādaṇḍa* version, the third line reads "not having to speak inferior (mean?) words."
70. *Prajñāśataka*, v. 24: "Whoever enjoys giving charity without any hope of reward will achieve fame in the human world."
71. In ancient Indian lore, the god Rāhu is said to occasionally eat the moon and the sun, thereby causing eclipses. Here the moon is being likened to the body, and Rāhu to Yama, the Lord of Death. Mipham is stating that so long as Rāhu has not found the moon (so long as death has not found one's body), one should continue to practice moral self-restraint for the sake of oneself and one's lineage.
72. Compare to *Prajñādaṇḍa*, v. 120, where only the last line—"It is appropriate to pursue one's own work"—is different from Mipham's.

So like the swans that suck the milk out of water,
focus on what is most dear.[73]

Focus on the *goals* to be accomplished.[74]
As a result, you will be rewarded with the glory you *desire*.
Those who gather together the pure *Dharma* of what is good in this life
and the next
will enjoy the fruit of *liberation*, everlasting happiness.

High rebirth, the highest good, cause, and effect—these four
are the so-called four aims, the sought-after goals of holy beings,
Wise ones who are conscientious
possess these fruits in large measure.
Even if they cultivate these for an exceedingly long time,
people who are foolish, careless, and unfortunate
are not happy, and their hopes for this life are shattered.
Any glory in the future life is also destroyed.
Therefore, wise rulers grow the wish-fulfilling tree
that bears the excellent fruit of these four aims, and their achievement
makes the entire expanse of the world virtuous.

73. The verse is identical to *Prajñādaṇḍa*, v. 140, and to Vararuci, *Śatagāthā*, v. 9.
74. In the Tibetan text, this verse contains words marked by dots, a common technique in Tibetan literature indicating that the words will together designate something (a name, phrase, or commonly known list of things). I have indicated this in the translation by underlining the words. In this case the four words—*don*, *'dod*, *chos*, and *thar*—refer to the four goals of human beings. However, Mipham reinterprets them somewhat. For example, the word *artha* (*don*), which usually means "wealth," can also mean "goal," and it is this latter sense that Mipham stresses in this verse. Likewise, *kāma* (*'dod pa*) means "pleasure," but it can also mean "desire," and again, it is this later sense that Mipham stresses. The third word *dharma* (*chos*), Mipham understands in its Buddhist sense as the Buddha's religion.

14. How to Protect the Kingdom

Once the king has learned how to protect himself [102]
through these four forms of spiritual nourishment,
so as to make his subjects happy,
he cares for them by nourishing them.
In the *Ten Wheels Kṣitigarbha Sūtra*[1]
this is taught using an example.

The intelligent ruler
who obtains the glory of kingship
examines the legal system of the rulers
of the past, present, and future,
and he gets the wise men who live in that kingdom
to apply them to the three "wheels of work."

1. *Daśacakrakṣitigarbha Sūtra*. Kṣitigarbha is a bodhisattva, and in the sūtra he imparts "ten wheels" of advice on all matter of topics, many of them having to do with politics. The work was translated into Tibetan from the Chinese during the imperial period by a Chinese monk named Zabmo (Profound) and the Tibetan translator Nampar Mitogpa (Nonconceptuality). Little work has been done on this important text in Western languages, but see Francis Wang, *Le Bodhisattva Kṣitigarbha en Chine du Ve au Xiiie siècle*; and Zhiru Ng, *The Making of Savior Bodhisattva*, especially chapter 1, and appendix 1 for an argument concerning the dating of the text. Zhiru does not rule out the possibility that portions of the work might have been composed in China. In Zhiru's words, "The core texts focus on the socio-political undercurrents Buddhism faced in medieval China. Its rhetoric is polemical and elevates the monastic vocation, arguing for monastic exemption from any form of state regulation." See also the interesting comments of Dzogchen Ponlop Rinpoche about the text, "Interview with Dzogchen Ponlop Rinpoche," *The Chronicle Project*, www.chronicleproject.com/stories_149.html.

The first, "wheel of political action," is the wheel
used to understand and to gain proficiency in the martial arts.
The second wheel involves training in the work
of farming, and architectural and construction work.
The third involves practicing the work
of various forms of commerce and art.
These three wheels
make people happy.

So as to bring happiness to that land—
with its many priests and artisans,
artist workshops and stores,
and ascetics and brahmins—
the king builds temples throughout the country.

He constructs images of the three jewels,[2]
and establishes traditions of scholarship and practice.
He worships the transcendental ones, the three jewels, and gives charity
to the common people.
In that country, which is constant in merit making,
goodness and virtue increase in abundance.

As a way of honoring
parents and the clan elders, [103]
he makes sure that all fashions, jewelry, and manners
follow the traditions of the righteous.

To bring joy to the world,
he creates parks, flower gardens,
and festival grounds for worshipping the gods,
and he establishes the arts of dance and music.

The king will never permit the slightest deterioration
of the sites that serve as homes to the country's nature spirits:

2. Compare to Nāgārjuna, *Ratnāvalī*, vv. 231–34, 310.

its fine rivers, lakes, mountains, and trees;
rather, he establishes them as scenic preserves.[3]

He does not permit evil people
to freely desecrate holy sites:
auspicious lands, high mountains,
and sacred power places.

Healers, astrologers, magicians,
exorcists, diviners, and shamans
are all committed to the welfare of the country;
and so he gets them to increase the food supply.

He establishes schools that train people
in the creation of amazingly beautiful objects—
various types of artistic workshops—
and builds markets where these goods can be sold.[4]

Strong armor and fortifications,
and various types of horses and weaponry
are amassed in the homes of every individual,
each of whom is courageous and knows the martial arts.

The king appoints smart, level-headed, and moral people
as the representatives of the national assemblies.
Soldiers and generals clad in armor will, when needed,
spring immediately to action without delay.

The royalty, knowing what prior preparations must be made
to achieve the kingdom's needs and goals, [104]
are able to tackle any task at just the right time
without impediment.

3. I've emended *bkod pas brgyan* to *bkod pa'i rgyan*.

4. Nāgārjuna, *Ratnāvalī*, v. 239, advises the king to provide estates for the upkeep of schools and the livelihood of teachers. Much more than that, however, Nāgārjuna advocates (vv. 240–49) for the creation of all manner of social institutions to help the populace (especially the poor): hospitals, barber shops, hostels, amusement centers, ponds, rest houses, medicine dispensaries, and so forth.

Even though sages are innately powerful,
they protect their opponents[5] with great care.
Even though fools are innately weak,
being vain in their ignorance, they live without fear.[6]

Fools only examine the present.
Wise people examine far into the future.
The wise are those who know beforehand
what benefits and harms await them.

Throughout the kingdom, each and every person
takes up the methods to increase good fortune and prosperity:
to make the rain fall, to reward the local spirits for their help,
to ward off plague, and to restore fertility to the land.

Because they are very experienced, and not being troubled
with too much work that is beyond their ability to do,
commoners get along with the intelligentsia,
and they each complete their work carefully and on time.

Just as a great cloud draws in
just enough water from the ocean
and constantly releases it upon the earth
so that the grasses, trees, and grain ripen,
likewise, the loving and intelligent king
redirects the lawful taxes and fines that he has collected
to the care of his subjects,
thus increasing the joy of all his people.

5. I've emended *pas rgol* to *phas rgol*.
6. It is not clear whether this verse and the next are referring to the sages and fools who live in this ideal kingdom, or whether they are meant as general observations, perhaps interpolated from some source other than the *Daśacakra*. In the former case, the verse might be read as claiming that whereas in other lands ignorant people pretend that they are wise—something that causes them fear and insecurity—in this kingdom, ignorant people acknowledge their ignorance, which gives them no reason to fear. But the verse, as I say, may just as likely be making a general observation.

From time to time he spies upon criminals, thieves,
cheats, and the like, and banishes them.
He controls the independence of the regions
and does not allow troublemakers[7] to remain.

Within all the regions that belong to him, [105]
the king should always employ strategies
that are conducive to the fearlessness and happiness of all beings
down to those that belong to the animal kingdom.

He makes arrangements for the needs of occasional guests.[8]
He builds boats, bridges, and roads as needed.[9]
He protects everyone equally
from the harm of enemies, thieves, and ferocious animals.

He is not abusive, but instead remains neutral
toward those who offend the laity,
toward those who deceive the world with a flood of lies, and so forth,
but he suppresses the worst bands of swindlers.

He appoints as national treasures
experts in the scriptures, those who maintain their vows,
accomplished yogis, and upholders of the Dharma,
respecting and praising them from afar.

He shows compassion for the meek,
and he reviles those who brandish military might inappropriately.
Even the gods rejoice in those places
where kingdoms are happy and free from anxiety.

He goes to other kingdoms from time to time
for the sake of trade and profit.

7. I've emended *phung dkrol* to *phung krol*.
8. The virtue of hospitality is touted in many texts. For example, Masūrākṣa, *Nītiśāstra*, v. 1.11b, also states that one should "properly greet occasional or unexpected guests."
9. I've emended *dge ba'i* to *dgos pa'i*.

Assembling his troops and in the company
of the generals who lead them, he travels with ease.

If little is accomplished, it is difficult to do anything about it.
If a lot is gathered, the king happily discusses
with the most capable people
how to dispose of the gains for their mutual benefit.

Getting people not to fight with one another,
and instead to support one another,
the king always uses the appropriate method,
whether gentle or tough.

In the individual nomadic regions,
people should harmoniously enjoy
the wealth from their own share of the land. [106]
Very greedy and partisan people are stopped through the law.

The people of the country must protect their own region
while also joining forces for their common welfare.
The country is protected
in a united way without dissension.

Ascetics and brahmins
are called the "roots" of the king.[10]
He should therefore protect the different divisions of the saṅgha
by respecting the saṅgha's property and so forth.[11]

10. Cāṇakya, *Rājanītiśāstra*, vv. 8.67, 8.69: "The king is the peak of righteousness. The root of righteousness are monks and brahmins. The fruit comes from the root. Therefore, do not harm the root.... The king is the tree and ascetics are the root. The ministers are the branches, and the townspeople the leaves. The tree does not wither so long as the root is protected. Therefore, protect ascetics and brahmins."

11. As Mipham explains in his *Entrance to Being Wise*, to steal or confiscate the wealth or property of the saṅgha is considered one of the "five secondary heinous sins" (*nye ba'i mtshams med pa lnga*). Stealing from the saṅgha—actually, from any of the three jewels—is also one of the downfalls in the bodhisattva's discipline. Obviously, only a powerful person such as a king or minister would have been in a position to confiscate the wealth or property of a monastery.

The lord of the land convenes discussions that,
taking time and place into account,
aim at determining the means of bringing about the happiness of
  the people.
He issues orders about what is beneficial based on these discussions.

Wishing the common people to flourish,
and diligent in what will bring them happiness,
he will not bring misfortune to even a single subject,
guarding everyone as if they were gold.
Due to their ignorance, most people
are unable to accomplish even minor goals.
Because he educates the ignorant,
the king is like their father.

Due to their hesitancy, most people
put forward little initiative.
Because he leads them and incites them to action,
the king is like their captain.

Like poisonous snakes, most people
harm others and are difficult to tame.
Because he uses various methods to discipline them,
the king is like a magician or snake charmer.

Because his compassionate mind
is always focused on his subjects
and strives solely to make them happy,
the king is like a mother. [107]

Taking great care to make inquiries and to examine
various aspects of his kingdom—the degree of its suffering and
  happiness,
and the extent of faults and good qualities—
the king is like a great watchman.

Because he gives solace to the frightened,
succor to those who suffer,

and joy to those who put their trust in him,
the king is like a wish-fulfilling tree.

Because he teaches others what to accept or reject,
distinguishes right and wrong for them,
and leads them to the good path,
the king is like an eye.

Because his glory
acts to ornament every direction,
and brings joy to the beings of his retinue,
the king is like a treasure of jewels.

Because he cannot be harmed by opponents,
makes the members of different parties feel at ease,
and intimidates all competing groups,
the king is like a great diamond fortress.

He enjoys high standing by virtue of his merit,
and splendor due to the gods and protector deities that back him.
The king who is victorious in all directions
is like a precious victory banner.

In this way, even without traveling to heaven,
the ruler who possesses the best qualities
can make the nectar-eating gods gather joyfully before him,
just like the four-faced Brahmā, the king of the gods.

Due to his glory, the king—this fine vase, wish-fulfilling tree, and
jewel—
the unrivaled, precious ruler,
acts as if all of the glory of the heavenly realms
rests within the very palm of his hand.

Word of his glory, majesty, and fame
circulates as far as the periphery of the oceans;
the glory of his matchless qualities blazes
like a second sun over this world.

15. On the Need for Consultation

It is best when the king accomplishes
the welfare of the people of his land
and the administration of just laws and so forth
in consultation with trustworthy people.

Even if you have the kind of mind that can analyze the details,
your work should be accomplished through consultation.
This is an excellent thing to do
whether or not you succeed in accomplishing your goal.[1]
When you are first contemplating something,
you ought to analyze what is reasonable and unreasonable
not only in the advice you receive from worthy ministers
but also in the opinions expressed by others.

There are many types of advice:
the mistaken counsel offered by someone of limited intellect;
the twisted advice of people out for their own self-interest;
the brash words of those who do not analyze the consequences
 of actions;
the hesitant words of someone whose self-confidence is weak.

The opposite of these are:
the words of very intelligent people that get to the heart of the matter;
the advice given with pure intention, unadulterated with self-interest;

1. The lines are identical to *Prajñādaṇḍa*, v. 5. They are also similar to Vararuci, *Śatagāthā*, v. 98; and to Cāṇakya, *Rājanītiśāstra*, v. 3.20.

the discourse of someone who understands the consequences of actions;
and the words that generate courage in the weak.

Once you have understood these distinctly without confusing them,
then, like a swan that sucks the milk out of water,
you adopt those forms of counsel that are meaningful. [109]
Intelligent people must decide for themselves what advice they will follow.[2]

Even when you know what to do and not do,
the work of the kingdom should still be subjected to consultation and scrutiny.
There will never be any regrets about a course of action
in which everyone is consulted and agrees.

The crooks of this degenerate age conceal their intrigues
and deceive the king by speaking in cahoots,
like the thieves who called the goat
that the brahmin was leading "a dog."[3]

Therefore, wise rulers must first understand
which parties are involved in intrigue.
Having done so, they obtain independence of mind.
Only then will rulers become experts in the law.

You should only trust someone who is truthful and dependable.
Don't always believe everyone.

2. Nāgārjuna, *Ratnāvalī*, v. 3.55ab: "You must first understand on your own what your ministers are telling you, and then always implement those policies that are going to be beneficial for the world."

3. The story is of a brahmin boy who is tricked out of his goat by some crafty thieves who convince him that he actually has a dog (and not a goat) on the leash. The thieves, who are working in cahoots, station themselves at different places along the road where the brahmin boy is walking with his goat. Each of them comment on the "dog" he has with him. By the time he comes to the last of the scoundrels, the boy is so perplexed that he abandons the goat and flees. The story is found in several sources, including the famous Indian collection of animal tales called *Hitopadeśa*. A reference to the tale is also found in Sakya Paṇḍita, *Sa skya legs bshad*, v. 150; Davenport, *Ordinary Wisdom*, 114.

Intelligent people do not seek the counsel
of suspicious crow-like individuals.[4]

When you question an intelligent person who can analyze things in
great detail,
you will obtain glory.
Even the powerful Rāma
enlisted the help of Hanuman.[5]

It is good to always rely
on those who have merit and who are powerful.
The sparrow frightened the nāgas of the ocean
by summoning Garuḍa.[6]

The advice of the wise can help you to discern
those aspects of your work that confuse you.
The water-purifying jewel can clean
rivers that have become cloudy with silt.[7]

Even if you're already intelligent,
you get new insights when you consult someone else,
just as King Prasenajit won the war
by hearing the words of the people of his city.[8]

4. The reference may be to the story of the crow who deceived the owls mentioned in chapter thirteen.
5. The reference is, of course, to the famous Indian epic *Rāmāyaṇa* where Rāma received the counsel and help of the monkey-king Hanuman in his quest to free his wife Sītā from the clutches of the demon Rāvaṇa. Sakya Paṇḍita, *Sa skya legs bshad*, v. 321, also refers to the *Rāmāyaṇa*, although to make a very different point.
6. The story of the little bird who frightened the nāgas with the help of Garuḍa is also found in Sakya Paṇḍita, *Sa skya legs bshad*, v. 282; Davenport, *Ordinary Wisdom*, 184–85, and n.142. According to one version of the story, the sparrow's nest and eggs are swept away by the sea. The little bird is determined to get them back and begins to scoop out the ocean's water a bit at a time. Garuḍa witnesses this and is so moved that he comes to the sparrow's rescue and torments the ocean nāgas until they return the sparrow's nest and eggs.
7. The metaphor of the water-purifying jewel is very common in *nīti* literature. It is also found in *Prajñādaṇḍa*, v. 168; in Vararuci, *Śatagāthā*, v. 92; and in Sakya Paṇḍita, *Sa skya legs bshad*, v. 12. In those works, however, it is used to illustrate another point. In any case, the wish-granting jewel (or *kataka*) is said to have the quality of being able to purify unclean water.
8. Prasenajit (ca. sixth century BCE) was the king of Kosala, with its capital at Śrāvastī. He

Unless you examine things well, [110]
problems can arise from just a few words.
The fox destroyed the great friendship
between the lion and the bull.[9]

You should not accept what people offer you
without first weighing its long-term benefits.
Just look at the loss that Sahasrayodhī had to suffer
as the result of the courtesy of being offered a bride.[10]

---

was a well-known lay disciple of the Buddha. He was also the uncle of the expansionist ruler Ajātaśatru, the king of Magadha. The uncle and nephew fought a famous war (sources differ as to the cause of the conflict). Ajātaśatru initially won, and the defeated Prasenajit returned to Śrāvastī disheartened. The rich merchant Anāthapiṇḍada then consoled him, gave him advice, and promised enough gold to raise another army. Prasenajit followed the merchant's advice, reengaged Ajātaśatru in battle, and this time emerged triumphant over his nephew, whose life he spared on the Buddha's advice.

9. The tale is found, for example, at the very beginning of the *Pañcatantra* (Book 1). The Buddhist version is found in the Pāli *Sandhibeda Jātaka* (Jātaka no. 349); E. B. Cowell, *The Jātaka*,, Book 4: 99–101. It is also found in the *Mūlasarvāstivāda Vinaya*; see F. Anton von Schiefner, and W. R. S. Ralson, *Tibetan Tales Derived from Indian and Buddhist Sources*, 325–28. A pregnant cow that is part of the royal herd is accidentally left behind in the forest and gives birth. The baby bull grows up beside a baby lion who had also just been born. The bull and lion become best of friends. In time, they are joined by a third animal, a jackal or fox. The jackal had eaten every type of animal flesh in the forest except for that of a lion and a bull. Motivated by his desire to experience new tastes, he sets out to split the two friends apart by secretly telling each of them the horrible things each was supposedly saying behind the other's back, and the story ends with the jackal feasting on the bodies of the two former friends.

10. It is unclear whether this is a reference to the story of Sahasrayodhī ("Able to Defeat a Thousand Men") found in the *Bhaiṣayjavastu* section of the *Mūlasarvāstivāda Vinaya*, which is part of the story of King Kuśa. The ugly King Kuśa had been wed to a princess, but when she saw his horrific looks, she absconded back to her native land. King Kuśa tried various means to get her back. In his last attempt, he poses as the brave Sahasrayodhī and finds work among the ministers in the princess's palace. In the meantime, another suitor presented himself to ask for the princess's hand, threatening to annihilate the kingdom unless his demand was met. Sahasrayodhī/Kuśa then wages war and defeats the rival prince. However, the story ends happily, since through Sahasrayodhī's bravery in battle he wins the princess's heart. If it is this story that Mipham has in mind, it is unclear what "the loss" might be—unless of course it is all the travails that Kuśa had to go through to get his wife to accept him. But then it is unclear why Mipham does not refer to him as Kuśa, since Sahasrayodhī is really just an alias, one of several that Kuśa uses in that tale.

Through just a slight pretense or disguise,
the wise can deceive even clever people.
Viṣṇu, having disguised himself using the body of a dwarf,
was able to bind Bali in the underworld.[11]

Someone who possesses the highest intellect
can defeat even a clever person.
Even Viṣṇu with his five mudrās
was skillfully forced into service by Legden Nagpo.[12]

Therefore, every deed should be accomplished
in consultation with those who are skillful.
It was the massive monkey army who, working together,
created the bridge over the ocean to Laṅka.[13]

The campa flower bends toward the sun.
The plantain tree grows where thunder roars.
You never know from where
helpful friends and good advice will emerge.

Rāvaṇa was killed on account of the wife he stole from Rāma;
and the capital of Laṅka was burned to the ground by monkeys.[14]

11. Vāmana the Dwarf is the fifth incarnation or avatar of the god Viṣṇu, who manifested in this dwarf form to defeat Bali, a king (or demon) who had usurped Indra's rule of the heavens. Vāmana presents himself before Bali and asks for as much land as he can take in three steps. Since he is a dwarf, the king agrees. Vāmana then grows to tremendous proportions, and in the first two steps traverses the heavens and earth, leaving Bali with only the underworld or Pātāla, which henceforth becomes Bali's dominion.
12. Legden Nagpo is a form of the deity Mahākāla. See René de Nebesky-Wojkowitz, *Oracles and Demons of Tibet*, 52. Khyab 'jug usually refers to Viṣṇu, but also to Rāhu; Nebesky-Wojkowitzw, *Oracles and Demons*, 115, 259, 260, and so on. I have found no reference, however, to a tale of either Viṣṇu or Rāhu being forced into submission by Legden Nagpo or Mahākāla.
13. The reference is to the great Indian epic *Rāmāyaṇa*. There is a chain of shoals at the tip of India extending to Sri Lanka that exists to this day called "Rāma's Bridge" (Rāmasetu), also sometimes referred to as Adam's Bridge. It is said to have been built by Rāma's army of monkeys who were created by the god Brahmā to help Rāma in his battle against the demon Rāvaṇa. In some versions of the epic, Rāma uses the bridge to reach Laṅka, Rāvaṇa's home, so as to rescue his wife Sītā from the demon's clutches.
14. Again, the reference is to the *Rāmāyaṇa*, in which the hero Rāma saves his wife Sītā from

It is unpredictable
from where harmful friends and bad advice will emerge.

For this reason, the wise abandon
unsuitable friends and advice.
Then, relying on suitable friends and advice,
their glory will never deteriorate.

Even[15] poor, isolated people consult someone. [111]
Everything up to the two accumulations of merit and wisdom depends on advice.
It is difficult to accomplish most of the work of the kingdom
without getting advice.

If, despite having a large retinue as numerous as the stars,
a stupid king doesn't consult anyone,
he will not be able to rise from his wretched condition
no matter who he is.

When you gather many people together and consult them,
even a great person will find it hard to defeat you.
As is well known, lion cubs can be killed
when swarmed by a horde of ants.[16]

Whether you wish to protect your own party,
or destroy the other party,
the wise recommend that you bring many people together
and engage in consultation.

Even if you are as affectionate as parents,
unless you engage in consultation,
how will others know the means you intend to use
to accomplish their welfare?

---

the demon Rāvaṇa. To do so, Rāma must invade the island of Laṅka, which he does with the help of his army of monkeys.

15. I've mended *su la* to *su la'ang*.

16. Compare to Sakya Paṇḍita, *Sa skya legs bshad*, v. 203.

Because people have so many different kinds of ideas
it is easy to find consensus in discussions
even in regard to unethical actions.
What need to say that consensus is possible when you consult about something worthwhile.

Whether they live near or far to each other,
those who have achieved consensus,
take up the task at hand as if they were doing it for their own sake.
Great deeds are accomplished through consultation.

From among the types of consultations, there is the one of "Drogjung"
spoken of in the tales of the scholars of old.
They didn't first engage in consultation,
and in the end regretted it, showing themselves to be fools.[17]

When people engage in proper consultation, a finer understanding arises.
No matter what goal they are working toward, when their purposes coincide, [112]
people easily achieve even the most difficult thing.
Therefore, how can those who have large retinues not consult their retinues?

Who succeeds in accomplishing an important goal without consultation,
simply by uttering some words, like a magician intoning a spell?
But there is no consultation about who is worthy of making the final decision,
and in this sense goals are accomplished through the words of rulers.[18]

17. I have not been able to find any reference to the tale related to Drogjung ('Grogs 'byung), and so the translation of this verse is tentative.

18. I suspect that some emendation is required to make sense of the last two lines of this verse, which read: *thag chod 'os pa'i gnas la gros med kyang/ sa bdag rnams kyi tshig gis 'grub par 'gyur*. Without getting into the technicalities of the Tibetan, I believe that its meaning is this: It is impossible to achieve a goal without consultation, simply by ordering it to be accomplished, as if one were uttering a spell that magically brings about the goal. So, kings engage in consultation. But when all is said and done, the final decision rests with the king alone. This is

Therefore, in everything they do, wise rulers
convene an assembly of their retinue,
and engage in proper analysis and consultation,
When they do this, even their most powerful opponents will not be
able to cause problems.

When the power and backing of many people is combined
and consensus is reached about what ought to be done,
it can attract everyone toward a well-deliberated goal,
like a magnet attracts iron.

---

his prerogative and is non-negotiable. It is ultimately the rulers' orders that must be followed, and in that sense, it is their words that accomplish goals.

16. How to Cultivate the Ten Virtues

When a king who is himself law abiding
enforces the laws among the subjects, this is pleasing.
When he himself transgresses the law,
how can it be appropriate for him to sit in judgment of others?

The unerring principles of karmic causality and dependent arising
are the general laws of the universe.
The punishment for those who act contrary to cause and effect
is suffering in the lower realms.[1]

If the king does not act in accordance with the Dharma,
he will become disreputable in this life
and his royal authority will be destroyed.
So he ought to personally observe the rules of the ten virtues.[2] [113]

Any of the ten nonvirtues
can lead to the three lower realms.
And even when you are eventually reborn into the higher realms,
you will experience horrible side effects that accord with the
nonvirtuous cause.[3]

1. According to Buddhist cosmology the universe consists of six realms. The three lower realms are the animal, hungry ghosts, and hell realms. The three upper realms are the realms of humans, demigods, and gods.

2. The ten virtues (and their opposite, the ten nonvirtues)—the basis for Buddhist ethics—are explained in numerous sources, but of the sources that Mipham mentions in his bibliography at the end of the book, they are treated in Nāgārjuna, *Ratnāvalī*, vv. 8–23, and Nāgārjuna, *Suhṛllekha*, v. 5.

3. These are explained in what follows. For example, people who murder are said to have

Killing

All living creatures value their own lives,
so the king must completely abandon killing.
Killing shortens one's own lifespan and increases illness.
That is why, throughout his kingdom, the king must, to the best of his ability,
bring an end to violence against any being, down to birds and wild animals.
He should protect the people and animals of his kingdom
so that they can live without fear.

For the sake of the welfare of the many,
he banishes hardened criminals.
If, no matter what method he uses, he cannot reform them,
there exists a kingly tradition that states that in this age of strife,
"The kingdom becomes happy when those who perpetrate
acts of violence on living beings are killed."[4]
But even in this case, the king
should never forsake compassion.[5]

Stealing

Being satisfied with your own wealth,
you should not unjustly confiscate the wealth of others.
Stealing causes poverty in future lives,
and results in others taking your possessions.
Even when you collect just taxes
and reasonable monetary fines for crimes,
you should maintain the attitude that wealth is injurious.
You should not allow yourself to become greedy.

---

short lifespans, people who steal are said to experience the loss of their property, and so on.

4. Earlier we saw that the *Satyaka Sūtra* forbids capital punishment. Mipham here seems to leave open the possibility of killing incorrigible criminals. However, the fact that he attributes this view to the "kingly tradition during the age of strife" indicates that he is not completely comfortable with this position.

5. Cāṇakya, *Rājanītiśāstra*, v. 3.18: "When you engage in some harmful act, you should never have a harmful intention, for this only causes your own collapse, like trees at the river's edge."

Without becoming corrupted by the evil of selfishness,
and for the sake of the kingdom's welfare,
the king will never lose his self-restraint
and harm and steal from his subjects.

Adultery

Delighting in your own wife,
you should not engage in adultery. [114]
By engaging in adultery, the retinue becomes unruly,
and there will be competition among your wives.[6]

Lying

Always speaking the truth
is the highest quality of the righteous.
Liars are really denigrated,
and themselves experience being deceived.

Divisive Speech

Abandoning divisive speech that creates rifts between others,
you should instead promote reconciliation.
Divisive speech creates disharmony in the retinue
and leads to having a bad retinue that quarrels.

Harsh Words

The ruler should always strive
to speak sweetly and pleasantly.
Those who use harsh words end up in quarrels
and as the object of unpleasant rumors.

6. Many classical sources identify these two things—an unruly retinue and competition among wives—as the result that adulterers experience in the next life. Mipham does not, however, qualify these as the future-life result of engaging in adultery. So the lines can be read in both a this-worldly and otherworldly context. The same applies to other nonvirtues in the verses that follow.

Idle Talk

Giving up meaningless idle talk,
let whatever you say have a real purpose.
Those who engage in idle chatter are not considered credible
and their fitness is questioned.

Covetousness

Whether someone else is wealthy or not, do not covet what they own,
but instead remain joyful for what you have.
Covetousness leads to the smashing of your expectations
and causes you to become greedy and unsatisfied.

Harmful Thoughts

Abandon thoughts of harming others,
and have a loving attitude toward everyone.
Harmful thoughts create tremendous pain
and cause you to be needlessly harmed by others.

Wrong View

Completely do away with wrong views,
like the belief that there is no karma and its effects.
If you do not get rid of wrong views now,
you will become a mendacious purveyor of wrong views in your
next life.

Those who come under the influence of wrong views
cannot grow in virtue
just as burned seeds cannot grow into sprouts.
Right view is the basis of the whole Dharma. [115]

Life is like a cascade falling from a steep mountain,
providing short-term sustenance, but not lasting very long.

You will quickly have to go to the next world,
so be conscientious and think about your future.

That karma leads to its effects is an inviolable truth; even when small,
karmic actions are never fruitless, nor do they simply vanish.
You will experience the result of whatever you do.
No one escapes this.

Therefore, living in unrighteous nations
is a preamble to hell.
Righteous nations, by contrast,
are stairways that take you to heaven.

Once the king and royalty
are in control of their society,
they should do everything in their power
to get people to enter the path of the ten virtues.

They should protect life, engage in charity,
stop adultery, and do away with lying, and so forth.
They should rejoice in others' wealth
and meditate on love and the right view.

They care for living beings
by collecting taxes, fines, and the like in a just way.
When one acts skillfully and compassionately,
these involve no moral faults, and can even create virtue.

If, committing yourself to the root of virtue,
you strive for unsurpassed enlightenment,
you will never violate the norms of the world,
nor transgress the way of the holy.

Those who properly care for living beings according to the Dharma
have the power to accomplish the two goals of self and other.

That is why the great bodhisattvas, the children of the Conqueror,
manifest in the form of kings. [116]

It is the king's responsibility to encourage respect
for parents, ascetics, brahmins, and so forth,
to encourage the worship of the three jewels,
and to bring an end to the stream of suffering, both in this life and
the next.

He who guides living beings to the tradition
of the multifaceted methods that lead to happiness
both in this world and the next
should be called "a righteous king."

17. The Laws of a Dharma King

The wise rightly praise someone
as a great Dharma king, when,
having become righteous himself,
he restrains others with the law of the ten virtues.

The ten nonvirtues are like poison.
They harm you in this life and bring suffering in the next.
Those who violate this moral code in thought or deed
are legally made to account for their actions by Dharma kings.

People who kill humans, steal wealth,
kidnap and rape others' wives,
deceive others through lies, divide others through slander,
or engage in speech that is purposeless or harsh
should be stopped through punishments
consistent with the nature of the offense:
with the extent of injury done to others,
with whether or not they are repeat offenders, and so forth.

By preventing their physical and verbal offenses,
their more subtle mental faults
automatically lose their power.
This is what is called, "institutionalizing the law of the ten virtues." [117]

When a powerful king stops those
who perpetrate acts of violence on sentient beings,
who harm the three jewels,
who lay waste to the king's districts,

or who cause the kingdom grief,
the kingdom experiences both general and specific forms of happiness.

When a kingdom has no righteous king, it is difficult
that other methods will succeed in making the kingdom happy.
In former times, when people had a conscience,
anyone who stole just one silver coin
would be sentenced to death.

In this way, theft was rare; but nowadays,
we live in an age in which it is very difficult to discipline evildoers.
If you killed people today simply for committing such an offense,
the country and retinue would ultimately be depleted of people.
That is why the penalties against those who violate the laws
are today more moderate and why they follow
the legal edicts of the wise kings of old.[1]

What we call "the law" is impartial:
as fair or "straight" as a plumb line descending from heaven.
It is, in that sense, similar to the operation of karma.
Hence, no one can change it.

When they violate it, even princes will lose.
When they follow it, even the city's poor will win.
Like a thunderbolt that can fall on anyone's head,
it is independent of one's social standing.

The royal laws are not lighter for the powerful and wealthy,
and not heavier for the humble and poor.
Instead, everyone is equal in the eyes of the law,
just as in a brothel all men are the same.

Prostitutes make their living off of their bodies.
Ascetics make their living off of the Dharma.
The royalty make their living from the laws. [118]

1. The Tibetan legal system evolved over many centuries from the imperial age until the modern period. For an overview, see Rebecca R. French, *The Golden Yoke*.

Brahmins make their living by protecting the paternal line.
Whenever the livelihood of each of these groups declines,
they have nothing else to protect them.
How can any other force protect you
when your essential life force ceases?

Someone obtains the title "king"
because he acts as custodian of the laws.
When the laws are not justly applied,
even if there's a king, it's as if there weren't any.

Having become the custodian of the laws,
your sentencing must be just, even in regard to enemies.
Even if someone has done you harm, you must set this aside.
The laws of the wise do not discriminate between friends and foes.

Wherever the law exists
the righteous feel at ease,
and the unrighteous are careful about their actions.
Good laws protect the world and act as its refuge.

Hearing that criminals
have been justly punished
makes good people feel relieved,
and it strikes fear into evil ones.

But hearing that criminals are not being punished
makes noble people worried,
and it sets the stage for malicious people
to start engaging in unscrupulous actions.

Good people lose heart when they hear
that the innocent have been punished.
The king's disrepute—that he is dishonest and vile—
will then reach as far as the heavens.

When an innocent person is acquitted,
those who know about that person's innocence

sing the king's praises,
and even the gods will rejoice. [119]

Assault and Murder

Using corporal punishment, the king should make an example
of those who harm the life of another.
You should stop them from repeating such acts
by beating them, striking them, and so forth.

Theft

Those who steal the wealth of others should be made to pay for
their crime
through fines and by compensating the victim.
Those who steal others' wives and slaves
should also be stopped through those same means.

If the king is too lenient,
criminals and thieves proliferate,
and the country becomes filled with vicious people.
Hence, as the *Satyaka Sūtra* states,
"Even though the king is compassionate,
he will impose timely and just punishments
on criminals, while also
showing mercy to the helpless and to animals."[2]

In the *Daśacakrakṣitigarbha Sūtra*,[3]
the Blessed One says

2. The *Satyaka Sūtra*'s advice to kings concerning the administration of the law was discussed in chapter six. Regarding this point, Mipham summarized the sūtra's position as follows: "There are some who have committed no fault, and there are many innocent beings—gods and herds of animals—that belong to their households. The king should not show enmity to these, and should not destroy or lay waste to them. This is how he protects the creatures that belong to the broader environment."
3. The discourse that the Buddha gives to the god Devagarbha—offered in response to the god's request for some advice on how kings may purify themselves and achieve liberation—is found at the end of the third chapter of the sūtra (fols. 256b–258b). However, the advice the

to the Mahābrahmika[4] god Devagarbha,
"When someone, with faith in the teachings,
becomes a monk—shaving his hair and beard,
and donning the saffron robes—
whether he keeps the discipline or breaks it,
I forbid gods, humans,
demigods, and so forth[5]
from treating him disparagingly,
as if he were a householder.
What need, then, to say that I also prohibit
cutting him with iron blades,[6]
beating him with sticks,
imprisoning, scolding, or rebuking him,
cutting off his limbs, or killing him.

Buddha gives in that section of the text does not correspond to the passage that Mipham is about to paraphrase. That is found in an earlier section of the sūtra in which the Buddha preaches to Mahā Brahmā the power that even monks who have broken their vows have to generate devotion in beings. "(fol. 214a) When sentient beings see them, they recollect the Buddha, and with respect, they generate an attitude of faith and devotion. . . . (215b) Son of a good family, when beings see someone who has ordained into my religion, even if his discipline has deteriorated, (216a) they generate, simply from seeing his body or his attire, ten special attitudes, and they obtain an infinite number of precious qualities. For this reason, kings, ministers, chiefs, and the like should not strike them and punish them with sticks, or imprison them, or scold and rebuke them, or cut off their limbs, or deprive them of their life. Mahā Brahmā, those who have gone for refuge in me and have ordained, even when their discipline has deteriorated, even when they engage in nonvirtue, when they are rotten inside and filled with excrement like the *kvala* bug, when they pretend to be ascetics although they aren't, or pretend to be celibate although they aren't. . . . In this way, even when a monk is no longer a vessel of the Dharma, by having cut off his hair and beard and donned the saffron robes, his attire and behavior resemble that of āryas." Elsewhere in the sūtra (starting on fol. 239b) we even find a king named "Victorious Over Enemies" (Dgra las rgyal) issuing the following edict: "From this day forward, let anyone in my kingdom who ridicules or harms a disciple of Buddha—whether that disciple is keeping the monastic discipline, has partially lost the discipline, or has completely lost the discipline—be put to death. So long as he has shaved his head and beard and wears the saffron robes, he may not be ridiculed or harmed."

4. The Mahābrahmika realm is the god realm ruled by the god Brahmā.

5. I've emended *la sogs pa yi* to *la sogs pa yis*.

6. It is possible that the expression *lcags gis gzhur ba* may refer not to cutting the body, but to the practice of shaving the head of a criminal—e.g., before execution (see below in this same chapter).

This applies not only to learned and disciplined monks,
but even when someone has ordained and his discipline degenerates—
when his nonvirtuous behavior makes him rotten to the core,
and when he does terrible things
such as pretending to be an ascetic when he's not— [120]
even then he is a treasure house of good qualities
and ought to be worshipped by the world and its gods."

When someone wears the attire of our teacher,
and people see him, there arises in them the good quality
of remembering the teacher, the discipline, and so forth,
for although it is said that "a fallen monk is like a corpse,"
he still possesses the power of residual good qualities,
just like bile still exists in the body of a dead bull,
and musk still exists in the corpse of a musk deer.

When it is necessary to prosecute the monk who has transgressed
his vows,
it should be the saṅgha council that expels him.
It is inappropriate for anyone who has gone for refuge to the Buddha—
the king, the ministers, or secular judges—
to punish someone who is wearing the robes
by striking him, beating him, and so forth.

The Buddha did not even give permission
for kings to strike or scold
a man who commits the five heinous sins[7]
while he is wearing monks' robes, even if fraudulently.

In the future, the royalty, behaving frivolously
and having no respect for righteous ascetics,
will denigrate the relics of the three jewels.
The gods will get angry at them
and will abandon them.

7. These are sometimes called "the sins of immediate retribution." They are: killing one's father, killing one's mother, killing an arhat, maliciously causing a Buddha to bleed, and creating a schism in the saṅgha.

Righteous individuals will despair and disperse to other places.
There will be turmoil both internally and externally.
There will be much suffering throughout that land.
The kingdom will decline, and sickness and so forth will arise.

When those members of the royalty die, they will go to the suffering realms.
Under advice from evil ascetics,
serving as the king's emissaries,
those future evil kings and ministers [121]
will steal the wealth of ascetics and of stūpas
and have no regard for the wealth of the three jewels.
As a result of these extremely heinous crimes, within this life,
they will suffer from diseases that are difficult to cure.[8]
and thereafter will burn in hell for a very long time.

Once upon a time, an elephant was pierced by a poisoned arrow,
but because the archers were wearing saffron robes,
the powerful elephant did not retaliate, but simply said,
"Although these men have deluded minds
their attire is like that of the Buddha's disciples.
It would be easy for me to kill them,
but it is not right for me to entertain such a sinful thought."
Hence, even those reborn as animals
can become enraptured at the mere sight of the robes.[9]

8. I've emended *gso ka'i* to *gso dka'i*.

9. The reference is to the *Jātaka of the Six-Tusked Elephant* (*Chaddanta/Ṣaḍdanta Jātaka*), which corresponds to Pāli Jātaka no. 514; E. B. Cowell, *The Jātaka*, Book V, 20–31. The tale is preserved in various Buddhist languages and has been depicted in a number of ancient Indian cave paintings and friezes (e.g., at Ajaṇṭā, Amaravātī, Barhut, Sanchi, etc.). The Tocharian version of the tale is in the form of a drama. In one version of the story, the king of a herd of elephants, white in color with six tusks (the Buddha in a former life) had two queens. One of the elephant queens became jealous over a trivial matter. She died shortly thereafter and was reborn as a human woman Bhadrā, who became queen of Benares. Still holding a grudge against her former elephant-husband, she sent a hunter to kill him and to bring his six tusks back as proof that he was dead. After a long search, the archer finally found the elephant and shot him with a poisoned arrow. The elephant was about to retaliate, but when he saw that the archer was wearing saffron colored robes, his respect for the Buddha prevented him from taking revenge. In some versions of the story, the hunter knows of the elephant's piety

The evil royalty of the future
will harm the followers of the Buddha.
Violating the injunctions
of the buddhas of the three times,
they will fall into the great hells.

In former times there was a king
named Victorious Over Enemies.
He sent a man to be executed
in a charnel ground that was an abode of demonesses.
The man's head was shaved,
and a piece of saffron cloth was wrapped around his neck.

A demoness called Weapon Eye,
surrounded by an entourage of 5,000, saw this,
and putting her hands at her heart in respect,
said to her sons, [122]
"Whoever has a nonvirtuous thought toward this man
who is wearing the saffron cloth that is like the 'banner of liberation'
of buddhas as numerous[10] as the sands of the Ganges,
will definitely fall into the hell of the heinous sinners."

Many demonesses then freed that man
and berated the king in this way,
"O king, you and your entourage
have done something amazingly stupid.
Are you true followers of the Buddha?
From this day forth, you should never,
even in jest, harm anyone
who wears the robes, even if they are fallen monks."
And the king proclaimed this as law.[11]

---

beforehand and purposely wears monks' robes to trick him. Before the elephant dies from the poison, he helps the repentant archer slice off his own tusks for the queen. See Léon Freer, "Le Chaddanta-Jataka," 31–85, 189–223; and Albert Foucher, "Essai de classement chronologique des diverses versions du Ṣaḍdanta-jātaka," in *Mélanges d'Indianisme oferts par ses élèves a M. Sylvain Lévi*, 231–36.

10. I've emended *bye sted* to *bye snyed.*

11. The story is found in the *Daśacakrakṣitigarbha Sūtra*, fols. 237a–240a.

Even a hungry ghost who was more malicious than the demonesses
also worshipped those who wore the saffron robes;
what need to mention those evil future kings and those beings
who are more vicious even than demons,
who are stupid and delusional,
and who disrespect, abuse, beat, and harm
the followers of Buddha.

Therefore, if someone steals the wealth of monks,
or abuses or torments them with punishments,
the gods who are sympathetic to the three jewels
will forsake him in favor of his rivals.
Any kingdom that imposes such punishments
will experience a lot of suffering
and its king will suffer from various terrible illnesses.

Sesame oil pressers,[12] prostitutes,
liquor sellers, and butchers each have sins
weightier than the previous one by a factor of ten.[13]
Even greater than those terrible sins
is the horrible crime of that vile king who abuses or kills monks,
and is thereby utterly despised.

But when a king protects [123]
those who have taken up the saffron robes,
he is performing a great act of worship of the three jewels,
and for that reason, the praises of his good qualities are innumerable."[14]

12. Oil pressers (*tailakāra* or *tailika*) were considered low caste in ancient India, a belief that persists to this day in some regions of the country. There have been moves to include oil pressers (*telis*) in the contemporary scheme of "Scheduled Tribes/Castes," an official Indian government designation given to historically disadvantaged classes for the purpose of affirmative action.

13. The relative gravity of abusing or beating monks (even monks who have broken their vows) vis-à-vis other sins is explained later in the *Daśacakrakṣitigarbha Sūtra* (fol. 257a). These same five occupations—oil pressers, prostitutes, liquor sellers, butchers, the king (presumably the king who abuses, beats or kills monks)—are listed, and each is said to be ten times more sinful than the previous one.

14. This portion of Mipham's text is drawn from different parts of the *Daśacakrakṣitigarbha Sūtra* (see the previous note), but chiefly from fols. 240a–b: "In previous times, a demoness

In like fashion,
sūtras such as the *Ākāśagarbha* and so forth,
state that our teacher, the Buddha,
prohibits the punishment of monks.
They state that if the followers of the Buddha
are subjected to legal punishments,
the power of the kingdom's merit diminishes
and becomes the reason for its destruction.

However, in this degenerate age,
there are many monks who are exceedingly unruly.
When they cannot be disciplined
through the saṅgha council's religious procedures,
then the king needs to do this.

Even when these monks are many in number,
the wise and effective king
will first recollect these words of our teacher,
and then will apply them to the rules of each community,
asking the saṅgha council to resolve the problem.

If an agreement can still not be reached,
then, together with the saṅgha,
and using the words of our teacher as the standard,
the king imposes his verdict on the saṅgha
and punishes those who do not comply by banishing them and so forth.

---

was born among the hungry ghosts. She was pale in color and ate meat and blood. She was attached to sin and had no compassion. Nonetheless, seeing a monk who had lost the discipline—who, although lapsed, had shaved hair and beard and had a piece of a monk's robe tied around his neck—she circumambulated him, revered him, venerated him, bowed down to him, worshipped him, and recited verses of praise to him. She had no thought of harming that fallen monk. But future evil kings, ministers, householders, merchants, ascetics, and evil brahmins who . . . harm them, abuse them, beat them . . . or kill them—whether or not the monks are true vessels of my monastic teachings—are violating the great ethical principles of the teachings of all the lord buddhas of the past, present, and future. Having burnt and destroyed their root of virtue, there is no doubt that they will fall into the hell reserved for those who perpetrate the most heinous sins."

The king should restore to the saṅgha any wealth
that might have been stolen from its members.
When he has done this,
with an attitude that cherishes the teachings of our teacher,
he worships and honors them,
and never harms the teachings. [124]

The righteous Dharma king is someone
who isolates those individuals who offend the laity
and who binds them to the law of Dharma
so that the Buddha's teachings won't degenerate.

Such a king worships
the three jewels of the three times.
His merit, glory, and splendor
fill the kingdom with happiness.

No one is exempt from
the golden yoke of the royal laws.[15]
That is why it is explained to "weigh heavily
upon the shoulders of all beings."

Those who are upright and moral
follow the path of goodness by their very nature.
They never have to suffer legal punishments.
Hence, for them the law is light.

The law is a way of making people happy,
for the wise do not consider it
a heavy burden,
or something that is difficult to follow.

15. The "golden yoke" refers to the royal legal system. Like the yoke that beasts of burden carry on their shoulders, it can feel heavy or light. For ethical and law-abiding people, it feels light. For criminals and miscreants, it is heavy. The golden yoke is contrasted with the "silk knot," which represents the system of religious laws. See French, *The Golden Yoke*, 1, and Carl Yamamoto, *Vision and Violence*, 201.

The legal system does not legislate against
minor improprieties that are the result of selfishness.
So just laws are exceedingly "light"
for the righteous person.

It is people who, afflicted by past karma,
commit crimes in this life
that think of the law as a heavy burden.
But that is their own fault.

Those who tread the path of the ten nonvirtuous actions
are setting themselves up for a karmic retribution
that is hundreds of thousands of times more severe
than the punishments they experience in this life under the king's law.

This is what it means to say that
"just royal laws are heavy yet light." [125]
Wherever such royal laws exist
everyone is happy.

The evil royalty of this degenerate age
are wholly focused on inappropriate actions:
assembling prostitutes, being obsessed with profit,
organizing hunting parties, falsely accusing one another, and stealing.
They inflict great torment on anyone who fails to pay
even a small fraction of their unjust levies and taxes.
Because of the heavy burden their legal system places
on the righteous and unrighteous alike, it should be considered unjust.

The same applies to the silk knot of the religious laws:
it can be either tight or loose.
When you bind yourself to the religious laws,
the source of happiness in this life and the next, they are liberating.
When you are loose about them and pay them no heed,
you will be tightly bound
by hundreds of terrible fetters.

The religious laws are what loosen these.
Therefore, even though the religious laws
make holy and righteous people
feel relaxed and at ease,
immoral people find them constricting.

Ethical religious laws
are like friends to the righteous.
Scoundrels see them as enemies,
but that is not the fault of the laws, but their own fault.

So the best of kings will renounce,
as if they were poison, laws established
by malicious and selfish people—
laws that are inconsistent with religion.

When the king properly upholds the joint temporal and religious
 legal tradition,
that brings happiness and benefit in this life and the next,
he achieves personal happiness, wealth, and fame [126]
spontaneously and without effort.

Possessing the power of the winds of his merit,
the ruler who can pilot the sun and moon of the good laws
that guide us to the fine, unbroken tradition
of worldly ethics and the path of the holy,
like the wheel of the starry path of space,
beautifies the crowns of the beings on the face of the earth.
Resting eternally on the shoulders of the mountain of ethics,
he radiates the light of happiness over all the land.

18. How to Conquer the World through Skill in Means

By properly caring for your own people through the law
and by sustaining their happiness in this way, four things—
your power, your merit, the renown of your retinue, and that of
your subjects—
increase as if they were competing with one another.

The ruler who is skilled in means,[1]
fittingly praised as being akin to a powerful yakṣa spirit,
is able to bring every land under his control
and to achieve victory in all directions.

Rulers who are skilled in means
know their own power and when to wield it,
and they know which strategies to employ.
This allows them to easily accomplish their objectives.

When you are rich and powerful,
you have many friends and no enemies.

1. In a Mahāyāna context, "skill in means" (*upāya-kauśalya*) is a technical doctrinal term that refers to the practice of the first five perfections or *pāramitās* (charity, moral discipline, patience, perseverance, and meditation), which together generate the merit the bodhisattva needs to advance on the path. But in a more general sense, to have skill in means or "to be skillful in one's methods" refers to cleverness or strategic skill—knowing which methods to use in particular situations and when to employ them.

Even those who have old deeply felt grudges against you
will hold their hands at their heart in respect and act nicely toward
you. [127]

When you're weak, many enemies arise,
even if there are no lurking grudges against you.
Therefore, if you wish to defeat your enemies,
you must first develop your own strength.

How can it be difficult to subjugate others when you possess
the power of courage and of perseverance—
just as the Paṇḍavas were able to conquer
the twelve garrisons of Duryodhana?[2]

So long as you are skillful in using wisdom to protect yourself
you cannot be harmed, even if you are not powerful—
just as a rabbit drove away a herd of elephants,[3]
and killed a lion.[4]

2. This is a reference to the great war that is the subject of the famous Indian epic Mahābhārata, in which two bands of cousins, the Paṇḍavas and Kauravas, fight each other for the throne of Hastinapura. Duryodhana is the eldest of the hundred sons of the blind king Dhṛtarāṣṭra, and the head of the Kaurava forces. The sons of Paṇḍu, despite being only five in number, win the war because of their greater courage and perseverance. Compare Mipham's verse to Sakya Paṇḍita, *Sa skya legs bshad*, v. 246.

3. This tale is found in a number of sources, including the *Pañcatantra* (Book 3); Viṣṇu Śarma, *The Panćatantra*, 284–90. Compare also to Sakya Paṇḍita, *Sa skya legs bshad*, v. 87. A herd of rabbits living next to a beautiful lake is trampled underfoot by a herd of elephants rushing to enter the water. A clever rabbit hatches a plan to get the elephants to leave and never return. The rabbit named Victory approaches the chief elephant and tells him that he is the envoy of the moon god, and that the god is angry because the elephants killed so many rabbits. In Indian lore, the moon is said to be marked by a rabbit. The rabbit tells the elephant that unless he and his herd desist, the moon god will withhold its cooling rays and the elephants will be scorched to death in the heat. Terrified, the elephant asks to meet the moon god to apologize. The rabbit takes him to the lake at night, and the elephant sees the reflection of the moon in the waters. Trying to touch it with his trunk, the waters ripple and many more moons appear on its surface. The rabbit convinces the elephant that this means that he has further enraged the moon god and that it is time for him to leave. The elephant apologizes and runs away, never to return.

4. *Prajñādaṇḍa*, v. 85, *Jantupoṣaṇabiṇḍu*, v. 22, and Sakya Paṇḍita, *Sa skya legs bshad*, v. 25, all make reference to this tale in which an old and clever rabbit who was destined to be the lion's next meal saves himself by tricking the lion into thinking that he has a competitor for

When their own side was weak
and the enemy was strong,
the crows got to remain in their nest and lived happily
without ever having to argue or fight with the snake.[5]

When you are living in other people's country,
and living off of others' food,
you have to bear their insults.
If you argue with them, you will be humiliated.[6]

You must know the minds, abilities, and power
of your enemies, as well as the right time to act against them.
An intelligent person will not wage war or quarrel
at an inappropriate time.

No task that you are trying to accomplish
poses any difficulty when it is done at the right time.
Those who know how to time their actions
are never confused about when to move forward and when to
change course.

---

the title of "King of the Forest"—another lion who lives in a well. When the lion sees his own reflection in the well, he becomes enraged, leaps into the well to attack his rival and is killed. The animals in the forest rejoice at the rabbit's cleverness. This tale too is found in the *Pañcatantra* (Book 1); Viṣṇu Śarma, *The Panćatantra*, 69–75.

5. This story is found in the *Pañcatantra* (Book 1); Viṣṇu Śarma, *The Panćatantra*, 62–69. A reference to the story is found in *Prajñādaṇḍa*, v. 84. Two crows are trying to raise their family of chicks in a tree, but each time a brood hatches, a snake who lives in a hole at the base of the tree eats them. The male crow consults his best friend, a crafty fox, who advises him to fly around until he sees some members of the royalty having a picnic. The crow is told to snatch away a piece of jewelry and to drop it into the hollow of the tree where the snake lives. This works and when the king's men go to retrieve the item that the crow had stolen, they come upon the snake and kill it. The crows live happily ever after in the tree, raising their chicks without any fear.

6. Compare to *Nāgarājabherī Gāthā*, v. 32, Lhasa ed., fol. 316a: "Those who abandon their home and country, and travel to others' lands, must put aside evil words, and have great patience." The identical verse is also found in *Jantupoṣaṇabinḍu*, v. 35. Compare also to Cāṇakya, *Rājanītiśāstra*, v. 8.4: "Staying in other people's homes—eating their food, wearing their clothes, living in their country, and having their women—can make even Indra's glory fade." Finally, consider *Jantupoṣaṇabinḍu*, v. 25: "When you have to live in other people's lands and be supported by them, you will find happiness only if you remain silent, no matter how much you are insulted."

Those who begin a task without first consulting
the texts of divination, astrology, and numerology
written by the great ascetics
are like blind men who go for a stroll in the jungle.[7]
Not knowing when the time is right and when it's not,
the people of this degenerate age,
ignorant about these insightful instructions, [128]
err even in regard to minor matters.[8]

People who possess merit
start their work at the appropriate time
by being aware of various auspicious omens
and of the signs revealed by protector deities.

You subjugate some people by caring for them;
others you need to destroy.
The man who is skillful in which method to use
accomplishes all his goals with little difficulty.

The greedy are deceived by wealth,
the proud by others' respect,
and fools by agreeing with them.[9]
Ordinary folk are happy with some food and drink,
and the poor with a little charity,
but gods, ascetics, saints, and sages
are satisfied only with one thing: the truth.[10]

7. The jungle was considered a dangerous place, and no one—much less the blind—would simply go for a leisurely stroll there without making the proper arrangements for their own protection.

8. Compare to Cāṇakya, *Rājanītiśāstra*, v. 8.50: "Simply reading the words and then further analyzing the meaning of the texts will allow you to avoid confusion about your actions."

9. Masūrākṣa, *Nītiśāstra*, v. 3.7. As Hugh Flick shows, the Tibetan translation misses the point of the Sanskrit. Mipham's version of the verse is actually closer to the Sanskrit; his source was probably Cāṇakya (see the following note). The Sanskrit, found in a number of sources, reads: "You captivate a greedy person with wealth, a proud man by showing him respect, a fool by acceding to his wishes, and a wise man by conforming to reality." See Flick, *Carrying Enemies*, 56.

10. The verse is very similar to Cāṇakya, *Rājanītiśāstra*, v. 2.12–13: "The greedy are captivated using wealth; the humble captivated by showing them respect. Fools are gladdened by

When you understand people's minds
and act accordingly, you can use this skill
to influence your opponent's thinking.
It will then not be hard to lead them wherever you wish,
like the wind blowing a bit of cotton around.

Until a danger actually arises,
you should fear that danger.
But once the danger actually manifests,
you should conquer it as if it were no danger at all.[11]

Really intelligent people triumph over the force of anger.
Evil people lose the fight from the very first moment of their rage.
How can one compare these evil-minded losers[12]
to the wise who practice patience?[13]

Attachment to the caress of a lover seems like water that you drink,
but once the heat is turned up, it can burn just like a fire.
When exceptional beings see this aspect of people's nature,
ordinary people become for them a cause for laughter. [129]

When your fortitude is as stable and vast as the earth,
and your perseverance pushes you as fiercely as the wind at the end
of time,
any enemy who opposes you
is destroyed like a ball of dust.

---

pleasantries; the wise are gladdened by the truth. Gods, brahmins, and the best of men are gladdened by the truth; ordinary people are gladdened by some food and drink." The word "deceived" (*bslu*) in the first line is found in all the different editions of Mipham's text, even though it diverges from "captivated" (*bsdu*) found in Cāṇakya. Compare also to Vararuci, *Śatagāthā*, v. 78, and to Sakya Paṇḍita, *Sa skya legs bshad*, v. 225. The sage's commitment to truth is also stressed in Amoghavarṣa, *Vimalapraśnottara*, v. 50.

11. Almost identical versions of the verse are found in *Prajñādaṇḍa*, v. 89, and in Masūrākṣa, *Nītiśāstra*, v. 2.6.

12. The Tibetan reads *pham pas pham par byas pa*, literally, "who have been defeated by one who has been defeated (or by defeat itself)."

13. The lines are identical to *Prajñādaṇḍa*, v. 67. See also Masūrākṣa, *Nītiśāstra*, v. 4.17: "One does not reveal to the enemy whether one's eyes are open or shut. When they insult you, pretend you're deaf. Then when the time is right, cut them with your blade."

When you always remain on the path of righteousness,
the power of the truth of your deeds delights the gods,
and the power of their righteous wrath destroys
any injustice that stands in your way. How amazing!

Due to his merit and the power of the protector deities that support him,
he always wears the armor of protection.
Armed with the weapons of fierce spells and curses,
the lion among men is victorious over all lands.

If he waits until his own strength has matured,
and then commences his campaign
with vigor and at just the right time,
what difficulties can he face in dealing with the enemy?

People who understand the right time to act
will reconcile with their enemies at the right time,
and will start friendships and wars at the right time.
Sometimes they begin an undertaking right away; at other times,
they delay.

Sometimes they act like the mute and the deaf,[14]
but when the time is right, they speak like a ruler.
Sometimes they are cool as a snow mountain,
but when the time is right, they blaze like a fire.

Sometimes they will be as pliant as grass,[15]
but when the time is right, they act like Mount Meru.

14. The next eleven lines beginning with this one are taken almost verbatim from the *Nāgarājabherī Gāthā*, vv. 63–64, 66, Lhasa ed., fols. 318a–b. The subject of these lines in the canonical version is not the king, but the sage or wise person (*mkhas pa*). Compare also to *Jantupoṣaṇabinḍu*, v. 24: "Sometimes, you should be as humble as grass. Sometimes, blaze like a fire. Sometimes, you should act like a snow mountain; and sometimes, like an invading army."

15. Mipham's text reads *rtsa* ("root"); the *Nāgarājabherī Gāthā* and *Jantupoṣaṇabiṇḍu* read *rtswa* ("grass").

Sometimes they will acquire as much as a king,[16]
but when the time is right, they will retreat to the forest like a
hermit. [130]

Sometimes they will amuse themselves in joyful song and dance,
and sometimes they will conceal themselves like deer,
but when the time is right, they manifest the prowess of a lion.[17]
Understanding the right and wrong times for various activities, they
behave in such ways.

Because of his knowledge of particular places, times, and people,
when the king challenges and opposes even his most powerful enemies,
he sometimes exacts
amazing retribution.
But despite the strength of the king and his army, because he takes into
account
factors like place, time, and the capacities of people,
there are also times when he is careful not to harm
even the weakest of his enemies.

Sometimes, when he sees that aggression is improper,
he will ignore a situation,
and with a gaze like that of a great elephant,
remains as if unaware of what is happening.
But in other instances, he quickly assesses
the machinations of the enemy, whose evil tradition
is spreading like a blight, and he exterminates it.
This is how the wise act.

Rulers with clear intellects will see
the precise extent of what their response should be
to various situations exemplified by those just mentioned.
How can fools understand this, even when they try?

16. Mipham's text reads *rgyal po lta bur 'byor bya zhing* ("they will acquire like a king"); the *Nāgarājabherī Gāthā* reads *rgyal po lta bur 'gyur bar bya* ("they act like a king").
17. Mipham's text reads *seng ge* ("lion"); the *Nāgarājabherī Gāthā* reads *gcan zan* ("wild animal").

Even if some information is completely true,
it will not sit well with others
unless it is the right place and time to share.
That is why speech that is timed just right is so stunning.

Even when he is at the peak of his powers,
he will not perform impossible acts of largesse.
Because people are under the influence of karma,
various ups and downs may still occur.

Even when he is really weak, [131]
he will not tolerate being bullied.
Who became whose slave
inside the vast belly of Kubera?[18]

Even when he is extremely poor,
he will not turn away from the Dharma.
When one acts according to Dharma,
frailties vanish like dreams.

Even when he is extremely powerful
he does not ignore others.
When one appropriately takes care of others,
one's own excellence increases.

Most things that are good on the surface
end up as bad hindrances. There are many such cases.
Most things that are bad on the surface
end up being advantageous. There are also such cases.

People are considered intelligent
when, without consulting others,
they use their own wisdom to analyze affairs
that are dangerous and extremely difficult to analyze.

18. Kubera (Nor 'dzin) is the god of wealth. He is portrayed as having a large stomach. But I know of no tale like the one that Mipham is alluding to here.

The charity that fools strive hard to accomplish,
the wise belittle and consider fools' attempts to impress people.
The anger and abuse that evil people spew out
simply elicit a smile for the wise.

Those who have skill in means become more focused even when they're tormented,
just as the elephant becomes more focused through the hook.
Unskillful people are repulsed by others even when they're being cared for by them,
viewing them as if they were some disgusting thing that they were being forced to eat.

The skillful use positive methods to accomplish negative ends,
and negative methods to accomplish positive ends.
The plans of people who have skill in means are accomplished
in a way that is unfathomable to others.

An image drawn in the mind may be invisible,
like a treasure buried in space, [132]
but when the time is right, all of its meanings
become as clear and distinct as the patterns in brocade.[19]

Someone who uses cunning to know people's innermost thoughts
is not said to be "skilled in means."
A deed of someone who possesses skill in means
is proclaimed by everyone as being truly amazing.

If gods, ascetics, and powerful kings
who have merit and skill in means
are able to really benefit or harm others simply through their words,
what need to mention what they can do through their actions.

19. The Tibetan tradition—and especially the Nyingma tradition of Mipham—speaks of certain treasures being concealed in space. For example, the deity Vajrapāṇi is sometimes said to have concealed the esoteric or tantric scriptures in space. When the time was right, they were revealed to King Jah, who was able to retrieve them through various dreams, and who then disseminated them in the world. See José I. Cabezón, *The Buddha's Doctrine and the Nine Vehicles*, 84–85.

When they first see the plans of the wise,
ignorant people deride them.
But when they finally see the completed result
everyone admires the wise.

Therefore, ordinary people's inability
to accept the deeds of the wise,
which are beyond their comprehension,
must be seen as a sign of their childishness.

When a great fire is engulfing the forest,
a huge hurricane only fuels it.[20]
No matter what harm the wisest people encounter,
it only benefits them.[21]

Most of the tasks that the ignorant consider to be heavy burdens
the wise consider to be light.
Enemies make skillful people flourish,
just as poison makes the bodies of peacocks more radiant.[22]

A hero is someone who defeats an army.
Killing your wife doesn't make you a hero.
Someone becomes a hero by prevailing in the face of a real danger,
and not simply by acting arrogantly in the royal court.

Horses, elephants, and humans
are superficially similar.
It is when someone applies his special inner qualities to a task
that we understand him to be human. [133]

Bribes, boons from the king, prostitutes' wages,
compliments, fare for passage on a ferry,

20. The metaphor (of the wind fueling the forest fire) is found in several sources—e.g., Vararuci, *Śatagāthā*, v. 20ab; and *Prajñādaṇḍa*, v. 41.
21. *Prajñāśataka*, v. 19: "Evil people cannot impede the plans of noble individuals. When a precious [magical] lamp is burning, a hurricane cannot put it out."
22. According to ancient Indian lore, peacocks have the unusual ability to eat poison. Instead of killing them, the poison makes their colors all the more brilliant.

and someone's share of the household inheritance—
need to be grabbed right away,
otherwise they'll be lost.[23]

Relying on the guidance of the holy, studying,
training in the arts, acquiring wealth,
accomplishing the deity, meditating in samādhi, and so forth—
require long-term effort; don't be impetuous about these.

The red banner of power is hoisted up
on a fierce sharp-tipped spear;
during the battle, this flag of victory over enemies
always remains in the hands of the greatest hero.

Anger at someone who is peaceful and disciplined is hard to bear.
When you rely on such an excellent person, you win; when you fight with them, you lose.
When you submit to them, they take care of you; when you compete with them, they destroy you.
The best of people possess many amazing qualities.

By taking a long view that looks far into the future,
those who have perfected their good qualities
reach ever higher accomplishments,
until they eclipse even the world of Brahmā.

Because their fame reaches such heights,
thinking that they're going to tear even through the top of space itself,
the mass of planets and stars that move through the deathless path of the sky
occasionally tremble with fear. When they witness this,
the mass of young flowers sitting on the lap
of Sītā, the daughter of Earth, open their eyes,
and displaying their strings of newborn saffron teeth,
they laugh in unison, thinking to themselves, "Perhaps they'll make it."

23. The verse is essentially identical to *Prajñādaṇḍa*, v. 9.

Dishonest people who are given to deceiving others [134]
can be recognized simply from the words they speak.
But no matter what strategies these crafty people use to deceive sages,
those wise ones are never tricked by them; this is a power they have.

The greedy, who crave wealth,
are deceived by that and do not realize
that it's their own choice to have been fettered by the wealth.
The wise focus on repaying others' kindness; this is a power they have.

Disciplined sages have this magical power:
when they experience harm due to someone's anger,
they stop the person harming them,
but think to themselves, "That was my fault."

Because the weapon of pride
causes the proud to become agitated,
intelligent people destroy the mountain of pride.
This is their highest accomplishment.

Those who have skill in means have this power:
when someone is jealous of them, they strengthen
the good qualities of the jealous person,
outshining their opponents without ever competing with them.

Whatever plans they undertake
they see through to the end.
They are triumphant over all opponents
and give solace to all factions.

Someone who has this level of skill in means—
like a cakravartin and like the sun—
can conquer the world alone
without needing any allies.

When he desires political power, he just claims it.
When he doesn't, he casts it aside even if he's obtained it.

He is totally independent of others.
He is the best of all men.

It is difficult to offer advice to him using words like,
"You should do such and such a thing in such and such a way." [135]
The power of his merit and the strength of his intellect
arise from his glory and from the blessing of the gods.

Whenever such incomparable individuals arise
in any clan or group,
it gives rise to goodness
that lasts until the end of time.

19. How to Contemplate the Dharma

The most intelligent rulers do not focus
simply on bringing about the happiness of this life,
which is as fleeting as the dance of lightning.

Foolish and childish people
become attached to fleeting pleasures
and then engage in sinful deeds to obtain them.
This brings them boundless suffering.

When a nation follows the holy Dharma,
the tradition of "the people's Dharma" arises as a byproduct,[1]
and the state's excellence increases
without ever being obstructed.

1. The tradition of "the people's Dharma" or *michö* (*mi chos*) generally refers to the customs that govern righteous conduct in society. The *michö* can also refer to a specific moral code set forth by the ancient kings of Tibet. For example, Songtsen Gampo (d. 649), who according to the Tibetan tradition was Tibet's first Buddhist king, is said to have created a code of conduct for his people called the "sixteen pure Dharmas for the people" (*mi chos gtsang ma bcu drug*): (1) having faith in the divine three jewels; (2) seeking out and practicing the holy Dharma; (3) repaying the kindness of parents; (4) honoring the learned; (5) showing respect for elders and people of high lineage; (6) helping one's neighbors and countrymen; (7) speaking truthfully and acting with humility; (8) being loyal to relatives and friends; (9) following in the footsteps of upright people and enduring in this; (10) moderation in food and wealth; (11) repaying those who have been kind; (12) repaying debts in a timely manner, and honesty in weights and measures; (13) not being too jealous of anyone; (14) ignoring bad advice and being independent; (15) speaking sweetly and not being verbose; (16) being far-sighted and having a broad outlook. Western scholars have questioned whether this code was in fact the work of Songtsen Gampo, but no one disputes that the tradition of *michö* is very old, since it is found among the Dunhuang documents. See appendix 1 concerning the *michö* in one such text, the *Elder Brother's Advice to the Younger Brother*.

When you properly practice the people's Dharma,
it won't be long before you reach heaven.
Ascending the staircase of gods and men,
you are then close to emancipation.[2]

Since you have obtained this human body, with its leisure and
 opportunities,[3]
that is so difficult to find, if you are not careful,
when the messengers of the Lord of Death come calling,
you will regret it; but what can you do about it at that point?[4]

2. The verse is identical to *Prajñāśataka*, v. 98.
3. A human rebirth is considered very rare and difficult to obtain, but a human rebirth that possesses the so-called leisures (*dal ba*) and opportunities (*'byor ba*) is considered extraordinary. Once attained, people who do not take full advantage of it are said to squander a very rare opportunity for spiritual practice. Generally speaking, the leisures and opportunities refer to being born as a human being with all one's faculties intact, and in a place and time that permits access to a buddha's teachings. The leisures and opportunities are explained in great detail in the *lam rim* or "stages of the path" literature. See, for example, Tsong-kha-pa, *The Great Treatise on the Stages of the Path to Enlightenment*, vol. 1, 117–128. In fact, most of what Mipham discusses in this chapter and the next is found in the *lam rim* literature—in texts like Tsongkhapa's *Great Treatise* (*Lam rim chen mo*) and in Patrul Rinpoche's *Revelations of Guru Samantabhadra* (*Kun bzang bla ma'i zhal lung*); Patrul Rinpoche, *The Words of My Perfect Teacher*. But many of these same topics—death and impermanence, the precious human rebirth, karma and the sufferings of the lower realms, compassion, the six perfections, and so forth—are also taken up in Nāgārjuna's *Ratnāvalī* and *Suhṛllekha*; many of these topics are also treated in the *Jantupoṣaṇabindu*, vv. 46–71. This chapter covers the *lam rim* doctrines up to the generation of "the mind of enlightenment" or *bodhicitta*. The next chapter covers the rest of the path, basically the six perfections. Mipham even includes, as many *lam rim* texts do, a very brief summary of Tantra.
4. Mātṛceta, *Kaniṣkalekha*, vv. 58–63, also contains advice to the king about when the Lord of Death comes calling. Leaving everything behind, the king's fate is determined by his past karma, just as it is for everyone else. This is also the main teaching of a Mahāyāna scripture *Instructions to the King* (*Rājadeśanāma Mahāyāna Sūtra*, Dpe sdur ma ed., 550–57), the recipient of which was King Bimbisāra. The sūtra deals with impermanence and the certainty of death, the transience of the body, youth, fame, and wealth, and the suffering that ensues from engaging in negative deeds. After hearing this, the king asks whether there is any happiness at all. The Buddha replies that nirvāṇa is the highest happiness. Hearing all this, King Bimbisāra "renounces saṃsāra, gives up his kingdom 'like spit,' and dedicates himself to achieving nirvāṇa." The Buddha concludes with this *subhāṣita* or elegant verse: "Of all footprints, the elephant's is supreme. Of all flowers, the white lotus is supreme. Of all recognitions, the recognition of impermanence is supreme. Of all thoughts, renunciation is supreme." *Rājadeśanāma*, Dpe sdur ma ed., 557.

Alas, all compounded things are impermanent;
They have the characteristic of constantly arising and ceasing.
Whatever is born dies. [136]
Anything that comes together falls apart.

Once born, your lifespan is quickly depleted,
like a waterfall flowing from a steep mountain.
The life of creatures lasts but a moment,
and then they go before the Lord of Death.

The Lord of Death won't wait or listen to such excuses as,
"I've finished this, but not that."
So engage in meritorious deeds
from this very day forward.[5]

Wealth fluctuates and youth ends in an instant.[6]
Life is lived in the fangs of the Lord of Death.
Alas, how amazing the behavior of people
who are lax about preparing for their next life.[7]

Abandon the bustle of this life;
but if you cannot do so,
then associate with holy people.
That is the medicine for the distracted life.[8]

Abandon desire,
but if you cannot do so,
then direct your desire toward being liberated.
That is the medicine for attachment to pleasure.[9]

5. Compare to Vararuci, *Śatagāthā*, v. 105; and to *Prajñādaṇḍa*, v. 324.
6. Amoghavarṣa, *Vimalapraśnottara*, v. 29: "What is unstable and quickly perishes? People's youth, wealth, and lifespan."
7. Compare to *Prajñādaṇḍa*, v. 214; to Vararuci, *Śatagāthā*, v. 102; and to Cāṇakya, *Rājanītiśāstra*, v. 8.14, which states, "In this world, life is unreliable. Wealth and youth are unreliable. Friendships are unreliable. Only righteousness, fame, and reputation are reliable."
8. The source of the verse is likely *Prajñādaṇḍa*, v. 187. But compare also to Vararuci, *Śatagāthā*, v. 12; and to Sakya Paṇḍita, *Sa skya legs bshad*, v. 435.
9. The verse is essentially identical to *Prajñādaṇḍa*, v. 188, and to Vararuci, *Śātagāthā*, v. 13.

If all these beings could see
the Lord of Death sitting on their head,
they would find no joy even in eating;
what need to speak about finding pleasure in other actions.[10]

The Lord of Death is already
sitting and waiting in front of you.
Who knows when he will strike,
like a bolt of lightning striking you on the head.[11]

People's lifespans are exceedingly short;
the night uses up half of its hours.
Sickness, old age, afflictive emotions, and fear
prevent us from living the other half happily.[12]

Alas, those who, deceived by frivolous distraction,
squander what little leisure and opportunity
they have in this momentary life,
will fall into the suffering realms. [137]

Can you really bear the sufferings
of the exceedingly hot and cold hells:
of being burned in raging fires
and being interred in pockets of snow?

The same applies to the suffering
of the poor, starving hungry ghosts,
and of the animals who experience the pain of being stupid,
of mutually harming one another, and of being exploited.

Those who fall into these three states of suffering
encounter horrific and long-lasting pain.

10. The verse is identical to *Prajñādaṇḍa*, v. 216, and to Vararuci, *Śatagāthā*, v. 104.
11. Amoghavarṣa, *Vimalapraśnottara*, v. 16: "What is to be feared in this life? Death, the end of life."
12. The verse is almost identical to Cāṇakya, *Rājanītiśāstra*, v. 8.15.

What self-aware person would enter
into such an abyss on purpose?

Even the higher realms of gods and humans
possess various kinds of suffering:
humans are born, grow old, get sick, and die;
gods too die and fall into the lower realms.

The world is permeated by the three forms of suffering:
the natural suffering of pain,
things that appear to be pleasant but that change into pain,
and the condition that acts as the cause of future suffering.[13]
Hence, there is no happiness within saṃsāra,
which is like a sweet-smelling swamp of excrement.

Childish beings constantly take rebirth,
cycling through these demonic lands and fire pits.
But what causes us to experience happiness and suffering
in the higher and lower realms?
The cause is virtuous and sinful deeds.
You experience the effect of each action you do; no doubt about it.
No matter how prosperous a kingdom may be,
old age, sickness, and death
are experienced by everyone in common.
How can anyone escape them?

When, ravaged by time, it is the king's turn to go,
his wealth, relatives, and friends do not follow him. [138]
Wherever individuals stay and wherever they go,
it is only karma that, like a shadow, follows them.[14]

13. These are the three forms of suffering listed and explained in many works: (1) suffering of suffering (ordinary pain, both physical and mental), (2) the suffering of change (things that on the surface appear to be pleasurable but that change into pain), and (3) the suffering that pervades all conditioned existence (the fundamental condition that leads to all of the other types of sufferings—having physical and mental "aggregates" that are produced by karma and mental afflictions).

14. Compare this verse to the *Ways of the World* (*Vajjālaga*) of the Jain scholar Jayavallabha: "Sons, relations, and even wealth desert a man, but there's something that doesn't—karma

The karma of embodied beings
never vanishes, even if a hundred eons go by.
When the proper conditions come together
and the time is right, it ripens into its result.[15]

Therefore, the belief in the infallibility
of cause and effect
is considered the mundane right view,
and the foundation of all positive qualities.[16]
Whatever great being
has acquired this mundane right view
will not go to the realms of suffering
even for a thousand lives.

Having understood the profound way of the interdependence of cause
and effect,
the master of living beings, the Buddha, taught the path of
emancipation.
There is no one comparable to our teacher,
the great ascetic, the highest refuge.

Likewise, no one else has a doctrine that is superior
to the one realized and taught by him—
a doctrine, the essence of which is the noble Eightfold Path,
that is a great cloud of peaceful, cooling, and blissful nectar.

Because their minds have absorbed the nectar of Dharma to satiety,
this holiest of fields,[17] the precious saṅgha,

earned in previous lives." Cited in T. R. Srinivasa Sharma et al, *Ancient Indian Literature: An Anthology*, vol. 2: 765–66.

15. Cāṇakya, *Rājanītiśāstra*, vv. 6.20–21: "Wherever the Lord of Death is, that is where you die. Wherever [the goddess] Śrī lives, that is where you find success. Wherever karma leads you, that is where you must go. Whatever acts—virtuous or nonvirtuous—you have done in the past, follow you, the actor."

16. Nāgārjuna, *Ratnāvalī*, vv. 1.43–44, discusses this in both negative and positive terms. Nihilism, the denial of karmic causality, he states, is a wrong view. The belief that actions (karma) lead to an effect is the "right view."

17. The saṅgha is called a field because when the seeds of virtuous actions are "planted" within it—for example, by giving alms to nuns and monks—they ripen into a harvest of happiness.

the basis of all good qualities, which is like the moon,
cannot be compared to any other community.

The white parasol renowned as the three jewels
is the source of all the goodness of this world and of the state of
  final peace.
Those who rely on them with trust and faith
will go from bliss to bliss and reach the highest enlightenment. [139]

People who are frightened
mostly go for refuge to the mountains, forests,
gardens, and to the great trees
that serve as the site for spirit worship.
But those are not the chief sources of refuge.
You will not free yourself of all suffering
by relying on those for protection.

To go for refuge to the Buddha,
the Dharma, and the Saṅgha,
means to use one's wisdom to examine
the four truths of the noble āryas,
who have reached the happiness of nirvāṇa—
the truths of suffering, the origin of suffering,
the transcendence of suffering,
and the noble Eightfold Path.
That is our true refuge.
Whoever relies on that refuge
will be liberated from suffering.

Out of his love and mercy, our supreme, incomparable teacher
took responsibility for all beings.
We too should train as he did to achieve
a state of immeasurable perfect qualities.

What self-reflective person would not want to generate
compassion for this mass of beings who, from beginningless time,

have been our mothers and fathers,
and who have been tormented, against their will, by the three types of suffering?

If you generate bodhicitta—the mind directed at enlightenment—
so as to bring beings as boundless as space
to a place of true happiness and beneficence, [140]
you will reach the other side of the ocean of good qualities.

Generating, from the start, the self-arisen mind,
the basis of enlightenment,
has been recommended innumerable times.
But even incomparable scholars cannot put this into words.[18]

18. Mipham seems to be making reference here to the teachings of Dzogchen, the Great Perfection, a practice aimed at generating the self-arisen mind (*rang byung sems*) or innate awareness (*rig pa*).

20. Meritorious Deeds

O father, this world is the site of karma;
beyond it lies the site of karmic result.
Whatever we have done in this life,
we will definitely experience in another.[1]

Even small virtues and sins
can have extensive results.
Having been born into this site of karma,
why not opt for planting virtuous seeds?

Holy people avoid even the smallest sin.
Evil people don't worry about even big ones.
The eye is careful to avoid just a speck of dust.
The hand dares to touch the fire.

Charity

The body is as fragile as a bubble.
Glory and wealth are as fleeting as clouds in an autumn sky.
Understanding the nature of the best that this unstable world has
to offer,
you must resolve to let it all go.[2]

After you die, there's no saying who will be the recipient
of the wealth that you have saved and never spent.

1. The source of the verse is *Prajñādaṇḍa*, v. 202.
2. Compare to Nāgārjuna, *Ratnāvalī*, v. 4.13; and to Vararuci, *Śatagāthā*, v. 61.

But if you give it away now, the result is great,
for that act of charity will then follow you into the next world.[3]

If you wish to turn your wealth
into a great treasure that is never lost,
engage in charity and rejoice in such acts of giving
without being stingy or greedy.[4]

Great wealth brings little benefit.
A little charity yields tremendous results. [141]
Although charity is the gateway to increasing wealth,
fools fear that it will exhaust their riches.[5]

The wise have no attachment
to the things that childish people crave.
The latter always look after this body
as if it were a beautiful royal chariot.

The wise have no attachment
to the things that foolish people crave.
The latter always obsess over their wealth
like bees over the honey they have accumulated.

When the good ruler, who is like a lotus pond,
fills every direction with the fragrance of his charity,
the flower eating bees, the people of the earth,
congregate before him and rejoice, dancing their happy dance.

3. Compare to Nāgārjuna, *Ratnāvalī*, vv. 4.14–16; to *Śatagātha*, v. 10; and to *Prajñādaṇḍa*, vv. 101, 197. Eventually we must give up our wealth—"you can't take it with you." It is better to do so voluntarily before we die since this constitutes an act of giving or generosity, and therefore creates merit, which is something that follows you into the next life.
4. Compare this verse and the next to Sakya Paṇḍita, *Sa skya legs bshad*, v. 256.
5. Compare to *Prajñādaṇḍa*, v. 198; to Sakya Paṇḍita, *Sa skya legs bshad*, v. 405; and to Cāṇakya, *Rājanītiśāstra*, vv. 6.9, 6.11: "Always be generous. A person should not be stingy. Using your wealth does not exhaust it, but [being stingy] does use up your good fortune. . . . When you give wealth away, it replenishes itself. Even if you take water out of a well, each day more will take its place."

Charity is the single best method to achieve
long life, wealth, fame, and the greatest forms of happiness
that belong to this life and the next; but evil-minded people
who are attached to their possessions are incapable of it.

No matter how tightly you hold on to things that are fleeting and
worthless,
sooner or later you will have to give them up—this is for sure.
Possessions are as fragile as bubbles of water.
So why not try and be charitable so as to acquire something that is
really worthwhile?

Charity is the ornament of the world.
Charity blocks rebirth in the realms of suffering.
Charity is the stairway to higher rebirth.
Charity is the virtue that brings peace.

If you want to obtain inexhaustible wealth,
you ought to take great interest in charity.
There's no need to mention its results in the next life,
but can't you see its benefits even in the here and now? [142]

Fools spend their lives enslaved in menial work
so as to accumulate wealth
with nothing to show for it except for suffering.
What is the point of such desires when you've grown old?

The delightful pastimes of the ruler
who amuses himself with a host of youths
and with his amazing wealth
is like a magic show that deceives children.[6]

Therefore, giving up attachment to wealth
make as many offerings and donations as you can.
Give the gift of a safe refuge
to those who have no protector.

6. Amoghavarṣa, *Vimalapraśnottara*, v. 52: "What brings grief? Attachment to wealth."

Kings should also bestow
the pure gift of the Dharma
so as to open the wisdom-eye
of worldly people who are like the blind.[7]

Thinking of the multitudes who, under the power of delusion,
experience so much involuntary suffering in saṃsāra,
great beings generate an attitude that reaches
to the very limits of space and time, thinking,
"Everything that I possess—
my body, my possessions, and so forth—
I will use to eradicate all their suffering
and to bring them happiness."

Moral Discipline

The ruler who, at the proper time,
takes the Mahāyāna precepts[8]
or who possesses a daily discipline
creates a kingdom like that of the gods in heaven.

Everything, both animate and inanimate,
exist in dependence on the earth.

7. These lines describe the three classical forms of charity: giving material things, giving protection, and giving the Dharma.
8. The Mahāyāna precepts (*mahāyāna poṣadha*, *theg chen gso sbyong*) are a special Mahāyāna form of a more general Buddhist practice called *upavāsa* taken by laypeople for a period of twenty-four hours. Both are often taken on auspicious days like the new and full moon. The Mahāyāna version is undertaken with the special Mahāyāna motivation of *bodhicitta*, the wish to attain enlightenment for the sake of others. The practitioner performs a brief ritual in the early morning and then vows to observe eight precepts until the sunrise of the next day: four of these are the first four of the five lay precepts (not killing, stealing, lying, or intoxicants). The fifth lay precept is avoiding sexual misconduct (adultery and so forth), but in the context of the twenty-four-hour Mahāyāna precepts, full celibacy is observed. The last three precepts are (6) fasting, (7) not using high seats or beds, and (8) not using perfumes or ointments or engaging in singing, dancing, or playing music. See Nāgārjuna, *Suhṛllekha*, vv. 10–11, and the commentary by Rendawa on these verses in Tharchin and Engle, *Nāgārjuna's Letter*, 44–45.

Likewise, all worldly and transcendental qualities
depend on moral discipline. So it is taught.

Guard your speech, control your mind well,
and do not engage in nonvirtues with your body.
When these three "paths of action" have been purified, [143]
you will obtain the path taught by the ascetic, the Buddha.

Maintain the discipline of the ten virtues yourself.
Get all the individuals of your retinue to do likewise.
Truly majestic rulers will always enact strategies
to bring about various forms of welfare and happiness.

Patience

Malicious beings who, like poisonous snakes,
are evil to their very core
abound among the people of these degenerate times.[9]
Who can possibly defeat them all?
But when you get rid of your own anger,[10]
it is like defeating all your enemies.[11]
Among all the forms of ascetic practice,
patience is praised as the best.[12]

People under the influence of anger act violently,
whether they want to or not.
But those who understand the nature of things
will not get even slightly angry.

In your next life patience gets you
a beautiful body the color of gold, held within a newborn lotus—

9. Compare to Cāṇakya, *Rājanītiśāstra*, v. 5.17: "Who would not fear people who are evil to the core, who are always saying bad things that are difficult to bear, who get terribly angry at you for no reason, and are like poisonous snakes?"
10. Masūrākṣa, *Nītiśāstra*, v. 1.3c.
11. *Prajñādaṇḍa*, v. 208.
12. Nāgārjuna, *Suhṛllekha*, v. 15ab: "There is no ascetic practice like patience. So do not give anger a chance to arise."

a supreme and incomparable body that is an ornament
for the eyes of the human and heavenly worlds.

Whoever can ignore every form of personal suffering,
who is dauntless in accomplishing great goals,
and who has the mental fortitude to reach the final profound reality
is the one who moves fearlessly in the world like a lion.

Perseverance

When you have the perseverance
to accomplish every excellence,
both mundane and transcendental,
there is nothing you will not achieve. [144]

When the mind that delights in the truth
burns like a raging fire,
even the most difficult tasks become like kindling
that fuels your practice.

The powerful deeds of a supreme lord[13]
are never inferior in their power and dexterity.
That is why the six perfections and four ways of attracting disciples
should be enhanced until they are as vast as the ocean and space.

Even if the people cast approving glances at you,
unless you destroy their ongoing poverty,
they will say, "He's not a supreme lord."
So leave behind a great legacy.

13. A "supreme lord" (*dang phyug dam pa*)—that is, a Buddha or an enlightened king (both readings are possible here)—possesses vast qualities and perform every deed in the best possible way. Those who aspire to these states of perfection—bodhisattvas and ordinary kings—must therefore attain the highest possible level of the six perfections and of the four ways of gathering disciplines. The latter refers to the methods that buddhas and bodhisattvas use to attract their students: giving them gifts, speaking sweetly to them, imparting teachings that meet their individual needs, and living in conformity with what they preach.

These are the ten Dharma activities:
writing scripture, worshipping, making offerings,
hearing, reading, memorizing,
explaining, reciting, contemplating,
and meditating on the teachings.
Rulers who exert themselves in these activities
so as to make their heap of merit infinite
ought to uphold the Conqueror's holy Dharma.

Everyone is alike in doing their own work.
But kings have this tremendous power
to get others to do things, and that is why they must establish
"the tradition of magnificent virtue."[14]

Samādhi

Like people carried away by a flooding river,
those whose minds are distracted
are disturbed by a host of afflictive emotions and sufferings.
Independence and happiness always eludes them.

What is the use of subjecting your body
to hundreds of dangerous hardships?
When the mind, the creator, is disciplined,
it is as if emancipation were close at hand.
When the mind is not disciplined, [145]
how can your evil thoughts be pacified
simply by wearing a fine saffron monks' shawl,
or a brahmin's thread, or by offering a bundle of kuśa grass?[15]

14. The "tradition of magnificent virtue" (*rlabs chen dge ba*) refers to the Mahāyāna, the path that leads to the highest accumulation of merit or virtue needed to achieve Buddhahood.
15. When the mind has not been tamed, neither wearing the monk's outward garb, nor bearing the physical symbol of high caste status (the brahmin's thread), nor rituals involving kuśa grass will help one to eliminate evil thoughts. Similar examples are used in Vararuci, *Śatagāthā*, v. 19, to make the case for the importance not of stabilizing meditation but of compassion. See also *Prajñādaṇḍa*, vv. 124–25.

Holy people are disciplined even when they live in the city;
the evil are wild even if they live in isolated monasteries.
A fine urban stallion is disciplined;
the wild animals of the forest are fierce.[16]

The mind resembles lightning, clouds, and wind.
It is like waves on the ocean.
It is deceitful and obsessed with every desirable object.
You must surely discipline it so that it does not stray and wander.

Once the mind has been made serviceable,
a vast multitude of good qualities, like the five supernormal powers,[17]
will appear within it,
just as the moon and stars appear on a still, clear lake.[18]

When you drink insatiably of the nectar
of the vast and profound Mahāyāna,
you increase the bodily strength of your learning,
and become crowned as "Lion of Speech."

Wisdom

By analyzing the meaning of what you've heard using the four forms of
reasoning,[19]
the rays of the wisdom-lamp of critical reflection
will dispel the dark gloom of the evil mind
and shine within the mind as if it were the sun.

16. Compare to Cāṇakya, *Rājanītiśāstra*, v. 6.6: "The lustful will give rise to faults even if they live in the forest. The holy control their senses even living in the household. Wild animals who live in the forest are fierce. The fine stallion who lives at home is restrained."
17. The five supernormal powers or *pañcābhijñā* (*mngon shes lnga*) are (1) divine sight (seeing things at far distances), (2) divine hearing (hearing things far away), (3) knowing others' minds, (4) remembering past lives, and (5) the ability to perform miracles. These and other superpowers are said to be the byproduct of attaining a high level of concentration.
18. I've emended *dwang pa'i mtsho* to *dwangs pa'i mtsho*.
19. The four forms of reasoning (*rigs pa bzhi*) are: (1) reasoning based on dependence (*ltos pa*), (2) reasoning based on how things function (*bya byed*), (3) reasoning based on valid knowledge (*tshad ma*), and (4) reasoning aiming at the highest reality (*chos nyid*).

By entering into single-pointed equipoise on reality,
the amazing wisdom-eye
that unites serenity and insight
will directly see the truth that is the reality of all phenomena.

Even the householders who bask in your glory can,
through the power of wisdom, quickly dry up the great ocean of saṃsāra,
making it the size of the water in a hoofprint, [146]
and travel to the site of highest emancipation.[20]

Those who see the world
as they see a water bubble
and as they see a mirage
will not be seen by the Lord of Death.

Whoever meditates on the noble truths
that are perfectly revealed by profound wisdom
cannot be frightened by any of the fears
that exist within this world.

These aggregates are like an illusory city.
The afflictive emotions are like arrangements of clouds.
Those who, devoid of pride, do not see any such thing as birth and death
will win the battle against the army of the four māras.[21]

They understand the conventional, appearing world,
which is like a dream, an illusion, and like the moon reflected in water.

20. Nāgārjuna, *Suhṛllekha*, v. 107: "There is no meditation without wisdom, and no wisdom without meditation. Whoever has both will turn the ocean of cyclic existence into a puddle the size of a hoofprint."

21. The four māras are: (1) the māras that are the afflictions (like anger, desire, etc.), (2) the māras that are our physical and mental constituents, the aggregates, (3) the māra who is the Lord of Death, and (4) the divine son māra. The first three are clear. The fourth, the "divine son māra," refers to any desire-realm spirit that impedes or obstructs virtue—the chief of these is Garab Wangchug, who is often equated with Kāma (the Indian Cupid), the god of love.

They understand the ultimate that, like space,
cannot be identified as anything whatsoever.

Tantra

Whoever understands the sphere of equality, the inseparability of the two truths,
the nonduality of appearances and emptiness,
the self-arisen, pure, radiant mind of enlightenment
will awaken to the highest enlightenment.

It is rare for buddhas to arise within this world,
and even rarer for the resultant vehicle
of the secret mantra to be taught.
But nowadays it shines like the sun.

Wise rulers, those fortunate ones,
who rely on this supreme path
that swiftly and easily frees one
as if they were in a magical trick, [147]
will quickly achieve the supreme fruit
as did King Indrabhūti,
who achieved enlightenment while playing
with the five sense pleasures to his heart's content.[22]

22. In the legend of King Indrabhūti, the Buddha appears magically before the king to teach him the path to emancipation, but the king asks for teachings that will not require him to forsake the pleasures of the world, and so the Buddha teaches him Tantra. See Cabezón, *The Buddha's Doctrine and the Nine Vehicles*, 87–88.

21. The Good Qualities of Being Ethical and the Good Qualities of This Treatise on Ethics

The king who follows the system of ethics
as explained herein will be appreciated
as an ornament by everyone
on the face of the earth, just like the sun.

In this degenerate age, it is difficult for
a king to possess all of these qualities,
but when this happens, he will single-handedly
bring all lands under his dominion.

Why not proclaim, as loudly as thunder in summertime,
the extent of the glory, wealth, and fame
of someone who has just achieved a measure
of most of the qualities explained above?

Wherever a king arises
who follows these ethical principles
many good qualities come together,
as if a cakravartin or a jewel had descended there.
That righteous king, the son of the gods,
becomes the lord of all people,
the father of his subjects, the friend of living creatures,
the shrine at which beings worship regardless of their religion.

Like a precious lord of mountains,
that king who, standing in the midst of men,
surpasses them because of his qualities,
is worshipped by the righteous
and he intimidates the unrighteous
whenever and wherever he arises. [148]

Even without having to try,
he benefits every land just by his nature.
In the realm of what is heard, he is praised and held up as a model.
In the realm of what is seen, he is looked at with fondness.

When others look at him and imitate him,
is it surprising that his own subjects should be devoted to him?
Even when jealous people compete
with fortunate individuals who are well liked,
because of the greatness of the good qualities of the latter,
they surpass everyone without intimidating them.

The conquerors, their children, and the protector deities of the world
all rejoice and grant him powerful blessings.
Hence, the power and might of that king
increase in each successive year.

Just as the earth gives rise to
flower, medicine, grains, and so forth,
likewise, among that king's subjects,
many kinds of auspicious signs appear.

There are men who have the splendor of heroism
as well as beautiful possessions.
Happiness, joy, marvels, and glory all increase
as if they were competing to outdo one another.

Without having to collect them,
wealth and population increase like clouds.
Everyone prays to this ruler,
"Please care for us for a long time."

The stainless *vaiḍūrya* of his renown,
becomes an ornament for the ears of exquisite women
from the shores of the oceans
to the peaks of the highest mountains.

Because every day both he and others
apply themselves to generating merit,
there is as much abundance there
as there are water and jewels in the inexhaustible ocean. [149]

Due to the power of his merit, everything that he wishes for
is accomplished effortlessly and naturally.
His kingdom is always happy,
as is the world beyond.

His good thoughts, political power, and glory
increase tremendously due to the power of his merit.
And through these same methods, his merit too
increases higher and higher.

Like the sun's inexorable power to rise, a river's to flow,
and the apocalyptic fire and wind to destroy the world,
no one can impede the awesome charismatic power
of the righteous king.

All religious and secular institutions
flourish and do not decline,
and in fact reach greater and greater levels of happiness—
this is a quality of living under a system of ethics.

He gathers together all the rivers of good explanations
of the manifold treatises on ethics.
How amazing is the ruler, the great ocean
that is the home and support of multitudes of powerful nāgas?[1]

1. Just as the ocean is the common home to all of the nāgas, likewise, the righteous king is the place where all of the exegetical lineages (the rivers) of the ethical treatises converge.

Although the things to be cultivated and avoided are infinite in
number,
some become clear by being explicitly taught,
others are realized through indirect means,
and still others are understood through works like this one.

Those who understand a single stanza
from this text and take it to heart
will experience a revitalization of their good qualities
as if they had taken an alchemically transformed medicine.

Everyone down to the heads of cities and households—
even if they are not born into the aristocracy—
becomes as resplendent as rulers
when they follow this system of Dharma.[2] [150]

Even those who live alone without companions
should engage in self-cultivation based on the Dharma of kings.
When one trains one's mind to care for living beings,
one eventually becomes a Dharma king.

Therefore, even when those who study these texts,
are not of royal blood,
their good qualities will definitely give them dominion
over a royal kingdom.

In accordance with the command of the holy prince,
who is an ornament on the face of this earth,
I have explained the treatises on ethics for kings
following the words of the bodhisattvas
and of the Lord Buddha, the Dharma king,
the constant caretaker of the entire world,
including its gods.

2. Here Mipham is following Nāgārjuna, who also ends his *Ratnāvalī* (v. 5.98) by stating that the doctrines that he has taught are not only helpful to kings but to all sentient beings.

When you hear it, it is the joy-producing drum of the gods;
when you contemplate it, it is the essence of the nectar of fine meaning;
when you meditate on it, it is the divine gem that increases abundance.
It is the supreme ornament of human kings and princes.

This is what causes rulers of kingdoms to attain
the glorious high status they have in the world,
and, if they do not fall from the path of Dharma,
it is what brings them the perfect fruit of enlightenment.

Like the sound of the gods' great drum
which is beaten when the gods and demigods fight,
the words of this text encourage the righteous
and bring dread to the unrighteous from the moment they hear them.

Who, except for the gods, ingest
the essence of the elixir that saves one from death? [151]
Likewise, unrighteous people oppose
these methods that have been adopted by the fortunate.

Those who adorn their bodies with the jewelry of the gods
acquire glory as bountiful as clouds.
Whoever practices the meaning of this text
definitely acquires the necessary religious and political requisites.

That is why, with a pure mind, I offer to you, royal prince,
these priceless aphorisms of good advice whose worth cannot be compared
even to a procession of hundreds and thousands
of precious horses and elephants.

Young lord who wishes to benefit everyone and has mercy for all,
please distribute shares
of this nectar of good advice
to future generations of righteous kings.

May you and other royalty, both present and future,
as well as the masses of people
who see, hear, or think about this text
come to possess all the good qualities explained herein.

Final Verses and Colophon

This garland that strings together the precious verses of good advice
of the Wise Conqueror and his children
should be worn around the necks of the royalty
and be read and contemplated on a daily basis. [152]

May the fine light of the moon of altruism not fade
even in Tibet, where the darkness of the degenerate age is great.
May the thoughts and activities of requesting and composing texts
benefit the teachings and beings in a timely way.

May they make the righteous king's empire flourish.
May this, in turn, increase the glory of the teachings and of beings.
And may this cause the multitude of living beings that pervade space
obtain the kingdom of a conqueror, a lord of Dharma.

When the time had arrived, and your fine prayers and merit ripened,
the latent seeds of goodness awakened in you even from the time you
were a child.
May you, who have been properly appointed as ruler by the gods,
achieve all life-affirming goals.[1]

O youthful one who is the color of a just-dawning orange sun,[2]
treasure-house of the knowledge of all the conquerors

1. This verse is undoubtedly referring to the prince of Dergé.
2. This verse is directed at Mañjuśrī, who is orange in color and is considered the manifestation of the Buddhas' wisdom.

whom the conquerors have prophesied to be the protector who tames
the royalty,
please bestow intelligence on those who uphold this text.

Through this narrative, may the fine light of mercy
of the Compassionate Lord, whose eyes never close,[3]
whose beauty surpasses that of a billion new moons,
easily penetrate the minds of living creatures.

Molten sky-blue in color, the splendor of your body is difficult to bear.
You who possess the vajra of gnosis that destroys the demons,
please generate courage and the power of universal conquest
in those who uphold this text.[4]

May the renowned protector Kṣitigarbha,
whose glorious light is as bright as a golden lamp, [153]
increase the great treasury of glory and wealth
in any land where this text is disseminated.

May the blessings of all the Buddhas and their children
bring about good fortune, happiness, and abundance
in those who see, hear, think about, touch, or uphold this work;
and may any wish they have that is consistent with the Dharma
be fulfilled.

This *Treatise on Ethics for Kings: An Ornament for Rulers* was written at the insistent requests of the lama-ruler of Dergé Dokham, Ngawang Jampel Rinchen,[5] who requested it together with the gift of a fine silk scarf. He had the wish that a work be written condensing the meaning of the treatises on royal ethics—a work that, even if lengthy, would be very accessible to anyone, whether high or low, and that would provide

3. The reference here is to Avalokiteśvara, the embodiment of the Buddha's compassion, whose eyes are perpetually open to the suffering of living beings.
4. The verse is a plea to Vajrapāṇi. With this verse, Mipham concludes three verses directed to the "three protectors" (*rigs gsum mgon po*)—that is, Mañjuśrī, Avalokiteśvara, and Vajrapāni.
5. On Ngawang Jampel Rinchen (1850–1920), the prince or king of Dergé, see the introduction.

beneficial nourishment for beings of this degenerate age. This ruler is a son of the Conqueror, a member of the royal line who took birth in the world through prayers equal in extent to the great sāla tree. From childhood, the nature of his holiness was manifest, without being concealed. He really exerted himself in the way of righteousness. He showed unrelenting effort and zeal for the holy Dharma. His wisdom-eye is supremely broad in scope. He has an utterly pure intention to benefit both sentient beings and the teachings, without any bias. Having the splendor of oceans of such praiseworthy qualities, the gods who protect virtue enthroned him on the fearless lion throne. [154]

Having obtained the eye of learning in regard to the fields of Sūtra, Tantra, and the cultural sciences, possessing a virtuous confidence that does not fear any literary task, and with a wish to accomplish the welfare of the teachings and beings that is not insignificant, I, Mipham Nampar Gyalwa, also known as Jampel Gyepé Dorje, with the crown of my head bowed in reverence at the lotus feet of the Buddha, the highest god, [155] have condensed into a single source all of the points concerning what is ethical and unethical as these are explained in the following scriptures of the Sugata:[6]

- *Ārya Suvarṇaprabhāsottama*
- *Daśacakrakṣitigarbha*
- *Smṛtyupasthāna Sūtra*
- *Bodhisattvagocaropāyaviṣayavikurāṇanirdeśa*
- *The Nāgarājabherī Gāthā*[7]

6. The first four sūtras in the list that follows—which have entire chapters dedicated to them in Mipham's text—have already been discussed extensively in earlier notes.

7. The *Nāgarājabherī Gāthā*, or *Stanzas of the Nāga King Bherī*, consists of 99 verses, all but two (vv. 95 and 96) quatrains. Mipham borrows, sometimes verbatim, from the text. Little scholarly work has been done on this text. Samdong Rinpoche, one of the few scholars to mention it, does so only briefly in "The Social and Political Strata in Buddhist Thought," 7. The work is written in the form of a *jātaka*. It begins by recounting how, during the Buddha's own lifetime, monks had gotten into the habit of verbally sparring and insulting one another, a situation that is also described in the Pāli *Kosambiya Sutta* (*Majjhima Nikāka* 48). Hearing an actual instance of such insults, the Buddha summons the monks together and tells them the story of three nāgas who had faced a similar problem in the past. The core of the sūtra consists of the advice given by the good nāga king Bherī (the Buddha in a former life) to his younger brother Upabherī (Ānanda) concerning why he should not retaliate against the evil nāga Bherīsvara (Devadatta) who had insulted them. This portion of the work reads like a typical *nītiśāstra*, offering moral advice on a wide range of topics: the importance of repaying

I have also consulted the following ethical treatises of the Ārya Nāgārjuna:[8]

- *Prajñadaṇḍa*[9]
- *Jantupoṣaṇabiṇḍu*[10]
- As well as prose works such as his *Ratnāvalī*.[11]

the kindness of others, of being a loyal friend, of knowing when to keep silent, the evils of pride and anger, the importance of properly timed actions, the importance of patience, the qualities and character of the wise, and so forth.

8. Mipham mentions in this section all of the works found in the *nītiśāstra* section of the Tibetan canon except for one work attributed to Nāgārjuna, the *Prajñāśataka*, or *Hundred Verses on Wisdom*. This is likely a minor oversight, for Mipham in fact relies on the *Prajñāśataka*, even including some of its verses verbatim in his work.

9. *Prajñādaṇḍa*, *Shes rab sdong bu—Tree of Wisdom*—is a work in some 260 stanzas. It was translated into Tibetan during the imperial period (eighth–ninth century). It was first edited and translated W. L. Campbell, a British Colonial officer, in *Shes-rab dong-bu*, and then again by C. T. Dorji, in *The Tree of Wisdom*. The standard academic edition and translation is by Michael Hahn (in three parts); it is this edition that I have used when referring to the text in this book. The work is also discussed in Suniti Kumar Pathak, *The Indian Nītiśāstras in Tibet*, 37–39, and in Hahn, "The Indian Nītiśāstras in the Tibetan Tanjur," an unpublished English translation and expanded version of "Die indischen Nītiśāstras im tibetischen Tanjur." Hahn states that "the fact that the *Prajñādaṇḍa* contains stanzas composed in the 7th or 8th century definitely rules out the possibility that it was compiled by Nāgārjuna."

10. *Jantupoṣaṇabiṇḍu* (Hahn prefers *Janapoṣaṇabiṇḍu*), *Lugs kyi bstan bcos skye bo gso ba'i thigs pa—Drop of Nourishment for the People*—a work in approximately ninety stanzas (of inconsistent length), was translated into Tibetan during the imperial period. It has been translated into English by Stanley Frye, *Nāgārjuna's a Drop of Nourishment for the People*. As Hahn has noted, "the greatest effect of the *Janapoṣaṇabiṇḍu* is the fact that is has transported many non-Buddhist Indian stories and motifs [e.g., from the *Pañcatantra*] to Tibet." The fact that two verses (84 and 86) make reference to Kālacakra leads Hahn to surmise that the work is rather late and therefore not a work of Nāgārjuna. It is possible, however, that the last portion of the text (beginning with verse 78) is a later addition—and that the rest of the work is old. That last portion of the text deals almost exclusively with apocalyptic themes like the decline of the Buddhist doctrine and is quite different from the rest of the work.

11. The full title is *A Sermon for the King: A Precious Garland*, *Rājaparikathāratnāvalī*, *Rgyal po la gtam bya ba rin po che'i phreng ba*. Unlike many other works attributed to him, the *Ratnāvalī* is generally considered to be an authentic work of the historical Nāgārjuna, the Madhyamaka philosopher. The Sanskrit text has been edited and published a number of times. A trilingual edition was published by Yukihiro Okada and Michael Hahn, *Nāgārjuna's Ratnāvalī*. The *Ratnāvalī* has been translated into English by Jeffrey Hopkins, *Nāgārjuna's Precious Garland*, and by John Dunne and Sara McClintock, *The Precious Garland*.

Also:

- *Kaniṣkalekha* of the master Mātṛceṭa[12]
- Buddhaguhya's *Letter to the King and Ministers of Tibet*[13]
- The *Gāthākośa* of Ravigupta[14]
- The *Śatagāthā* of Vararuci[15]
- The *Nītiśāstra* of Masūrākṣa[16] [155]

12. The full title is *A Letter to the Great King Kaniṣka*, *Mahārājakaniṣkalekha*, *Rgyal po chen po ka nis ka la springs pa'i spring yig*. A work in eighty-five verses, it has been edited and translated in Hahn, *Invitation to Enlightenment*, 6–49. Hahn dates Mātṛceta to the second century CE, and considers him a younger contemporary of Nāgārjuna.

13. *Bod rje 'bangs dang btsun rnams la spring yig*. A critical edition, English translation, and study is currently being undertaken by Jake Nagasawa. But see also Siglinde Dietz, *Die buddhistische Briefliteratur Indiens*.

14. *Gāthākośa*, *Tshigs su bcad pa'i mdzod—Treasury of Verses*—is also known as *Āryākośa*, *Noble Treasury*. Ravigupta, the author of the work, flourished in the eighth century; he was born in Kashmir and also composed works of philosophy, medicine, and Tantra. Thanks to the work of Nilanjana Shah, 142 of the 145 stanzas of the *Gāthākośa* have been found embedded in a longer work of Ravigupta called the *Lokasaṃvyavahārapravṛtti*, which exists in Sanskrit; Hahn, "The Indian Nītiśastras," 15, n. 28. This permitted Hahn to publish an edition and English translation of the entire *Lokasaṃvyavahārapravṛtti*: "Ravigupta and his Nīti Stanzas (I)," and "Ravigupta and his Nīti Stanzas (II)." See also Ludwik Sternbach, "Ravigiupta and his Gnomic Verses."

15. Vararuci's dates are not known with certainty. He may have flourished around the fourth century CE, but some tales put him in the court of Vikramaditya, whose dates are also uncertain, but who may have lived as early as the first century BCE. Vararuci's *Śatagāthā*, (*Tshig bcad brgya pa*) or *Hundred Stanzas*, has been edited in Tibetan, restored into Sanskrit, and translated into English and Hindi by Losang Norbu Shastri in *Śatagāthā of Ācārya Vararuci*.

16. Masūrākṣa claims to have written his *Nītiśāstra* (*Lugs kyi bstan bcos*), or *Treatise on Ethics*—a work of approximately 130 stanzas in seven chapters—based on previously extant "*arthaśāstras*" but it is possible that many of the verses may have been his own. This work was first studied by Sunitikumar Pathak, *Nîtiśāstra of Masūrākṣa*. More recently, it has been edited and translated by Hugh Meredith Flick, Jr., *Carrying Enemies on Your Shoulders*. Both translations need to be revised. Flick dates Masūrākṣa, whom he identifies as a Pāla dynasty regent, to the beginning of the ninth century. Some useful tables at the end of Flick's book show the texts from which some of Masūrākṣa's verses may have derived; other tables show later texts (especially the collections of *subhāṣita* or elegant verses) in which stanzas found in Masūrākṣa are anthologized. Leonard van der Kuijp has mentioned a recently discovered Tibetan commentary on Masūrākṣa's work by a certain Lodrö Bepa (1400–1475), a student of Duldzin Dragpa Gyaltshan (1374–1436). See van der Kuijp's "Review of *Dge ldan legs bshad*," 618.

- The *Rājanītiśāstra* of Cāṇakya[17]
- The *Vimalapraśnottara Ratnamālā* of Amoghovarṣa[18]

Finally, I also consulted the various *nītiśāstras* composed by Indian and Tibetan sages, like the *Eloquent Verses* of the glorious Sakya Paṇḍita.

Having condensed into a single source all of the explanations of what is ethical and unethical from what was taught in various treatises, like the final testaments of the Dharma kings of the land of Tibet, I began this work during a time when virtue is important—that is, during the best of astrological periods, on the fourteenth day of the waxing of the month of miracles in the female wood sheep year[19] of *rab tshes* [i.e., the fifteenth year of the

17. As explained in appendix 1, Cāṇakya or Kauṭilya (ca. 350–275 BCE), whose given name was apparently Viṣṇu Gupta, was the author of the most important work of Indian political-economics, the *Arthaśāstra* or *Treatise on Wealth*. Cāṇakya was counselor to king Candragupta Maurya, and after him to his son Bindusāra, the father of the famous Buddhist king Aśoka. Besides the *Arthaśāstra*, which is mostly written in prose with interpolated verses, a number of purely verse works of the *nīti* genre purportedly written by Cāṇakya circulated in India. One of these *nīti* texts, *A Treatise on Ethics for Kings*, or *Rājanītiśāstra*, is preserved in Tibetan, *Tsa na ka'i rgyal po'i lugs kyi bstan bcos*. This is the text known to Mipham. It contains eight chapters and some 260 verses (the vast majority the standard four line verses, but some longer). The colophon states that it was compiled from other *nīti* treatises by "Śrīpāla, son of Kāti" (or per Michael Hahn, by Bālakātyāyana). Hahn, "The Indian Nītiśāstras," 4, states that 85 percent of the verses in the Tibetan version of Cāṇakya exist in Sanskrit. The work has apparently been edited and translated in a master's thesis by Hahn's student, Maria Cinque, but that work was unavailable to me. On the Tibetan version of Cāṇakya's aphorisms and their relationship to other Indic *nīti* works, see also Pathak, *The Indian Nītiśastras in Tibet*, 33–34.

18. *Vimalapraśnottara Ratnamālā, Dri ma med pa'i dris lan rin po che phrang ba—Stainless Answers to Questions: A Precious Garland*—is the work of Amoghavarṣa (Don yod 'char), a Jain scholar-king who flourished in the middle of the ninth century CE. The Tibetan version of the work (in forty to fifty-six verses, depending on how one parses them), was translated into Tibetan in the eleventh century by Kamalagupta and Rinchen Zangpo (d. 1055). It is unusual among the *nīti* texts insofar as it is in question-answer format. "Q: Lord, what is to be taken up? A: The meaning-laden words of the guru. Q: What is to be abandoned? A: All evil deeds."—and so forth. The text was edited in Tibetan with German translation by Anton Schiefner, "Carminis Indici '*Vimalapraçnottararatnamālam*' Versio Tibetica." The Sanskrit was found later and edited with French translation by Phillipe E. Foucaux, *La guirlande précieuse des demandes et des réponses*. See also Albrecht Weber, "Über die Praçnottararatnamālā, Juwelenkranz der Fragen und Antworten."

19. This corresponds to the year 1895. This was the year in which the thirteenth Dalai Lama assumed political leadership of Tibet. It was also the date of an uprising against the Qing in Si ling and several other sites in Amdo.

rab byung cycle]—at the court of the Dharma king, the great palace known as the glorious Lhundrub Teng, the great meeting place of one hundred systems of Dharma and government.

This text was requested, with fine prayers, by the divine ruler, the precious master Ngawang Jampel Rinchen and others. It was written during the breaks of teachings I gave on the cycle of Maitreya's texts. It was completed during a period when virtue should be enacted, at an astrologically auspicious time, on the *dga' ba gnyis pa* [i.e., sixth or twenty-first day] of the following, that is, the second Tibetan month. The scribe was Sönam Peldrup, a priest who has clear intelligence in regard to the texts of the cultural sciences.

May this work act as the cause of truly vast benefit for the teachings and for sentient beings equal in numbers to space.[20] [156]

20. There follow verses of prayer written at the time of the printing of the text, but as these were not part of Mipham's work, they have not been translated here.

Appendix 1: Indian and Tibetan Precursors to Mipham's *Treatise*

Indian Antecedents

Mipham's *Treatise,* in twenty-one chapters and 150 folio sides, is one of the longest classical works on the theory and practice of Buddhist kingship ever written in any Buddhist language. It is a complex work that deals with ethical self-cultivation, education, administration, law, punishment, taxation, rules of war, and much else. Amazingly, the *Treatise* is written entirely in verse. What would lead a Tibetan monk-scholar to write such a long and complex work on kingship? What would cause him to write it in verse? To answer these questions, we need to explore the Indian literary antecedents to Mipham's *Treatise.*

Mipham's work—*A Treatise on Ethics for Kings: An Ornament for Rulers*—belongs, as the title implies, to an Indo-Tibetan literary genre of verse works on practical morality called "treatises on ethics," known as *nītiśāstra* in Sanskrit and *lugki tenchö* (*lugs kyi bstan bcos*) in Tibetan. The Sanskrit noun *nīti* (pronounced "neetee") comes from the verb *nī,* which means "to lead" or "to guide." In the present context, *nīti* refers to moral and practical guidance. Hence, a *nītiśāstra,* a "treatise on *nīti,*" is a work that provides guidance on how to lead an ethical, successful, and joyful life. It is sometimes said that among the four classical Indian "goals of life" or *puruṣārthas*—duty or righteousness (*dharma*), wealth (*artha*), sexual pleasure (*kāma*), and liberation (*mokṣa*)—the *nīti* literature is mostly concerned with the first two. I find this useful as a rule of thumb.

Nīti treatises are works on ethics or moral righteousness as well as on wealth, power, and the general material aspects of human flourishing. They deal only tangentially with love or sex, and although they frequently allude to religious ideals, they are not concerned with complex doctrinal issues. From the earliest times, some of the *nīti* literature dealt with kingship and statecraft: how kings in particular should lead their lives, and especially how they could become effective and just rulers. *Nīti* treatises often included explanations of the intellectual and moral qualities that a king should cultivate, the ethical principles that should guide him, and the ideals that ought to prevail in his kingdom. But the *nīti* works often included much else: theories of the origin of the institution of kingship, advice on how to constitute a functional administration and conduct foreign relations, the art of war, and so forth.

Sometimes, these polity-oriented *nīti* works were called *rājanīti*, or "ethics for kings." However, some of the *nīti* texts on statecraft are simply called *nīti*, and contrariwise some of the texts bearing the title *rājanīti* are often as much aphoristic collections of folk wisdom as they are treatises on kingship and polity. For example, the *Essence of Ethics* (*Nītisāra*) by the scholar Kāmandaki,[1] is mostly about polity and governance despite lacking any reference to kings (*rāja*) in its title, whereas *Cāṇakya's Treatise on Ethics for Kings* (*Cāṇakya Rājanītiśāstra*)[2] is, despite its title, as much a compendium of worldly wisdom as it is a treatise on statecraft. Mipham designates his text as a *rāja-nīti* work, a "treatise on ethics for kings," and in this case the title is apt, for the work is almost entirely concerned with the theory and

1. Mitra and Mitra, *The Nītisāra by Kāmandaki*, and Manmatha Nath Dutt, *Kamandakiya Nitisara, or The Elements of Polity*. The dates of the work are contested. Some claim that Kāmandaki (or Kāmadaka) was a direct disciple of Cāṇakya, which if true would mean that the work belongs to the third century BCE. Others date the *Nītisāra* to the Gupta age, that is, to the fourth century CE or later. See K. V. Rangaswami Aiyangar, *Rājadharma*, 85.

2. This work is preserved in Tibetan, having been translated in the tenth century. It is one of a number of collections of aphorisms attributed to Cāṇakya (fourth century BCE) in Sanskrit. The different editions of Cāṇakya's aphorisms have been studied by various scholars, including the great Ludwik Sternbach in his *Cāṇakya-nīti-Text Tradition*, 5 vols. See also Sternbach, *Cāṇakya-Rāja-Nīti*. Scholars are dubious of whether the aphorisms attributed to Cāṇakya were actually written by the author of the *Arthaśastra*, the great Sanskrit treatise on politics. Sternbach has shown that most of the stanzas found in the Tibetan version of the *Cāṇakya Rājanītiśāstra* are also found in the *Garuḍa Purāṇa* (ca. tenth century) and in the *Bṛhaspati Saṃhita* (seventh century?), a version of which is found in the *Garuḍa Purāṇa* (in sections 1.108–115). See Sternbach, "The Tibetan Cāṇakya-Rāja-Nīti-Śāstram," 99–122. Sternbach also discusses all prior scholarship on the Tibetan *Cāṇakya Rājanītiśastra*.

practice of kingship, and what general moral guidance it provides is mostly directed at the ruler.

Some of the oldest Indian literature contains speculation about the origins of kings. Ancient texts also suggest that kings often turned to sages or wise men for advice on affairs of state.[3] Even the Buddha is described in the scriptures as occasionally giving advice to the rulers of his day.[4] But all of these early accounts, both Buddhist and non-Buddhist, are relatively brief and nontechnical. This all changes in the fourth century BCE with the composition of the first major work of political theory, Cāṇakya's *Arthaśāstra*, ostensibly a treatise (*śāstra*) on wealth (*artha*), but actually an encyclopedic text that covers all aspects of statecraft: economics, law, bureaucratic administration, foreign relations, military strategy, the management of spies, the design of the palace, and so forth.[5] The *Arthaśāsatra*, which is mostly written in prose with some interspersed verses, is one of the great classics of Indian literature. It is the most important source for all subsequent Indian

3. For a list of early Indian texts that discuss the origin of kingship, see Deborah P. Bhattacharyya, "Theories of Kingship in Ancient Sanskrit Literature," 111.

4. Some of these sermons—especially the ones preserved in Pāli—are realistic and practical. Others, like the Mahāyāna sūtra called *Instructions to the King—Rājadeśanāma Mahāyāna Sūtra, Rgyal pa la gdams pa zhes bya ba theg pa chen po'i mdo* (Toh. no. 214)—which is a teaching to Bimbisāra on impermanence, karma, and nirvāṇa as the highest felicity, are of a more religious and idealistic character. Another sūtra by this same name, *Advice to the King* (*Rājadeśa*, Toh. no. 215), is even more idealistic and even supernaturalistic. In this second work, the Buddha sees that the time has come to convert Udāyana, the king of Vatsa, and goes to meet him just as he is about to wage war against the kingdom of Kanakavatī. Udāyana gets angry at the Buddha for meddling, and considers his presence on the battlefield to be inauspicious. So, in anger, he shoots an arrow at the Buddha to kill him! The arrow circles in the sky instead of hitting its target, and as it whirls in space, it sounds out a verse: "Anger only generates suffering. In this life, fighting and quarrel just exhaust you. In the next life, they bring about the suffering of hell. So abandon anger, fighting, and quarrels." When Udāyana witnesses this miracle, he generates faith in the Buddha, who then preaches to him a sermon on the evils of warfare—which he calls "the fight against the little enemy"—and on the necessity of defeating the true enemies, the mental afflictions, and the grasping at self.

5. Cāṇakya (a.k.a. Kauṭilya) and his *Arthaśastra* are often dated to the reign of Candragupta Maurya (r. 321–297 BCE), the grandfather of the Buddhist king Aśoka (r. 268–232 BCE). However, like most important classical Indian works, the *Arthaśāstra* was likely modified and expanded throughout the centuries. The work has been edited and translated by R. P. Kangle, *The Kauṭilīya Arthaśāstra*, 3 vols.; and more recently by Patrick Olivelle, *King, Governance, and Law in Ancient India: Kauṭilya's Arthaśāstra*.

writings on statecraft and governance,[6] including the *nīti* literature. *Nīti* texts are almost always verse works.

Treatises on kingship written in verse do not begin to appear until the turn of the common era. For example, the great Indian epic Mahābhārata contains embedded within its "Peace Chapter" (*Śāntiparva*)—probably compiled in the first centuries CE—a long section on the duties of kings (*rājadharma*).[7] Dating to around this time, the *Hundred Verses on Ethics* (*Nītiśataka*) is attributed to the great grammarian and poet Bhartṛhari.[8] Classical Indian scholars continued to write *nītiśāstras* throughout the medieval period and into modern times. For example, Somadeva Sūri's *Nectar of Ethical Discourse* (*Nītivākyāmṛta*) dates to the tenth century,[9] and the *Ethics of Śukra* (*Śukranīti*), whose eponymous title suggests its author to be the ancient, pre-Cāṇakyan sage Śukrācārya, was actually written, it seems, in the nineteenth century.[10]

All of these works were written in Sanskrit, and none of them were translated into Tibetan. However, several other Indian *nītiśastras* did make it into the Tengyur, the section of the Tibetan Buddhist canon that contains the translations of Indian treatises. One of these texts we have already mentioned, *Cāṇakya's Treatise on Ethics for Kings*. Another is the *Treatise*

6. This is not to say that there did not exist earlier Sanskrit works on polity. Cāṇakya acknowledges earlier schools of political thought—e.g., those of Bhṛgu and Śukra, and of Aṅgiras and Bṛhaspati—but these figures are quasi-mythological and whatever work has survived that bears their names is of questionable authorship.

7. Some portions of the purāṇas also contain sections on ethics and the duties of kings, although these works are much later. The classical tradition also considers didactic fables like the *Pañcatantra* and the *Hitopadeśa* to be *nītiśastras*, although as McComas Taylor notes, "if we take the mainstream members of the *nītiśāstra* genre as a guide, it [the *Pañcatantra*] can at best be considered a distant outlier of the nītiśastric archipelago." McComas Taylor, *The Fall of the Indigo Jackal*, 129.

8. Kamayani Mahodaya, ed. and trans., *Bhartṛhari's Śatakatrayaṃ* (Delhi: Chaukhamba Sanskrit Pratishthan, 2011), 4–50. The dates of the work range from the first century BCE to the first century CE, although some scholars claim that it belongs to the fifth century CE or even later. See M. R. Kale, *The Nīti and Vairagya Śatakas of Bhartṛhari*, viii–xi. Unlike the *Arthaśāstra* and the *rājadharma* section of the Mahābhārata, Bhartṛhari's *Nītiśataka* has little to do with politics, being instead a more general work on ethics and worldly wisdom.

9. The work has been edited and translated in Sudhir Kumar Gupta, *Nitivakyamritam*.

10. A *Śukra Nītiśāstra* in some 2200 verses has come down to us, but it is now widely considered to be a nineteenth century "forgery." See K. Satchidananda Murty, "Sanskrit and Philosophical Thought in the Vasco da Gama Epoch," 794. The *Śukranīti* has been translated into English by Benoy Kumar Sarkar, *The Sukranīti*.

on Ethics of Masūrākṣa (ninth century). Mipham explicitly tells us that he relied on both of these works as sources. The Indian *nīti* literature—like the *Arthaśāstra*, on which the genre is based—is diverse, containing general advice, specific rules, and different strategies for success in everything from health to conquest. Here are some verses drawn from Kāmandaki's *Essence of Ethics*, one of the earliest works of advice to kings. The stanzas give one a taste for the diverse materials contained in these works.

> The king should administer his state with equity and justice,
> augmenting his treasury through lawful means.
> He should deal sternly with persons
> obstructing the cause of law. (6.6)
>
> He should bathe in water
> purified of poisons through antidotes;
> use gems and jewels
> capable of neutralizing poisons;
> and eat food
> only after it has been examined
> in the presence
> of toxicologists and physicians. (7.9–10)
>
> He should never falsely accuse his allies
> based on the allegations of others.
> All those who create rifts among allies
> should be forsaken. (8.79)[11]

Kāmandaki was not a Buddhist but a follower of the Brahmanical or "Hindu" tradition. His *Essence of Ethics* is concerned with lofty ideals (equity and justice), but also with nitty-gritty matters like protection of the king from assassins, foreign relations, and military strategies. Buddhist *nīti* works are much more concerned with broad ethical principles than with the world of *realpolitik*, although their insistence that the king not take undue

11. The translation of these verses are slightly modified versions of those found in Mitra and Mitra, *The Nītisāra by Kāmandaki*.

risks and their ground rules for the conquest of other kingdoms also hint at the latter.[12]

McComas Taylor has noted that "*nītiśastras* fall into two broad and overlapping classes: practical textbooks on governance that resemble the *Arthaśāstra*, and collections of gnomic verses."[13] To understand the *nīti* literature, it is therefore necessary to understand what is meant by gnomic verses (*subhāṣita*). Gnomic or wise sayings—sometimes called "well-spoken" or "well-turned" verses—are clever stanzas of worldly wisdom that set forth fundamental truths about life and offer practical moral advice. Ludwik Sternbach describes *subhāṣitas* as:

> pithy epigrams of proverbial philosophy—miniature word-paintings which contain deep thoughts masterfully incorporated into verse. They are scattered throughout Sanskrit literature. These epigrams, aphorisms, wise sayings, maxims and adages, however quaintly expressed, contain the essence of some moral truths or practical lessons. They are drawn from real life and give the fruit of philosophy grafted from the stem of experience.[14]

Bhartṛhari's *Hundred Verses* is an example of a *nīti* work written entirely in the form of *subhāṣita* verses. It is a collection of gnomic aphorisms that have little to do with kingship or polity.

Consider this example of a *subhāṣita* from Mipham's *Treatise*, a stanza based on almost identical verses found in several Sanskrit *subhāṣita* texts:

> The mind should be trained while one is still young.
> The cow should be nourished during winter.
> The fields should be sown when they are moist and warm.
> These three are the conditions that ensure a good result.

The verse stresses the importance of starting to study while one is still young and the mind is flexible. The poet uses two examples drawn from pastoral

12. Skilling, "King *Sangha*, and Brahmans," 195, has noted that in Thailand there are a number of works (not actually called *nīti*, by the way) that are concerned with things like troop formations, and how to achieve victory in war. Interestingly, some of these texts refer to Kāmandaki's *Nītisāra* as their source.

13. Taylor, *The Fall of the Indigo Jackal*, 128.

14. Ludwik Sternbach, *Subhāṣita, Gnomic and Didactic Literature*, fasc. 1, 1.

life to drive the point home. Also, consider these two verses from *Cāṇakya's Treatise on Ethics for Kings* in the version preserved in the Tibetan canon:

> Someone who helps you is a relative even if he's a stranger.
> Someone who harms you is a stranger even if he's a relative.
> Someone who helps you is a rare medicine.
> Someone who harms you is an illness growing in your body. (1.10)
>
> The one who brings you joy is your wife.
> The one makes you happy is your son.
> The one who is trustworthy is your friend.
> The place that nurtures you is your country. (1.12)

On the surface, the verses appear to be descriptive, but in actuality they challenge our ordinary understanding of what constitutes a stranger, a relative, and one's homeland. They suggest that someone is a *true* relative or friend according to their deeds—whether they are helpful, bring you joy, are trustworthy, and so forth—and not because they happen to be related to you by blood or through a long acquaintance. Likewise, your true homeland is the one that nurtures and makes you flourish—and implicitly not the one in which you happen to be born.

A *subhāṣita* is a stand-alone verse. Other types of verses—for example, those found in narrative or philosophical literature—are part of storylines or arguments, and to understand their meaning requires an understanding of their context.[15] But a *subhāṣita* can generally be understood on its own. There are tens of thousands of Sanskrit *subhāṣitas*. These verses floated freely, being passed down from one generation to the next, often orally.[16] Erudition in classical India was measured, at least in part, by a person's ability to recite a *subhāṣita* appropriate to a given situation. Later, the verses

15. As Daniel Ingalls states, "a *subhāṣita* (well-turned verse) is a rather special product. . . . Not only should a *subhāsita* carry mood [*rāsa*] and suggestion [*dhvani*]; it should carry them even when torn from its context. The requirement of mood and suggestion rules out didactic and narrative verse, of which Sanskrit contains a vast amount. The second requirement [i.e., context independence] rules out still more." Daniel H. H. Ingalls, *An Anthology of Sanskrit Court Poetry: Vidyākara's "Subhāṣitaratnakoṣa,"* 88.
16. In a real tour de force, Ludwik Sternbach and his colleagues have attempted to compile all known *subhāṣitas* into their own compendium, detailing where each verse is found. This is the *Mahā-subhāṣita-saṃgraha*, 8 vols.

were compiled into anthologies (*saṃgraha*), which often grouped them into chapters according to themes: women, friends, food, learning, love, worthy people, villains, and so on.[17] One of the most famous *subhāṣita* anthologies, *The Jewel Treasury of Elegant Verse* (*Subhāṣitaratnakoṣa*), was compiled by Vidyākara, a Buddhist monk (perhaps a hierarch) of the Jagaddala monastery in Bengal during the latter half of the eleventh century.[18] Some anthologies (or their commentaries) identify the poets who composed specific verses, although there is often disagreement regarding who wrote which verses. More often than not, however, the authorship of individual verses was lost to time.

The dividing line between the *nīti* and *subhāṣita* literature is blurry at best, and many texts are referred to under both rubrics. Most of this literature was written in Sanskrit, but *nīti* and *subhāṣita* texts also exist in Prakrit, Tamil, Pāli, and other Indic languages.[19] From India, the literature spread to Sri Lanka, Burma, and the rest of Southeast Asia, and of course to Tibet and Mongolia.[20] None of the Indian *subhāṣita* anthologies were translated into Tibetan. But two important *subhāṣita* texts attributed to single authors—Ravigupta's *Treasury of Stanzas* (*Gāthākośa*) and Vararuci's *Hundred Stanzas* (*Śatagāthā*)—made their way into Tibetan. Mipham tells us that he consulted both works while writing his *Treatise*.[21]

17. Most of these anthologies are quite late, dating to the second millennium CE. As an example, see A. N. D. Haksar, *Subhāshitāvali*. The compiler of this work was a certain Vallabhadeva, and the anthology is usually dated to the fifteenth century.
18. The work has been translated into English by Ingalls, *An Anthology of Sanskrit Court Poetry*.
19. Prakrit collections of *subhāṣita* verses include the *Seven Hundred Stanzas* (*Sattasaī*) of Hāla (its dates are unknown, but it was probably written between the third and seventh centuries). The *Ways of the World* (*Vajjālaga*)—originally compiled by the Jain scholar Jayavallabha (eighth century) but likely added to over the centuries—was influenced by the work of Hāla. Sternbach (*Subhāṣita*, 10) considers these two works "the oldest *subhāṣita-saṃgraha* known to exist in India." The *Tirukkuraḷ* of the Tamil poet and philosopher Thiruvalluvar (first centuries BCE) is an important and early work of the *nīti-subhāṣita* genre. Its three parts provide guidance in (1) ethics or virtue, (2) "property," meaning "worldly affairs," which includes sections on kingship and polity, and (3) love or matters of the heart. Although purportedly a single-author work, Sternbach (*Subhāṣita*, 41) states that the Tirukkuṛal and the other Tamil *subhāṣita* collections *Nālaṭiyār* and *Nīti-venpā* "contain many verses of Sanskrit origin," which suggests borrowing.
20. See Sternbach, *Subhāsita*, 41–3 for an overview. The Pāli *Lokanīti* of Burma has been translated in James B. Gray, *Ancient Proverbs and Maxims from Burmese Sources, or the Nīti Literature of Burma*.
21. As we have seen, Mipham lists all of the works that he consults at the end of the *Treatise*.

To sum up, the Indian antecedents to Mipham's *Treatise* are the Sanskrit *nīti* and *subhāṣita* texts, didactic verse works on how to live a moral life and achieve success in worldly matters. Some of the *nīti* texts contained sections on polity, and in several cases were almost entirely concerned with kingship and matters of statecraft. Although Mipham calls his own *Treatise* a *nītiśāstra*, the work also contains many verses typical of the *subhāṣita* genre. Indeed, the *Treatise* is sometimes classified as a *subhāṣita* work.[22] We now know, in any case, why Mipham wrote his *Treatise on Ethics for Kings* in verse: he was following the model of the Indian *nīti* and *subhāṣita* texts. Writing the work in verse was simply a requirement of the genre.

All of the texts just mentioned—the *nīti* aphorisms of Cāṇakya and Masūrākṣa and the *subhāṣita* texts of Vararuci and Ravigupta—are non-Buddhist works. Why then should they have been translated into Tibetan and incorporated into the Buddhist canon? And why should Mipham have consulted these heterodox works? The fact that these texts were written by "Hindus" does not mean that they were unacceptable to Buddhists. The editors of the Tibetan canon placed them into a section of the Tengyur called "Common or Shared Treatises" precisely because, belonging to a shared tradition of moral and political speculation, most of what they teach is acceptable to Buddhists and non-Buddhists alike.

That is not to say that *everything* we find in the Hindu political or gnomic treatises is acceptable to Buddhists. For example, caste plays an important role in the Hindu *nīti* texts, but much less so (or not at all) in their Buddhist counterparts. The Hindu texts also generally sanction capital punishment, whereas Buddhist works are much more circumspect about such forms of punishment. Hindu works like Kāmandaki's also pay a great deal of attention to topics like the protection of princes, the cultivation of allies, the management of spies, the different sections of the armed forces, and military strategy. Buddhist texts are much less concerned with these subjects. That said, the Hindu and Buddhist political and gnomic literatures do have a lot in common, so it is understandable that Mipham should have considered it appropriate to consult non-Buddhist texts.

Not *all* Indian literature on kingship and polity is, however, Hindu.

The reader will find more information about each of these works in the notes to that portion of the book.

22. For instance, Mipham's *Treatise* is anthologized in a recent collection of *subhāṣita* literature published in Tibet: *Legs bshad bstan bcos phyogs bsgrigs*, 6 vols.

Several Indian Buddhist texts also discuss these topics.[23] Some of these works—specifically the sūtras (Pāli suttas)—have the status of "buddha's word" (*buddha vacana*). Other texts were written by later Indian Buddhist scholars. Turning first to the Pāli Buddhist tradition, the *Sutta on Beginnings* (*Aggañña Sutta*) describes how human society devolves from a utopian state at the beginning of a cosmic cycle to an age in which crime (initially theft) necessitates the election of the first king, the "Great Elect" (*mahāsammata*), who is contracted to enforce the laws. The *Sutta on Beginnings*' cosmogonic ideas are also found in the *Sutta of the Lion's Roar of the Cakkavati* (*Cakkavatti Sīhanāda Sutta*). But instead of elaborating a "contractual theory" of kingship as the *Aggañña Sutta* does, the *Cakkavati Sīhanāda* outlines the duties of another kind of king called a cakravartin (*cakkavatti*), the universal monarch or "wheel turning" king. This is how such a king is admonished in that latter text:

> Arrange proper shelter, protection, and defense for your family, for the army, for your noble warrior vassal(-kings), for brahmin householders, for town dwellers and country folk, for ascetics and brahmin(-renouncers), and for animals and birds. Let no wrongdoing take place in your territory; if there are poor people in your land, give them money. Go from time to time to the [righteous] ascetics and brahmins in your kingdom . . . and ask, "What, sir, is good? What is not good? What is blameworthy, what blameless? What is to be done, what not? What would lead to happiness and benefit for me in the long run? You should listen to them, and avoid what is bad; and instead take up what is good and do that.[24]

According to the *Sutta*, when a king disregards these principles, or when people exploit the king's generosity and use the wealth they have received

23. For a brief overview, see Pankaj Mohan, "Kingship," in Robert E. Buswell, Jr., *Encyclopedia of Buddhism*, vol. 1: 467–68.

24. The translation is slightly adapted from that found in Steven Collins, *Nirvana and other Buddhist Felicities: Utopias of the Pāli Imaginaire*, 604. See also Ven. Dr. Mahinda Deegalle, "The Analysis of Social Conflicts in Three Pāli Canonical Discourses," www.undv.org/vesak2015/paper/analysis_social_conflicts.pdf. Deegalle also discusses the Kūṭadanta Sutta (Dīgha Nikāya 5, PTS I, 127–49), which advocates for the "fair distribution of resources . . . aimed at eliminating poverty through the promotion of agriculture."

to selfish ends, violence increases and the society crumbles. Elsewhere, the Pāli scriptures speak of seven things that make a kingdom stable and invulnerable to external attack: having frequent meetings that are well attended, harmoniously attending to the affairs of state, adhering to the ancient traditions and laws, having respect for elders, respecting and protecting women, venerating shrines, and protecting and venerating saints.[25] This tradition, which presumes a more diffuse model of political power, stresses social consensus and cultural continuity rather than putting the entire onus for the kingdom's prosperity on the king.

The Mahāyāna scriptures, which generally postdate their Pāli counterparts, contain their own myths about the origin of the monarchy. They also elaborate typologies of kings and describe the ideal king's qualities and duties. Mipham devotes three chapters of the *Treatise* to analyzing the political, economic, and ethical ideals found in three important Mahāyāna scriptures:

- The *Sūtra on the Revelations of the Bodhisattva Truth-Teller* (*Satyakavyākaraṇa Sūtra*)
- The *Sūtra Establishing Recollection* (*Smṛtyupasthāna Sūtra*)
- The *Sūtra of the Perfect Golden Light* (*Suvarṇaprabhāsottama Sūtra*)

Mipham also offers a lucid summary of a portion of the *Ten Wheels Kṣitigarbha Sūtra* (*Daśacakra Kṣitigarbha Sūtra*) that, among other things, prohibits the punishment of monks; and he incorporates into the *Treatise* some of the ideas found in *Stanzas of the Nāga King Bheri* (*Nāgarāja Bheri Gathā*), a text that contains, embedded within it, an important and little studied collection of Buddhist *nīti* verses. Mipham does not discuss kingship and statecraft in the Buddhist tantric or esoteric tradition. This is probably due to the genre. The Buddhist *rājanīti* literature is almost exclusively exoteric in nature. It would have been odd to write a *nīti* work that described how to obtain sovereignty over a kingdom using esoteric or magical means. In any case, Mipham's synthesis of the Buddhist sūtra literature provides us with an unparalleled description of kingship and statecraft in exoteric Mahāyāna Buddhism.[26] To my knowledge, no other work, Indian or Tibetan, ancient or modern, does such a thorough job of digesting this material.

25. See, for example, *Mahāparinibbāna Sutta* (Dīgha Nikāya 16, PTS 2.72–78).
26. Mipham also mentions three other canonical works in passing as relevant for the study of

In addition to the sūtras, the later Buddhist scholars of India—its great commentators, philosophers, and poets—also wrote on kingship, statecraft, and political ethics. These topics are treated in scholastic compendiums, in narrative literature, in texts of the *nīti* and *subhāṣita* genres, and in epistles (*lekha*). Many of these works date to the fourth or fifth century CE, the Gupta period, a time of great intellectual efflorescence in India. For example, Vasubandhu's *Treasury of Metaphysics* (*Abhidharmakośa*), an important Buddhist scholastic treatise, describes four types of cakravartins, those who possess wheels made of iron, bronze, silver, and gold. They conquer from one to four "continents," respectively, with the golden wheel king conquering all four human continents. The first two of these four kings conquer through the power of their charisma; while the last two must put on a display of their martial prowess to get people to submit, but end up conquering "without causing harm" (*avadha*).[27] Another scholastic work of this same period, the *Stages of the Bodhisattva Path* (*Bodhisattvabhūmi*) attributed to Asaṅga, explains that bodhisattvas take rebirth as kings in the world in order to help those in need—for example, to protect beings who are under attack by a hostile army.[28] More important, the *Bodhisattvabhūmi* sets forth these brief ethical guidelines for bodhisattva kings:

> Bodhisattvas who are sovereigns rule their subjects without punishments and weapons.[29] They collect revenue in a just manner. They enjoy the kingdom that they have inherited and do not forcefully and without warning invade a foreign country. Using all their abilities and powers, they cause beings to turn away from evil. They act as a parent to their subjects. They are naturally

Mahāyāna views of kingship, statecraft, and ethics: the *Ratnaketu Dhāraṇī*, the *Root Tantra of Mañjuśrī* (*Mañjuśrī Mūla Tantra*), and the *Ākāśagarbha Sūtra*.

27. The discussion is found in the third chapter of the *Kośa*, vv. 94–96. See *Abhidharmakośa-Bhāṣya of Vasubandhu*, French translation by Louis de la Vallee Poussin, English translation by Gelong Lodrö Sangpo, vol. 2, 1100–05.

28. Ārya Asaṅga, *The Bodhisattva Path to Unsurpassed Enlightenment*, translation by Artemus B. Engle, 583–84. Even then, the text continues, the bodhisattva king will repel the attack "peacefully and using skillful means." All of the translations I cite here are Engle's. The *Bodhisattvabhūmi* also states (p. 212) that although bodhisattva kings may engage in vast acts of generosity, they never give "the child or wife that belongs to one person . . . to someone else," nor do they "offer to someone from another [kingdom] an entire village or town."

29. The Indian commentary glosses this as "without confiscating property or putting subjects to death."

> disposed to share wealth even with strangers, needless to say with those who are their own dependents. They avoid doing injury and speak truthfully. They have given up such forms of harm to sentient beings as killing, imprisoning, punishing, cutting off [limbs], and beating, etc.[30]

As we shall see, Mipham will not go quite as far as the *Bodhisattvabhūmi* in limiting the kinds of legal punishments that a king can use—for instance, he permits imprisonment and even corporal punishment (beating, etc.)—but then again, the *Bodhisattvabhūmi*'s somewhat idealistic stance is meant to govern the actions of not just any king, but of a bodhisattva king.

Like these scholastic sources, works of the narrative genre also treat the subject of kingship. These texts include the *Tale of Aśoka* (*Aśokāvadāna*),[31] the story of the famous king of the Maurya dynasty who converted to Buddhism after conquering almost all of India in the third century BCE. Some contemporary scholars believe that the ideal of the cakravartin is modeled on him. The *Tale of Aśoka* is unusual in that its protagonist is a historical ruler, but there are countless other tales in which a mythical king figures prominently. Āryaśūra's *Jātakamāla*, that dates to around the fourth century CE, is a collection of tales about the Buddha's former lives. Many of them center on the figure of a king (often the Buddha in a past life) and take place in a royal court.[32] The *Jātakamāla* is of mixed genre, containing both prose and verse. Many of its verses have a distinctively *nīti* flavor to them. Consider, for example, these verses from Āryaśūra's *Jātaka* no. 22, the "Tale of the Goose King":

> Virtues bring joy and are blessed by praise.
> There is no such prosperity in the perils of vice.
> Knowing the nature of virtue and vice,
> what sane person would stray from the path of benefit?

30. Asaṅga, *The Bodhisattva Path*, 588, with minor modifications to the translation on my part.
31. See John S. Strong, *The Legend of King Aśoka*.
32. To give another example of the centrality of kings to the Jātaka literature, in a collection of 150 Jātakas compiled by the Tibetan scholar Loter Wangpo (Blo gter dbang po, 1847–1914), one of Mipham's teachers, roughly 40 percent of the all of the tales have some reference to royalty (king, prince, etc.) in their title. Skilling ("King, Sangha, and Brahmans," 195) has also noted that the Jātakas are an important source for royal policy in Thailand.

Neither power, treasury, nor good policy
can bring a king to the same position
as he reaches through the path of virtue,
however great his effort or expenses.

The glorious king of the gods himself heeds virtues.
Humility exists even in those eminent in virtues.
It is from virtues that fame arises.
The majesty of power depends on them.

Virtues are lovelier than the moon's splendor.
They alone can appease the hearts of enemies,
however hardened by anger and pride,
however their envy is entrenched by deep hatred.

Protect the earth, guardian of the land,
her proud kings subdued by your power,
and use your discipline and other bright virtues
to awaken in creatures a passion for morality.

A king's highest duty is the welfare of his people.
This path brings prosperity in this world and the next.
It will arise in a king devoted to goodness.
For people tend to follow the behavior of their king.[33]

Most of the ideas expressed in these lines—the importance of virtue, the fact that the king's status depends on his moral qualities, the importance of the sovereign acting as a model of virtue for his subjects, and so forth—are all found in the *nīti* literature, and indeed in Mipham's text.

Mipham does not mention any scholastic treatises or narrative works as source material for his book, although he draws from the *jātakas* and *avadānas*—and even from Hindu didactic tales—to illustrate various points. He does, however, explicitly mention several of the Buddhist *nīti/subhāṣita*

33. Āryaśūra, *Garland of the Buddha's Past Lives*, vol. 2, 76–77. I have cited Meiland's translation from the Sanskrit here, but for the Tibetan—which suggests some alternative readings of the Sanskrit—see *Skyes pa'i rabs kyi rgyud*, Sde dge ed., fol. 81a.

works that he consulted. Three of these are attributed to Nāgārjuna (second century CE):

- The *Tree of Wisdom* (*Prajñādaṇḍa*)
- *A Drop of Nourishment for the People* (*Jantupoṣaṇabiṇḍu*)
- The *Hundred Verses on Wisdom* (*Prajñāśataka*)

Mipham also mentions as sources three epistles:

- Nāgārjuna's *Precious Garland* (*Ratnāvalī*)
- Matṛceta's *Letter to King Kaniṣka* (*Mahārājakaniṣkalekha*)
- Buddhaguhya's *Letter to the King and Ministers of Tibet*

Mipham does not specifically mention Nāgārjuna's *Letter to a Friend* (*Suhṛllekha*), but I have shown in the notes to the translation that he seems to draw on this work as well. Contemporary Western scholars are skeptical about the authorship of some of these works, but whoever may have written them, there is no doubt that, with the possible exception of Buddhaguhya's letter, they all have an Indic pedigree.

A great deal more could be said about the Indian antecedents to Mipham's work, but this brief overview should suffice to give the reader a sense of the richness of this literature and of Mipham's tremendous command of it. Only a scholar of Mipham's erudition could have synthesized such a vast and diverse body of Indian texts, both Buddhist and non-Buddhist, into a clear and coherent whole. It has often occurred to me while reading through the *Treatise* how much it has in common with modern Buddhological scholarship, which, like Mipham's work, is committed to the systematic examination of a wide array of texts and to the documentation of those sources.

Tibetan Antecedents

As is well known, Tibetans scrupulously followed the Indian tradition in religious and literary matters. During the height of Tibet's imperial period (mid-eighth to mid-ninth century), most of the energy of the Buddhist Church went into translating Indian texts. As a result, Tibetans wrote few texts of their own during this period. But as the empire collapsed and imperial sponsorship of translations ceased, Tibetans began to compose their own works. On the subject of ethics, one of the earliest such works, which might date to the ninth century, is a Dunhuang document called *The Elder*

Brother's Advice to the Younger Brother (*Phu bos nu bos btams*). Among other things, the text explains the *michö* (*mi chos*), literally the "people's Dharma," which is to say the tradition of worldly ethics.[34] The work is written in the form of a dialogue between a younger brother (the questioner) and an elder brother (the respondent):

> *Younger Brother:* What does it mean to be ethical and unethical?
> *Elder Brother:* To be ethical means to be upright and respectful, to be gentle and mild, to be compassionate, not to put others down, and to have honor and a sense of decency. It means to be humble and really diligent; to be wise and to consider things carefully. Whoever acts in these ways is held in high esteem and is trusted by everyone. To be unethical means to be crafty and cruel; to lack modesty, decency, and honor."

The younger brother then inquires about what it means to be "upright," "loving," "compassionate," "brave," "noble," and so on. The elder brother replies to each question in turn: "To be upright means to respect all the king's righteous laws," and so forth.

Elder Brother's Advice also teaches worldly wisdom and ethical principles through comparisons: "An honest poor man is more noble than a rich [cheat]. It is better to be destitute than to be a thief." Some of these comparisons have a witty, riddle-like, and even comical quality to them, reminiscent of what we sometimes find in *nīti* literature:

34. The discussion that follows, and the passages from the text that I translate, are based on the analysis and sample passages cited in Chab 'gag rta mgrin's very valuable *Bod bstan po'i dus kyi rtsom rig*, chapter 2. The *Elder Brother's Advice* is written in prose and not in verse, but Chab 'gag rta mgrin goes on (p. 215f) to discuss a different Dunhuang text that he also considers another early Tibetan *nīti* work, namely *Teachings of the Magical Monk to Later Generations* (*'Phrul gyi byig shus phyi ma la bstan pa'i mdo*), which is written entirely in verse. It deals with such topics as forsaking power and wealth in favor of virtue, the inevitability of death, the uselessness of piling wealth in tombs, the law of karma, the importance of practicing virtue so as to experience happiness in the next life, avoiding the ten nonvirtues, not killing living beings, not drinking alcohol, being respectful to parents, and so forth. Is this work a text of the *nīti* genre? While the *Teachings of the Magical Monk* is written in verse and clearly has an ethical agenda, it strikes me as being more of a catechism than a *nīti* or even *proto-nīti* work.

> Q: What is the best and worst that one can find on one's bed?
> A: On the daybed, the best that you can find is a king, a chief, a wise man, an honest man, a scholar, a brave man, a great artist, a poet, and an orator. On the night-bed, the best is a good wife. On the daybed, the worst is a thief, an insincere person, a prostitute, a crook, a madman, a dissolute man, a coward, and a weakling. On the night-bed, the worst is a young virgin girl.

Some of the text's discussions deal directly with politics and the law.

> Q: What is the measure of an honest or upright man? How can you determine this without error?
> A: Someone is called "honest" if he respects the king's righteous laws. But even if you can't figure this out from his attitude toward the laws, examine him to see whether he brags or exaggerates. This is how you determine unerringly [whether he is honest]. If you want to be a leader of men, be as impartial as the sky, and as honest or straight as the lever on a scale. Take no pleasure in exaggerating or boasting. Help everyone equally.

The text also urges tolerance when underage and immature people violate ethical norms or the law; but if someone is of age and mentally mature, punishment is permitted. The text even has sections on education and on the different types of honest occupations (commerce, farming, and so on). An important work that belongs to the earliest period of Tibetan indigenous literature, *Elder Brother's Advice to the Younger Brother* has unfortunately received little scholarly attention in the West. There is no reason to believe that Mipham had access to this work, but many of the ideas found within it, forming part of the pan-Tibetan ethical tradition known as the "people's Dharma," are certainly consistent with a lot of what we find in Mipham's *Treatise*.

Throughout the centuries, Tibetan lamas have written advice (*gdams pa*, *bslab bya*) to their disciples—sometimes even to kings. These short works can be in prose or in verse. Contemporary Tibetan scholars have sometimes considered this advice literature as a whole to belong to the *nīti* tradition. However, most advice texts are of a strictly religious and technical nature. They are the lama's instructions—often in response to a disciple's query—on how to understand a particularly difficult point of doctrine, how to practice a particular technique of meditation, how to understand a particular sign or vision, and so forth. Generally speaking, therefore, these works do not belong to the *nīti* literature, which is of a more mundane and worldly character. Atiśa's advice to the Tibetan king Janchub Ö[35]—written in elegant and unusually long (fifteen syllable) lines—is an example of such an "advice" text. Here are some of the more practical lines in that work:

> Educate yourself by paying respect to the learned and not being jealous of them.
> Do not examine others' faults, but rather examine your own faults, and expurgate yourself of them as if getting rid of bad blood.
> Do not think about your own virtues; think about others' virtues. Act respectfully toward everyone as if you were their servant. . . .
> Always speak to others sincerely, without anger, and with a smiling face and a loving mind.
> If you engage in too much senseless speech, you become confused, so speak in a timely way and in moderation. . . .
> Because you have to leave your accumulated wealth behind, do not accumulate sin for the sake of wealth.[36]

However, apart from these few lines, most of the rest of Atiśa's text is of a specialized religious nature, dealing principally with the tradition of "mind training" or *lojong* (*blo sbyong*). Therefore, generally speaking, the advice literature does not fall under the rubric of *nīti*.

There are, however, some notable exceptions. One is a beautiful work attributed to Atiśa's main disciple, Dromtön Gyalwey Jungné (1004–1064) called *Garland of the Main Points of the People's Dharma*,[37] which

35. Atiśa was one of the greatest Indian Buddhist scholars of his day. He was invited to the court of Gugé-Purang in western Tibet by King Yeshé Ö (ca. 959–1040). Traditional accounts state that the king died before Atiśa arrived. The letter was requested by Yeshé Ö's grandnephew, Jangchub Ö on the eve of Atiśa's departure back to India. *Mnyam med jo bo chen po rgya gar la phebs khar lha bla ma byang chub 'od la zhal gdams su btsal ba*, 367–74.

36. *Mnyam med jo bo chen po lha bla ma byang chub 'od la zhal gdams*, 371–73.

37. 'Brom ston rgyal ba'i 'byung gnas, *Mi chos gnad kyi phreng ba*. It was requested by Nagtso, another of Atiśa's main students, who said, "Give me something practical to think about on the road," as Dromtönpa was escorting him at the time of his departure. The work is found in Cha ris skal bzang thogs med and Ngag dbang snyin pa, eds., *Blo sbyong nyer mkho phyogs bsgrigs*, 374–80.

is written in a style that is distinctively Tibetan. Here are some lines from the work:

> No matter where or in which direction you go,
> no matter where you settle or call home,
> no matter what friends you have or cultivate,
> getting along with others is the root of worldly ethics.
>
> It is said to be the basis of all goals, so listen!
> It is the ground rule of all activities, so listen!
> It is said to be a teaching that pacifies gods and nāgas, so listen!
> Among the teachings, it is the best one on worldly ethics. . . .
>
> No matter what virtues you may have,
> lessen despising others and treating them with contempt.
> Even if you have great attachment to wealth,
> decrease your tendency to quarrel over others' wealth.
>
> Even if you are skilled in works and plans,
> lessen your disregard for the general laws.
> Even if it is money that you yourself have saved,
> diminish your tendency to horde it by hiding it from others.
>
> Even if others consider you authoritative,
> lessen the pride that thinks, "That's me."
> Even if you are superior to all others,
> get rid of your arrogance, at least a little.

Infused with both a distinctively Tibetan voice and with the spirit of the Kadampa tradition that Dromtönpa founded, the *Garland* is an example of an advice text that could easily be considered a part of the *nīti* tradition.

Another early and important collection of advice texts that falls under the *nīti* rubric is a group of works by the Sakya hierarch Pagpa Lodrö Gyaltsen (1235–1280) written in the form of counsel to various Mongol princes.[38] A

38. The Tibetan texts are found in 'Phags pa blo gros rgyal mtshan, *'Gro mgon chos rgyal 'phags pa'i gsung 'bum*, Dpe sdur ma ed., fol. 115. Excerpts from some of these works have been translated in Christopher Wilkinson, *Chogyal Phagpa: The Emperor's Guru*, 203–29.

some verses drawn from his *Advice to Prince Jibig Temür* give one a sense of Pagpa's style:

> Because you are already so rich,
> what is the point of offering you the gift of wealth?
> Instead, I offer you the gift of Dharma,
> which is like jasmine illuminated in the winter moon,
>
> No matter how much wealth you possess,
> unless you have the wealth of Dharma,
> it is like eating good food mixed with poison;
> it only brings you suffering.
>
> And even when one possesses the wealth of Dharma,
> if one lacks material wealth,
> like a precious stone that is rough or uncut,
> it cannot serve the welfare of others.
>
> But whoever possesses both kinds of wealth
> can accomplish both great goals.
> A gem that has been skillfully polished
> beautifies both self and other.
>
> Thus, focus your mind on what I have said,
> so that, possessing both religious and material wealth,
> you achieve the result in its totality.[39]

Or consider these verses from Pagpa's *Advice to Prince Maṅgala*:

> Immediately repay the kindness
> of your parents, your clan,
> and anyone who has helped you in the least.

Adam Krug's study of one of these works, "History, Ideology, and the Construction of a Tibetan Buddhist State Identity in 'Phags pa's Advice to Prince Jibik Temür," is forthcoming in a special issue on kingship in *Cahier d'Extrême Asie*.

39. 'Phas pa blo gros rgyal mtshan, *Rgyal bu ji big de mur la gtam du bya ba nor bu'i phreng ba*, in 'Gro mgon chos rgyal 'phags pa'i gsung 'bum, Dpe sdur ma ed., vol. 4: 115–16.

Not only does this increase the virtues you already have,
but because others will follow your example,
it increases everyone's virtues, both your own and others'. . . .

The practices of worldly virtue—
not drinking beer, having a pure livelihood,
never harming anyone, worshipping who or what is worthy of
worship,
and protecting the poor through acts of charity—
were all taught by Ārya Nāgārjuna himself.

Use your conscience and sense of shame to restrain yourself.
Abandon the activities that everyone despises;
and exert yourself in acts that are praised.
When people see these remarkable deeds,
it will cause their hair to stand on end in amazement.

When you do not harm anyone, help everyone,
and build temples, stūpas, gardens,
and dwellings for the poor,
your banner will fly in the ten directions.[40]

They are not the kind of specialized religious advice that a lama might offer to a monastic disciple. They are the kind of practical ethical counsel to royalty that is characteristic of the *rājanīti* literature. Mipham's *Treatise* advises Buddhist kings in much the same ways as Pagpa does in these verses.

Neither the Dunhuang texts, nor Dromtönpa, nor Pagpa call their works *nītiśastras*. As far as I know, the first Tibetan work to explicitly use the words *nītiśastra* in its title is the *Treatise on Ethics: An Analysis of Fools* written by the great Bodong Paṇchen (1376–1451), the most prolific scholar in Tibetan history.[41] Bodong's *nīti* work, which is in ten chapters, is about one third the size of Mipham's text. A little-known work, it is currently being translated and studied by Miguel Alvarez Ortega. Is it a coincidence that two of the

40. 'Phags pa blo gros rgyal mtshan, *Rgyal bu mangga la la gtam du bya ba*, in 'Gro mgon chos rgyal 'phags pa'i gsung 'bum, Dpe sdur ma ed., 136–37.
41. The full Tibetan title of the work *Byis pa 'jug pa'i sems kyi bslab pa bstan par lugs kyi bstan bcos blun po brtag pa*, and it is found in Bodong's *Collected Works*.

most prolific authors in Tibetan history—Bodong and Mipham—should have written texts that they explicitly identify as *nītiśāstras*? Probably not. Both Bodong and Mipham were polymaths. Their writings cover all of the subjects of classical Indian learning. *Not* to have written at least one text of the *nīti* genre would have represented a lacuna in their oeuvre. One wonders, therefore, whether they saw the composition of such a text as a kind of requirement, for the completeness they both sought (whether intentionally or not) to achieve in their literary life's work required the composition of at least one *nīti* text.

From the time of Bodong up to the time of Mipham, few Tibetans wrote any texts that they actually called *nītiśāstras*,[42] but despite that, a number of works clearly fall into this genre, or into its sister genre, the *subhāṣita* or *legshé* (*legs bshad*) literature. Interestingly, one of these works is ascribed to a Tibetan Muslim: *Advice of Khache Palu*.[43] But this is the exception. All of the other *subhāṣita* texts in Tibet were written by Buddhists. In fact, most were written by Gelugpa scholars who hailed from the Amdo region of eastern Tibet. I will not discuss these works in any detail because an anthology containing translations of several of them will appear shortly in *The Library of Tibetan Classics*. The following list, which is by no means exhaustive, highlights some important examples:

- Panchen Sönam Dragpa (1478–1554) was an important early Gelug scholar who was the fifteenth Holder of the Ganden Throne, or Ganden Tripa, as well as abbot of Drepung Monastery. He was the author of *A Cluster of White Lotuses: Eloquent Verses of the Geden Tradition, a Treatise Examining the Wise and*

42. There is a work preserved in the collection of the Library of Tibetan Works and Archives called *Inexhaustible Treasure: A Treatise on Ethics (Nītiśāstra), Precious Instructions to All of Humanity* (*Skye bo kun la gdams pa'i rin chen lugs kyi bstan bcos mi zad pa'i gter*). The work is missing the final page, so we do not know who wrote it or when it was written. It is a long work, over 160 folio sides in small pecha (*dpe thung*) format. I received the images of the text just as this book was going to print, so I have only had a chance to glance at it, but from this brief perusal, it seems to be a compilation of several works and is not a continuous *nīti* treatise. My thanks to Lobsang Shastri for making the images of the work available to me.

43. The dates of the author are unknown. The full title of the work is *Palu-the-Muslim's Advice on Evaluating the Effects of Actions in the World*. It is perhaps the only premodern Tibetan work written by a Tibetan Muslim. The text has been translated in Dawa Norbu, *Khache Phalu's Advice on Art of Living*. For references to other literature on this text, see http://tibetica.blogspot.com/2006/06/khache-phalu-tells-it.html.

the Foolish (*Mkhas pa dang blun po brtag pa'i bstan bcos dge ldan legs bshad padma dkar po'i chun po*). The work, in some 125 stanzas, is the earliest *legshé* text of the Gelug tradition.

- Changkya Ngawang Lozang Chöden (1642–1714) was the second Changkya incarnation, abbot of Gönlung Monastery in Amdo, and imperial preceptor to the Chinese Kangxi Emperor from 1693 to 1697. He wrote *Eighteen Delightful Admonitions That Clarify What to Accept and Reject in the Two Systems* (*Lugs gnyis kyi glang dor gsal bar byed pa'i bslab bya gces pa bco brgyad*).
- Sumpa Khenpo Yeshé Peljor (1704–1788), abbot of Gönlung Monastery in Amdo, was author of *A Beautiful Flower Garland: An Ethical Treatise on the People's Dharma* (*Mi chos lugs kyi bstan bcos me tog phreng mdzes*). It is the only one of these Gelug works that contains the word *nītiśastra* in its title.
- Gungtang Könchog Tenpey Dronmé (1762–1823), the third Gungtang Rinpoche and the twenty-first abbot of Labrang Monastery in Amdo, composed: (1) *Wood Treatise: The Two Systems with Its Hundred Leaves and Branches* (*Shing gi bstan bcos lugs gnyis yal 'dab brgya ldan*), and (2) *Water Treatise* (*Chu'i bstan bcos*), with the same subtitle.
- Ngulchu Dharma Bhadra (1772–1851), an important Gelug scholar and hermit, wrote *Crystal Mirror of Precious Advice, Providing Unerring Instructions on What to Accept and Reject as Regards the Joint System* (*Lugs zung gi blang dor 'dzom med du 'doms pa'i bslab bya rin po che'i do shal*).
- Lozang Jinpa (1821–1891), a scholar of Trashi Lhunpo Monastery in Tsang, and the abbot of Kyilkhang Monastery, was the author of two texts: (1) the *Air Treatise: Elegant Verses to Make the Banner of the Joint System Flutter* (*Lugs zung ba dan g.yo ba'i legs bshad rlung gi bstan bcos*), modeled, according to the author, on Gungtang's *Water Treatise* and on Namgyal Zöpa's *Earth Treatise* and *Fire Treatise*.[44] Lozang Jinpa states that he composed the *Air Treatise* to complete the quartet of works based on the four elements (earth, fire, water, and air) started by his predecessors;

44. It is unclear to me who Namgyal Zöpa (Rnam rgyal bzod pa) might be. Lozang Jinpa writes about him as if he were his teacher. Nor have I found texts with the names *Earth* and *Fire Treatise* that predate Lozang Jinpa.

(2) *Moon Treatise: Elegant Verses That Clearly Expound Advice Related to the Worldly People's Dharma* (*'Jig rten mi chos dang 'brel ba'i bslab bya gsal bar ston pa'i legs bshad zla ba'i bstan bcos*), which he states is modeled on Gungtang's *Wood Treatise.*

- The Sixth Paṇchen Lama, Lozang Tubten Chökyi Nyima (1883–1937), authored *Wood Treatise: A Garland of Jewels Radiating Light onto the Two Systems* (*Sa'i bstan bcos lugs gnyis 'od brgya 'bar ba'i dbyig gi phreng ba*).
- Ngawang Lozang Tendzin Gyatso (1882–1954), abbot of Yershong Monastery in Amdo, was the author of three *legshé* texts: (1) *Jewel Treatise* (*Rin po che'i bstan bcos*), (2) *Fire Treatise* (*Me'i bstan bcos*), and (3) *Iron Treatise* (*Lcag kyi bstan bcos*)

All of these works except for the first were written after the Gelugpa consolidation of power under the fifth Dalai Lama in 1642. The "two systems" or "joint system" spoken of in several of these titles can refer to worldly and religious ethics, or more specifically to religion and politics. The Ganden Potrang, the government of the Dalai Lamas from the time of the Fifth Dalai Lama, considered itself, just as prior regimes had, to be the "union" of Buddhism and politics.[45] It is not surprising to see Gelug authors preoccupied with the two systems from the late seventeenth century, when the Gelug Church came to dominate the political affairs of Tibet.[46] That so many of these writers hailed from Amdo is due, on the one hand, to the flourishing of the literary arts in that part of the Tibetan world, something that is true even today; on the other hand, several of these figures had ties

45. An excellent resource for understanding the Tibetan notion of the "union of politics and Dharma," is the recently published collection of essays, Christoph Cüppers, *The Relationship Between Religion and States (*chos srid zung 'brel*) in Traditional Tibet.*

46. Max Oidtmann has shown, for example, that the "two systems" was very much on the minds of Amdo Gelugpa hierarchs in the early nineteenth century because of new forms of Manchu political intervention in Tibetan affairs. Max Oidtmann, "A Case for Gelukpa Governance: The Historians of Labrang, Amdo, and the Manchu Rulers of China," in *Greater Tibet*, 111–48. Oidtmann shows how in 1819 Belmang Paṇḍita (1764–1863), the twenty-fourth abbot of Labrang and a contemporary of Gungtang, was arguing for a form of government based on a system of Buddhist laws. He sees Belmang's famous *History*, where he laid out these arguments, as a kind of "prince's manual"—in part a response to Qing policies, and in part an attempt to show why the Gelug Church ought to be privileged in the administration of the political affairs of Tibet.

to both the Ganden Potrang and to the Qing court, which means that questions of religion and political power were always on the horizon for them.

All of the authors in the above list, except for the last two, predate Mipham. Whether Mipham was familiar with any of these earlier Gelugpa *legshés*, or whether the later Gelug authors were familiar with Mipham's *Treatise* is something that remains to be investigated. Clear parallels exist between several of these *legshé* texts and Mipham's *Treatise*, but Mipham does not mention any of these scholars or their texts by name. In fact, the only *legshé* text that Mipham acknowledges is the *Elegant Verses of the Sakya Tradition*,[47] written by Sakya Paṇḍita Kunga Gyaltsen (1182–1251), the uncle of Pagpa and one of the greatest scholars in Tibetan history. The *Sakya Legshé*, containing more than 450 verses, is the first book-length *subhāṣita* work written by a Tibetan; its influence on all subsequent Tibetan *legshé* literature cannot be overestimated.

I have offered this admittedly incomplete overview of the indigenous Tibetan *nīti* and *subhāṣita* literature to give the reader a sense of the richness of this tradition prior to Mipham's time. Apart from the *Sakya Legshé*, Mipham tells us only that he consulted "various *nītiśastras* composed by Tibetan sages." The task of determining precisely who those "Tibetan sages" were still lies ahead.

47. This is the famous *Sakya Legshé* (*Sa skya legs bshad*), which has been translated with commentary in Davenport, *Ordinary Wisdom*.

Appendix 2: The Thirty-Five Duties of a King as Taught in the *Smṛtyupasthāna Sūtra*

THIS LIST FORMS the basis for Mipham's seventh chapter. It is an important Indian Buddhist source for the duties of kings. To my knowledge, it has not been discussed in Western scholarship, so I expand on it in this appendix.

The sūtra first presents the list in order; it then comments on each of the items. I have included exemplary passages from the sūtra's glosses after each item. The folio numbers for each item are provided in parentheses before each extract. Two phrases are typically found at the beginning and/or end of each of the glosses and act as markers to divide the thirty-five topics: "A warrior-caste king who has been consecrated on his crown does X"; and "When a warrior class king who has been consecrated on his crown does X, he will always experience its benefits, and when his body is no more, he will be reborn in heaven, and becomes the ruler of the Aviha world." The initial, abbreviated list is found in folios 402b–403a of the *Smṛtyupasthāna Sūtra* (Lha sa bka' 'gyur edition); the glosses on each of the items immediately follow that.

1. འདིའི་རང་གི་སྐྱེ་བོ་གཙང་བར་གྱུར་པ་དང་། (His innate nature is pure.)[1]

Commentary (fols. 403a5–404a2): "He brings vast numbers of people to

1. The Tibetan translation is less than clear, but I take the expression *rang gi skye bo* to be translating something like *svajā* ("self-born" or "innate"). This is supported by the gloss. The point, it seems, is to stress that this is the king's natural condition or innate propensity. Mipham

the pure life, and in this way is exceedingly helpful to others. He is extremely scrupulous in protecting righteousness. He guards his commitments and is never dissolute. . . . He guards the kingdom righteously. He only speaks about beneficial and helpful things. He fasts at the appropriate times. He never ridicules those who are honest. . . . He is not motivated by desire and pride. In no instance does he allow his commitment to the Dharma to diminish. He is always interested in discussions of the afterlife. He fears saṃsāra. He does not deny that karma gives rise to results. He abandons the three types of misdeeds and does not accustom himself to them. He does not enjoy imposing fines."

2. དཔྱ་རྣམས་རིས་པར་བྱས་ནས་ཟ་བར་བྱེད་པ་དང་། (He does not tax people beyond what has been determined.)

Commentary (fols. 404a3–404a7): "Taxes are determined in regard to the times and occasions in which they are collected in the country, cities, villages, and markets, and for the king to violate this precise schedule is a fault related to time. But even when this is done correctly from the viewpoint of time, if he steadily increases the amount, and appropriates an improper share for himself, then this is a violation related to the measure or amount. . . . The king consumes only what has been determined. He does not harm beings."

3. བཟོད་པ་དང་ལྡན་པ་དང་། (He is patient.)

Commentary (fols. 404b1–404b7): "He makes all living beings rejoice. How? By being patient. When something makes him angry, he overcomes this. Even after becoming king he does not give himself permission to act in this way. He is not intolerant of others' wealth. He does not retaliate even against cities that are at fault. He never speaks harsh words to his friends. When he does become angry, he pacifies it through patience. He speaks sweetly. . . . In this way, he has compassion on every occasion, in all circumstances, and at all times. He does this naturally, and not motivated by some interest."

---

understands item no. 1 somewhat differently, seeing *rang gi skye bo* as referring to the fact that both the king himself (*rang*) and his entourage (his *skye bo* or men) are pure.

4. ལུགས་ལས་ཕྱོགས་འཛིན་མེད་པ་དང་། (He is impartial because he is just.)

Commentary (fols. 404b7–405a7): "Because of the evenness of his unexcelled virtuous thought, the king is like a mother and father to his country. He does not consider what wealth people have provided him, or how they have benefitted him. He does not rule thinking that these are his people, that they have benefitted him, that he is related to them, that he is the lord of these people, or that he is their military leader. In no instance does he act with partiality. When he administers justice, he treats friends and non-friends equally. When he acts in this way, the king's country never declines, nor does his reputation. His cities never become kingless. There is no fear of others' armies, nor do other kings criticize him. He will rule for a long time."

5. བླ་མ་མཆོད་པར་བྱེད་པ་དང་། (He makes offerings to the guru.)

Commentary (fols. 405a7–405b6): "A guru is someone who perfectly teaches the truth. He is ethical, wise, and possesses ascetic discipline. He is skilled in leading sentient beings to what benefits them. He is singularly virtuous. His actions of body and speech are pacified. This is the type of stainless person—someone who dedicates himself to leading others—that the king ought to cultivate as his guru. He listens to his sermons. He acts as the guru himself acts."

6. སྤར་ཉིད་[2] སྦྱེར་བར་བྱེད་པ་ཡིན། (He performs acts of charity himself.)[3]

Commentary (fols. 406a5–407a2):[4] "The generous king experiences the fruits of his generosity even in this life. How so? Because of the fame he enjoys, his cities and country become prosperous. They will not revolt against him. He receives unexcelled offerings from other lands. Witnessing these things, the armies of his opponents will not rise up against him. Enemies do not have the slightest opportunity to oppose him. He has the best of cities. Even kings who have not cultivated any pious motivation will

2. I have emended to the text to read *rang nyid* rather than *sngar nyid*.

3. In the gloss, the topic is simply called "giving" (*sbyin pa*).

4. In the commentarial portion of the text, nos. 6 and 7 are reversed, with the gloss for no. 7 preceding that for no. 6, but here I have maintained the order of the original list as it first appears in the text.

experience such results of charity in this life. What need to mention those who actually give fields and wealth with an excellent motivation. . . . There are three types of giving: the giving of material things, the giving of fearlessness, and the giving of Dharma. When a king gives these to mendicants and brahmins, as the result of that, once his body is no more he becomes the lord of the heavenly Aviha world."

(There follows at this point a passage which is almost word-for-word identical to one found under point no. 8 concerning the fact that the king does not support the unrighteous, which I do not include here because it is translated later.)

7. སྔར་བྱིན་པར་གྱུར་ནས་བྱིན་ཀྱང་སྟེར་བར་བྱེད་པ་ཡིན། (He gives again what has already been given.)

Commentary (fols. 405b6–406a5): "With a mind that is unsullied and free of mixed motives—with a beneficial intention and the highest faith—he rejoices in whatever fields or wealth may have been given in the past by his father, or by any of his ancestors, distant ancestors, or others. He praises those past acts of charity. He follows their example by giving other things."

8. ཆོས་ལ་ཡིན་པ་འཛིན་པར་མི་བྱེད་པ་ཡིན།[5] (He does not support the unrighteous.)[6]

Commentary (fols. 407a2–408a1): "He does not support those who are unrighteous. What makes a king, a member of the warrior caste, righteous or dharmic? What makes him a follower of the Dharma? It is the fact . . . that he does not support within his country those who are unrighteous: those who, using impure chants and with wrong views, 'deliver'[7] wild animals; those who engage in sacrifices[8] and kill domesticated animals; and he does

5. Following the gloss, I have emended the wording of this line to read *chos ma yin pa 'dzin pa mi byed pa*.
6. Mipham understands this to mean that the king eliminates (*spang*) them from the land, suggesting that he banishes them.
7. The text reads *ri dwags kyi 'khor ba 'grol ba* ("liberate [from] saṃsāra"), which I take to be a euphemism for some kind of ritual sacrifice, just as *sgrol ba* (a homonym of *'grol ba*) was understood in later tantric traditions as the "liberation" or "deliverance" of a being—usually an "enemy of Dharma" (*bstan dgra*)—through an act of ritual killing.
8. The Tibetan reads *mchod sbyin*, which translates a variety of Sanskrit words: *yajña*, *kratu*, *yajus*, *yajña*, *yāga*, *iṣṭi*, and so forth.

not support within his country debased men, men who uphold mistaken ways, like those who do not respect their parents.

"Other people, even those who have a virtuous mind, are laid to waste as a result of the error of associating with these teachings. Being laid to waste due to the error of those teachings, their kingdoms also decline. Rains fall at the wrong time. The gods raise the temperature at the wrong time. The harvest ripens at the wrong time. The country is destroyed—all due to the great fault of those sinners. For that reason, the king only supports those who are righteous. By giving his full support to those who are righteous, the gods make the rains fall at the right time, make the winds blow at the right time, make the harvest ripen at the right time. The kingdom is not destroyed, and beings live free from fear, torment, and terror. The individuals who master those true doctrines destroy the suffering of all conditioned things. So, he supports and relies upon those individuals who are righteous, the highest essence of which is the celibate life."

9. སྡིག་པའི་གྲོགས་པོ་དང་སྟེན་པར་བྱེད་པ་མ་ཡིན། (He does not cultivate sinful friends.)

Commentary (fols. 408a1–408b7): "There are eight types of evil friends:[9] (1) The first are nihilists. They deny the need for oblations[10] and charity, the existence of the world, or the world beyond. (2) The second are those who claim that there are no women who are off-limits sexually, that there is no point to celibacy, and that it is permissible to have sex with women even during their menstrual periods. (3) The third type of evil friend discourages giving to sentient beings and discourages the practice of priests making offerings into the sacrificial fire. (4) The fourth type of sinful friend claims that people exist for the length of their lives, and once they die, whatever good or evil they have done dissipates like clouds or fog so there is no retribution for their actions. The merit and sin of living beings, they say, is just like that. (5) The fifth type of sinful friend is one who claims that one's

9. As will become clear, many of these "evil friends" are nihilists of various kinds insofar as they deny fundamental Indian metaphysical truths, moral norms, or religious practices. The relationship of these various views to those typically ascribed to the Indian materialists—the Cārvāka or Lokāyatas—is a subject worth exploring further.

10. The word *sbyin sreg* translates the Sanskrit *homa*, *huta*, or *yāga*. Although these terms refer to a form of sacrifice, given what the text has just finished saying about the sacrifice of animals—that it is an unrighteous act—we must probably understand by this a more benign form of sacrifice that does not require the taking of life.

mother and father are to be abandoned and that one should free oneself of any sense of devotion to them. (6) The sixth type of sinful friend claims that the elderly, the blind, the protectorless, and the poor ought to be killed, for once they have died, they will find happiness in the afterlife. (7) The seventh sinful friend claims that everything is eventually destroyed by wind or burnt by fire; that this is the end of the world for beings and at that point they move to other worlds.[11] (8) The eighth type of sinful friend claims that God made everything, and that there is no law of karmic cause and effect.

"These eight types of sinful friends ought to be forsaken; they ought to be abandoned; they ought to be banned from the country. The king ought to support those individuals who correctly advocate cause and affect; he ought to support their holy Dharma."

10. བུད་མེད་ཀྱི་དབང་དུ་འགྲོ་བ་མ་ཡིན། (He is not controlled by women.)

Commentary (fols. 408b7–410a1): "Ordinary beings who are controlled by women are reviled by the people of the world; how much more is a controlled king, who is born into the highest and most magnificent lineage. All women are divisive by nature. They cause the king to become estranged from his country and from all of his vast districts. They win him over through desire and then point out the faults of his close associates. Being obsessed with wealth, they block his acts of charity. . . . When a man is completely concerned with thoughts of sex, he forgets about his own goals or affairs. Women cause divisiveness even among religious men. They are also a source of calumny, pride, and jealousy, and they all have this same nature. Anyone who becomes subservient to a woman deteriorates just as if he were dependent on a poisonous black snake. Therefore, the king renounces subservience to women."[12]

11. I suspect some textual error here, since the position as outlined actually resembles a cosmological doctrine found in a number of Buddhist works.

12. The misogyny found in passages like this are unfortunately not that uncommon. Although often attributed to the fact that these texts were written by monks who feared women because of the threat they posed to their celibacy, attitudes like this are found even in Brahmanical texts written by non-monks. They are therefore pan-Indian and not unique to an ascetic, religious worldview.

11. ཐམས་ཅད་ཀྱི་ཚིག་ལ་དད་པར་བྱེད་པ་མ་ཡིན། (He does not believe what everyone says.)

Commentary (fols. 410a1–410b5): "The living beings of the world are all of different minds—they mutually disagree about almost everything: their natures are different; their reasons are different; their motives are different; and their impurities are, by nature, different. They are always quarreling. They are always arguing. . . . The king does not become enmeshed in these disagreements. Some people speak in ways contrary to reason—there are contradictions between earlier and later portions of what someone says. Others have evil intentions toward one another: they speak from a partisan position; they speak out of a desire to curry favor; they portray the good that someone else did as harmful; they speak to the king motivated by the desire to fleece others of their property. All of these are cases of speech motivated by people's hostility to one another. In all of these cases, the king will not trust what people tell him. In this way his kingdom will not be destroyed. He does not get angry at people's improprieties, but he does not trust those who are trying to cause divisions. That king, who possesses special qualities, does not come under others' influence; instead he acts according to his own wishes. He has little anger, and is a comrade to all men and gods."

12. སྙན་པར་གྲགས་པ་ལ་འདོད་པ་སྐྱེད་པ་ཡིན་གྱི་ནོར་ལ་འདོད་པ་ཅན་མ་ཡིན་ནོ། (He has a desire for a good reputation, but not for wealth.)

Commentary (fols. 410b6–411b4): "He craves a good reputation, but not wealth. He is not greedy. He is not a miser: he is not tight-fisted; his face is not scrunched up; his eyes are not beady. He has few desires. He is not easily angered, nor is he quick to trust. His retinue is very stable. Although he possesses both wealth and reputation, he does not care about wealth, but the king works to achieve a good reputation among men. As a result, enemies cannot vanquish him, and instead they join his side. He obtains a good reputation through ten causes: speaking sweet words, having a pleasant disposition, and so forth."

13. ལོག་པར་ལྟ་བ་དང་ལྡན་པ་མ་ཡིན། (He does not have false views.)

Commentary (fols. 411b4–412a5): "False view is the root of all faults. Incorrect and mistaken views disparage and deny causality. The king does not tolerate such views. They make him very angry. He reviles them. He eliminates them. A king who has false views is abhorrent to everyone. Being abhorrent, everyone in his kingdom constantly revolts against him. He is not tolerated. The righteous gods too rise up against him. . . . The king who has right view is committed to the welfare of living beings. All countries worship him. The righteous gods do not forsake him. All of the regions of his empire are loyal. All of his plans come to excellent fruition."

14. གཏོང་བ་ཅན་ཡིན། (He is charitable.)

Commentary (fols. 412a6–413b4): "The root of that king's profound sense of morality is giving; this is the way he achieves the welfare of the world. All goodness—both mundane and supramundane—derives from giving. When someone engages in charity—whether it is the king who does this or one of his ministers—all of the districts will naturally hold the charitable person in the highest regard. They will not revolt against him; they will not revile him; they will not insult him; they will not transfer their allegiance to another kingdom. When he takes on another body after death, this thought occurs to everyone: 'There goes a charitable king.' . . . In this way, giving is praised for its abilities to achieve the goals of this world, but also of the world to come. . . . Other qualities in this life also arise from giving. What are these? Charitable people destroy pride, destroy avarice, destroy jealousy, and destroy ignorance; they have faith in causes and conditions; they have faith in the results of karma; they do not cast doubts on the next life; they make offerings to the guru; their mind is serene."

15. མཐུན་པར་བྱེད་པ་དང་ངག་སྙན་པར་སྒྲུར་བ་ཡིན། (He is agreeable and sweet-spoken.)

Commentary (fols. 413b.4–414a.7) "The king speaks sweetly and agreeably because he is perfectly just. It is in his nature to act lovingly toward everyone. What he accomplishes by speaking sweet and loving words cannot be accomplished through giving material things. The happiness that he brings to the country through his sweet words is reciprocated through the people's friendliness toward him. He does not give instant gratification to all people of the country,[13] and for that reason too his speech is sweet. . . . When even

13. The phrase is not altogether clear: *skye bo rnam thams cad shin tu myur bar rab tu tshim par byed pa ni/ yod pa ma yin*. I read this as suggesting that the king does not tell people what they want to hear in the moment—literally, what satisfies them very quickly.

enemies become the allies of the sweet-spoken king, what need to mention neutral or friendly parties."

16. བདེན་པར་སྨྲ་བ་ཡིན། (He speaks the truth.)

Commentary (fols. 414a7–416b1) "He acts as the cause of emancipation for all people bound within saṃsāra. He creates a priceless treasury of inexhaustible spiritual wealth for his people, thereby becoming the cause of special essential wealth. He becomes a source of refuge—both in the here and hereafter—for all holy beings, who are the greatest and most beautiful precious things in the land. He becomes the steward of those striving for nirvāṇa. He does not allow those committed to achieving good qualities to become extinct. This truth-speaker—the destroyer of want, the creator of faith, the demolisher of poverty—is the wealthiest of men even if he is completely devoid of wealth. Why? Because he is illuminated by the light of truth. Even when he belongs to the lowest of all the social classes, he is superior to the leaders of all the social classes. . . . Everyone sees him as a friend, and wherever he goes he is worshipped as a king and as mother . . . and even in the invisible world, the gods proclaim his fame. . . . The gods pursue and worship those who engage in virtue. They even destroy their nightmares. The chief of the gods worship them as if they were gods. . . . 'Truth speakers' are immovable; no one can move them. They cannot be swayed by friends; they cannot be swayed by non-friends. They are unshakeable. . . . Even in the absence of water, due to their essential truthfulness, these bathers on the shores of the highest pure truth achieve the highest form of cleanliness. Even when they have no clothes, they are constantly clothed in superior swaths of the unwoven pure white cloth of truth. Even when they are dirty, the sweet smell of their moral discipline pervades all the major and minor directions."

17. ནོར་གཞིས་རྣམས་འཕེལ་བ་དང་འགྲིབ་པར་གློ་བུར་དུ་མི་བྱེད་པ་ཡིན། (He does not capriciously increase or decrease wealth and landholdings.)[14]

Commentary (fols. 416b.1–417b.2): "That king is steadfast. Knowing that,

14. In the entire Tibetan Buddhist canon, the phrase *nor gzhis* is found only in this particular portion of the *Smṛtyupasthāna*. I have not found any Sanskrit equivalent. I have translated *nor gzhis* as "wealth and landholdings," but it is possible that it simply means "wealth in the

the wise men who oversee justice and the affairs of state rest easily. Those who act only after having examined situations in great detail will become king; those who do not engage in such analysis will not. Any king that, after some superficial analysis, increases or decreases wealth and landholdings will not be king, or if he is, he will not be for long. He will be a king in name only, for he does not act based on proper analysis. He will be considered foolish, a loose cannon, and unstable. He does not trust in anything that his ancestors have said. That lying king, who does as he pleases, will be thwarted in his desires, and another king will be put in his place. Understanding these faults, he will not lie. . . . When he does not act truthfully, he will capriciously cause wealth and landholdings to increase or decrease. Anyone who acts truthfully would always be self-disciplined, and he would never capriciously cause wealth and landholdings to increase or decrease. . . . A king whose mind is constant, unchanging, singular in its determination, and who is dedicated to giving happiness to all will, after his body is no more, be reborn in a higher realm as the lord of Aviha."

18. མིའི་ཁྱད་པར་ཤེས་པ་ཡིན། (He knows peoples' qualities.)

Commentary (fols. 417b.2–419a): "Someone who knows people's qualities knows something great indeed. That king is considered a worthy recipient of the whole world. Others will not be able to achieve this. . . . The king who knows people's qualities does not support unrighteous people. . . . Instead, he supports those who can be effective by virtue of having the opposite qualities, like not being hostile to the world, not having wrong views, not being deceitful. But a king does not consider people holy simply because they lack negative qualities, but because . . . they do not always commit strong sins, are not revolutionaries, do not speak deceitfully, are not naturally dissatisfied, are not useless to the world, do not get others to sin, are not proud, are not enemies, are not in torment, do not have uncontrolled speech or uncontrolled minds. Rather, the king supports those who have positive

---

form of landholdings"—that is, the estates or land grants given by kings to individuals and institutions (like Buddhist monasteries). In any case, one can perhaps see in this "practice of a king" the saṅgha's concern with maintaining its property and estates. The text is urging the king not to act capriciously by confiscating wealth and landholdings without justification and serious consideration. Since the Buddhist monastic community was an important land holder, it is not farfetched to see this as monks attempting to encourage kings to honor the endowments that their ancestors made to monasteries.

qualities: people who are righteous . . . humble, who speak the truth, who are wise, trustworthy, stable, who do not torment others, who are honest, who avoid deceit, who worship the three jewels as the highest religion, who know satisfaction, who are self-controlled, who continuously contemplate karma, whom the world finds agreeable, who are compassionate, who are attached to people's praise, who have the right view. . . . It is individuals with these qualities that the king supports; and these are the qualities he seeks to know in people. Whatever king joins himself to such individuals will not be able to be deposed by others, will not be able to be controlled, and will be wealthy. Thus having become wealthy and a righteous follower of the Dharma, he will engage in acts of charity. He will engage in acts of merit. He will make offerings to the three jewels."

19. དུས་ངེས་པར་ལེགས་པར་སྟོན་པར་བྱེད་པ་པོ་ཡིན། (He is someone who teaches the highest doctrine of emancipation at specific times.)

Commentary (fols. 419a1–419b4): "The king who teaches at specific times will rule for a long time. He will not experience distress. He will know people's qualities. He does not do what is unrighteous. Having made his country as strong as possible, he averts its decline. The king who takes great care to look after these things will be wealthy . . . and by being wealthy, he will not be dependent on others. He will also be righteous; he will follow the Dharma, and will make offerings to mendicants and brahmins. By listening to the Dharma from them, his Dharma practice will flourish. To whatever extent he practices the Dharma by teaching the highest doctrine, to that extent will he be wealthy. Having become wealthy, he engages in acts of charity. He creates merit. He becomes moral. No one can control him. Those good qualities are possible for him. For this reason, the king ought to teach at specific times."

20. གཉིད་ཆེ་བ་མ་ཡིན། (He does not sleep too much.)

Commentary (fols. 419b.4–420a.5): "He should not enjoy sleep. The king who controls his sleep can properly contemplate what ought to be contemplated. His mind will not be too attached, nor too deluded. The enemy will not be able to defeat him. He will be focused. He will possess fixed objectives, and possessing fixed objectives, he will engage in the proper analysis of those objectives. Having properly analyzed those, he knows which person will be able to bring his objectives to fruition, and he accomplishes these goals in a short time, achieving them quickly. He is self-controlled. Being self-controlled, he will live a long life. . . . He will be wealthy. . . . He will safeguard moral discipline."

21. ལེ་ལོ་མེད་པ་ཡིན། (He is not lazy.)

Commentary (fols 420a.5–421a.2): "The king who is not lazy employs reasoning that is characterized by stable perseverance and so he triumphs over all of his works—perfecting them, achieving them, and mastering them. He cannot be vanquished and his mind is, in every circumstance, naturally happy, joyful, affectionate, and loving. His country, with its cities, towns, hamlets, and markets, achieve a high level of excellence. The king who is not lazy and who possesses stable perseverance will subdue his opponents. He accomplishes every work that he commences. Why? Those who are not lazy use reasoning to determine the best place and time to undertake an action."

22. གྲོགས་པོ་བརྟན་པ་ཡིན། (He is a steadfast friend.)

Commentary (fols. 421a2–422b5): "The king who is a stable friend is exceedingly well liked and enjoys a long reign. . . . Like a tree, he is very stable and hence immovable; he cannot be swayed by evil people. His friendship is very stable like the forest, which stays just as it is even when the wind blows through it. Because of his very fine nature he is the most loving of companions. He has thirteen mundane qualities that characterize his stable friendship: when something occurs to rupture a friendship between two people, he conceals it. . . . He does not forsake someone even at the cost of his life. . . . He rejoices whenever something good occurs in the life of his friend. He commiserates when tragedy strikes. His demeanor never changes, even when someone gets really angry at him. . . . He will give away anything that he has in his house without any regrets, and so forth. . . . There are also ten qualities of his friendship related to his delight in the supramundane path and his commitment to achieving these aims: (1) Whenever someone does something unrighteous, he stops it, (2) he gets them to engage in charity, and (3) to accustom themselves to moral discipline. (4) He gets them to give up evil friends. (5) He teaches the results of karma. (6) He converts to the right path those who are following evil paths. (7) He gets people to give up even the smallest violation of moral discipline. (8) He reconciles people with their parents. (9) Always and with great effort, he incites people to the highest felicity of nirvāṇa. These are the special qualities of his friendship that are supramundane. Furthermore, (10) he protects people from wrong ways of acting. He is like a father and mother. . . . This is how the king will practice stable friendship."

23. མི་ཕན་པ་རྗེས་སུ་སྟེན་པར་བྱེད་པ་མ་ཡིན། (He does not rely on those who are unhelpful.)

Commentary (fols. 422b.5–423a.7): "He does not rely on unfriendly people, those who are not involved in doing good—for example, those who teach a wrong path with the sole intention of deceiving everyone, those who teach the cultivation of evil thoughts, or those who have given themselves over to great evil. The root of these destructive people is twofold: ideological nihilism and immoral behavior. Ideological nihilists are deceivers of the world—people who, having no faith, and making use of false logic, deny the existence of karma; who deceive both themselves and others with the thorny logic of the heterodox, like the peddlers of fake goods; who deny the afterlife; who take up the accoutrements of piousness but who are actually evildoers. It is natural that the king may come into contact and speak with these "thieves," but he will not make any offerings to them; what need to say that he will not befriend them. He will even distance himself from their associates."

24. ཁྲོ་བའི་ཤུགས་དང་དགའ་བ་ལ་ཡ་བོ་སྡོམ་པར་བྱེད་པ་ཡིན། (He controls the force of his rage and his excitement.)[15]

Commentary (fols. 423a7–424a3): "There are two other qualities that the king ought to avoid at all costs: rage and excitement. These must be controlled. The king who controls his rage and excitement will have a stable kingdom. . . . Kings who control their rage and excitement do not act without first thinking, suddenly move from one place to another, beat servants, openly speak about what should be kept secret, reward or punish people, become ebullient about something pleasant, nor do their goals change when they become depressed. They do not associate with unholy beings. Their

15. The gloss replaces *dga' ba* ("joy") with *rgod pa* ("restlessness," "agitation," or "excitement"). I have adopted that latter reading in the translation of this line.

minds are stable. The king who controls his rage and excitement in this way is praised in regard to his mundane achievements. How is he praised . . . in regard to his supramundane aspirations? By controlling his rage, he controls one saṃsāric stain. Whoever controls the force of excitement is also controlling the force of desire. Whoever controls both of those forceful stains also controls the force of delusion. The control of the force of these three stains brings knowledge, brings patience, brings mental stability, and ensures that one has a controlled intelligence that is focused. When these prior causes and conditions ripen and his body is no more, he is reborn in heaven as the ruler of the Aviha world."

25. ཟས་དང་སྐོམ་ལ་ཤིན་ཏུ་ཀུན་ནས་ཆགས་པའི་རང་བཞིན་ཅན་མ་ཡིན། (He is not overly attached to food and drink.)

Commentary (fols. 424a3–425b5): "A king who is overly concerned with food and drink becomes distracted due to his longings. He is obsessed with the thought of satiating his appetites. As a result of his natural cravings, he thinks of only this one thing, like an animal. He cannot think about anything else but food and drink. . . . He does not care about the country or the people. He does not think about the goals of the state . . . and as these goals deteriorate, the country's wealth declines and, as a result, food and drink disappear."

26. ལེགས་པར་བསམ་པར་བྱ་བ་རྣམས་སེམས་པའི་ཡིན། (He engages in proper reflection.)

Commentary (fols. 425b2–426a3): "He reflects about good deeds, engaging in proper reflection. Why? Because this is what accomplishes the welfare of beings both in this life and in the next. Why? Because these are the good qualities of mind. Whoever reflects properly in this life and the next achieves the highest happiness. But he also thinks about destroying faults, also bearing this in mind. He explains that the stains of desire and so forth always lead to the lower realms, and he thinks about eradicating them through their antidotes: eradicating desire through the contemplation of foulness, eradicating anger through love, and eradicating delusion through wisdom. . . . Even worldly things are achieved through proper reflection."

27. དོན་དུས་རིང་དུ་བསྐོར་བར་བྱེད་པ་མ་ཡིན། (He does not procrastinate.)

Commentary (fols. 426a3–427a1): "Procrastinators can never achieve any goals—whether worldly or spiritual, whether beneficial or not. So do not be complacent in regard to those goals. It is just like the case of an illness: the quicker you treat it, the better. But those who procrastinate will not be able to achieve the cure and the illness consumes them. Likewise, those who do not tackle their various other goals quickly will not be able to take them up at some later time and they get nowhere. The same thing applies to the eradication of the afflictions, which are like illnesses, and which lead to the lower realms; due to the fault of procrastination, you get nowhere on the spiritual path. . . . A procrastinator—whether it be a king, a monk, a wealthy person, or anyone else—never has a good reputation; no one ever sings his praise. On the other hand, those who do not procrastinate—who deal with their faults in the very moment—will relinquish them, destroy them, eradicate them, destroy them from the root. . . . Faults, like noxious weeds, only increase with time, leading to many other problems. So vanquish them in the moment."

28. ཆོས་ལ་སྐྱེ་རྒྱུ་རབ་ཏུ་འགོད་པར་བྱེད་པ་ཡིན། (He leads living beings to righteousness.)

Commentary (fols. 427a1–427b6): "He rules living beings with righteousness and not with unrighteousness. The superior righteous king benefits both himself and others. . . . An ethical king never rules living beings unrighteously. This also benefits him. . . . By ruling them in the proper way, he attains righteousness, his goals, and a good reputation. If, from the outset, through his righteousness, he introduces them to the supreme felicity of nirvāṇa, how could they ever be unrighteous? The king achieves his goal. . . . The king who properly rules living beings achieves the love of his cities, and his reputation and fame are proclaimed in all directions."

29. དགེ་བ་བཅུའི་ལས་ཀྱི་ལམ་གྱི་དགེ་བ་རྣམས་བྱེད་པར་འགྱུར་བ་ཡིན། (He practices the path of the ten virtuous actions.)

Commentary (fols. 427b6–430b3): "These acts bring him the highest happiness. The path of the ten virtues are divided into three: actions of the body, of the speech, and of the mind. The acts of the body are those that avoid killing, stealing, and sexual misconduct; the acts of speech are those that avoid lying, divisive speech, harsh words, and nonsensical talk; and the acts of the mind are those that avoid coveting, harmful thoughts, and wrong views. When the king and people practice these, the gods will protect them. The country will experience no fear of weapons or famine. In their country, the harvests are timely and of excellent quality. The sun and moon shine their light on the country as they should. All needs are met and the country becomes excellent."

30. རྒྱུ་དང་རྐྱེན་ལེགས་པར་སྟོན་པར་བྱེད་པ་ཡིན། (He properly contemplates cause and effect.)[16]

Commentary (fols. 430b3–431b4): "The king, or even a minister, who properly contemplates cause and effect will not be confused. His mind will constantly dwell on karma and its effects. He will not disregard the affairs of the country. The word *cause* refers to the seed; *conditions* refers to the collection of other factors like the season and the soil. Those who do not denigrate causes and who do not denigrate effects will witness the truth of cause and effect. They will not engage in sinful karma. They will be no more confused about the ripening of results from karma than they are about the causal process of seeds and sprouts. The virtuous and nonvirtuous karma that one accumulates in one birth transforms into the various aspects of happiness and suffering experienced in one round of birth after another. . . . The king who contemplates cause and effect will not be overcome by faults. Terrified by the fear of faults, he will not engage in nonvirtuous actions and will always do what is virtuous."

31. ལྷ་དག་མཆོད་པར་བྱེད་པ་ཡིན། (He worships the gods.)

Commentary (fols. 431b4–432b1): "The gods who do good works will, of their own accord, help him in his good works. They will not create any obstacles to virtue. Those who worship the gods with offerings both day and night will achieve mastery over all of their work. Those gods will correctly

16. The phrasing in the original list is different: "He properly teaches causes and conditions." The phrasing found in the gloss—which I follow here—substitutes "contemplates" (*blta*) for "teaches" (*ston par byed pa*), and "cause and effect" (*rgyu dang 'bras bu*) for "causes and conditions" (*rgyu dang rkyen*).

reveal to him, in his dreams, the good and bad that he will experience in the future.

"They will protect the country from any danger that it may encounter. They will always encourage the king in virtuous acts. . . . Therefore, the virtuous gods ought to be worshipped using many methods just as if they were one's parents. The king constantly worships the gods through dharmic rituals, through commitments, and by avoiding sinful actions. He worships them nonviolently, and he does not seek the intervention of the deities of people who have wrong views. . . . With the help of the virtuous gods, the pious king will not fail to achieve his goals. . . . Living beings increase in goodness; cities flourish; and so too does the king himself."

32a.[17] ལེགས་པར་སྐྱེ་རྒྱུ་རྣམས་བསྐྱང་བར་བྱེད། (He properly takes care of living beings.)

Commentary (fols. 432b1–433a4): "The king who properly takes care of living beings practices the Dharma; he follows the Dharma; he provides freedom from fear to his mother, father, and so forth. . . . All of the city dwellers become attached to him, and as a result of that attachment, he achieves his goals, wealth, and fame. He is happy both day and night. The king who follows such a policy increases his control because of his commitment to the welfare of all sentient beings. As his sovereignty flourishes, the crops properly grow. As his cities flourish, the king too flourishes. In this way, the king who takes care of living beings constantly achieves the Dharma, wealth, and fame."

32. བུ་དང་བུ་མོ་ཡང་དག་པས་བདེ་བར་ཡོངས་སུ་སྐྱོང་བར་བྱེད་པ་ཡིན། (He properly takes care of his sons and daughters.)

Commentary (fols. 433a4–434a5): "Any king or queen, or even minister, who pays attention to the real happiness of their sons and daughters will continuously increase their merit in many ways. . . . A king gives his children money, food, drink, clothing, hugs, and sweet words; he gives them whatever makes them trusting and joyful, and he gives them freedom from fear. Whatever actions are done on behalf of his sons and daughters result in great merit. Great and manifold merit arises for that household. How does

17. The commentary adds, before the thirty-second point, this item not found in the initial list.

he take care of them? Out of a sense of compassion, he ensures that they do not suffer from poverty, and are not oppressed by want. Having provided them with monetary support, he takes great care to select their bodyguards.

"Those who are unable to ordain out of faith ought to take up raising sons and daughters. Those who are able to ordain but who do not support their sons and daughters because of their poverty are neither householders nor monks. Therefore, monks who ordained after having children should make arrangements for their children's material support.[18] The king or king's minister accustoms himself to moral discipline, and then inculcates moral discipline in his sons and daughters; he gets them to engage in charity; he gets them to meditate on wisdom.

33. རྟག་པར་ཡང་ཤེས་རབ་སྒོམས་པར་བྱེད་པའི་རང་བཞིན་ཅན་ཡིན། (He is naturally given to constantly meditating on wisdom.)

Commentary (fols. 434a5–436a1): "How does he meditate on wisdom? He meditates, in every possible way, on the cause that extricates one from the whole of saṃsāra—that destroys all suffering. Wisdom is the lamp that lights the way for those who have fallen into great darkness—for those who grope about in the darkness of a multitude of sufferings. It is wealth for those stricken with the poverty of saṃsāra. It is the eye for the blind, power for the powerless, a friend for the friendless, a protector for those lacking protection. It is medicine for living beings suffering from illness. It is the guide for lost travelers. For those stuck in the deserts of saṃsāra and suffering from thirst, it is cool water. It is the cause that extricates those bound in the prison of saṃsāra. . . . That is why wisdom is so exceedingly important. Kye ho! Whether in this life, in the next, or in any other, from time immemorial, there has never been a cause like this one for the advancement of living beings. Through wisdom, all good qualities are perfectly united into one, and by properly meditating on that, the highest path is realized. . . . In this way the king enjoys a long reign. The city dwellers delight in him. The kings of other kingdoms are unable to defeat him. He will live a long life, will not experience suffering, and will enjoy many forms of happiness over a long period of time."

18. The *Arthaśāstra* (2.1.29) states that a man who abandons his home to become an ascetic without first making arrangements for the financial support of his wife and children is subject to legal penalties such as a fine.

34. ཡུལ་གྱིས་དགྲི་བར་འགྱུར་བ་མ་ཡིན། (He is not ensnared by sense objects.)

Commentary (fols 436a1–437b4): "He is not like those who are enticed by objects. Those kings who are captivated by the finest of things—the sounds, touchable things, tastes, forms, and smells that are considered most excellent—as a result of their various preoccupations, are unable to create virtue. Their countries will not be properly governed. They will lose their supreme status in their own countries, and as this occurs, their righteousness, wealth, and reputation will deteriorate. As a result of this deterioration, rival kings harass them, and as a result of those harassments, the city dwellers become unhappy and the empire crumbles. . . . Therefore, the king should not put a lot of emphasis on objects. The king who does not put a lot of emphasis on objects safeguards his own righteousness, and his mind also becomes exceedingly calm. He will not be enticed by sounds, touchable things, tastes, forms, and smells. When such a king rules living beings, he always possesses righteousness, wealth, and a good reputation. . . . He always desires the welfare of living beings, has no ill will and no covetous thoughts, and when his body is no more, he will be reborn in heaven as the lord of the Aviha gods."

34a. གདུལ་དཀའ་བ་རྣམས་ཡུལ་དུ་འཛིན་པར་བྱེད་པའོ། (He does not support within his country people who are hard to tame.)[19]

Commentary (fols. 436b6–437b4): "Whatever individual, having become king, supports within his country immoral people—sinful evildoers who are hard to tame—will, in short order, fall into the great fault that those evil people have committed. Their grave faults will cause the destruction of the kingdom and will bring about the demise of the ruler. Harvests will not ripen; virtuous acts will disappear; living beings are not protected. . . . The gods of that country will show no mercy. Hard to tame people make highly disciplined men hard to tame. How so? By associating with them; when moral people associate with others who are not, they become spoiled. That is why the king will not support those who are hard to tame. . . . So the king only protects what is righteous; he supports only what is righteous; he assists only what is righteous."

19. This item is found in the glosses but not in the original list.

35. རིགས་པ་དང་ལྡན་པའི་རང་བཞིན་རྣམས་ཀྱི་རིགས་ཀྱིས་གཞི་སྦྱིན་པར་གཏོང་ངོ། (He gives resources to his dependents in a way that is just and that accords with the standard.)[20]

Commentary (fols. 437b.4–438b.6): "The land, wealth, and charity given to dependents[21] for their present use is given by the king to those dependents according to the rules for households. This naturally prevents their directing their displeasure at the king; it prevents the king's dependents from competing with one another; and it prevents dissatisfaction. When there is a proper division of resources, there will be no deceit. The king who creates no cause for doubts about the division of resources is celebrated more than the most celebrated.

"He does not get involved in commercial activities. Even though he is the most powerful person, he does not harm even the least powerful. He does not get impassioned about dharmas.[22] He is satisfied—satisfied with what he has produced through his own labor.

"The gods do not send untimely rains to his districts. The sun does not get hot at the wrong times. There are no famines, no conflicts involving weapons, and no disturbances of wind. The gods do not abandon the country and shift their allegiances to other countries. Other gods do not empty the country of people and destroy it. . . . Realizing the problems that ensue, the king does not support sinful people. Wherever people practice virtue—in whatever countries the best of these practices, the best righteous activity, are supported—the gods offer their protection and support. As a result of this support, the hosts of gods and the other gods of neighboring countries cannot create obstacles, and in fact will protect that country."

Whatever king upholds these thirty-five Dharmas will be well supported. He will perfect all of his good qualities. He will live continuously experiencing one form of happiness greater than the last.

20. In the glosses, the wording of this item is quite different: "The king acts with great diligence and possesses righteousness; he is, by nature, someone who does not have attachments."
21. The word *bran* (Skt. *dāsa, bhṛtya*), which I am here translating "dependent," can also mean "servant."
22. The line reads *chos rnams la 'dod pa can yang ma yin*. The meaning is not completely clear.

Appendix 3: The Order of the Thirty-Five Practices in Mipham's *Treatise* and in the *Smṛtyupasthāna Sūtra*

In his discussion of the *Smṛtyupasthāna*'s thirty-five practices (see appendix 2), Mipham follows a different order than the one found in the *Sūtra*. This table compares the order of the two lists.

Subject	Number in Mipham's Text	Number in the Sūtra
Meditating on wisdom	1	33
Proper reflection	2	26
Worshipping the guru	3	5
Avoiding sinful friends	4	9
Not denying karma	5	13
Right knowledge of causality	6	30
Knowing people's qualities	7	18
Not trusting everyone	8	11
Cultivating steadfast friends	9	22
Avoiding untrustworthy friends	10	23
King/retinue is purified	11	1
Charity, sweet speech, good deeds	12	12

Subject	Number in Mipham's Text	Number in the Sūtra
Eliminating laziness	13	21
Not procrastinating	14	27
Moderation in food and drink	15	25
Not sleeping excessively	16	20
Not being controlled by women	17	10
Nor being ensnared by five senses	18	34
Controlling rage and excitement	19	24
Being patient	20	3
Sweet words	21	15
Speaking the truth	22	16
Impartiality	23	4
Not changing landholdings	24	17
Fixed taxes	25	2
Not supporting the unrighteous	26	8
Not changing endowments	27	7
Giving	28	6
Generosity	29	14
Offerings to the gods	30	31
Support of children	31	32
Proper support of subjects/serfs	32	35
Leading beings to happiness	33	28
Practicing the ten virtues	34	29
Teaches the Dharma	35	19

Bibliography

Aiyangar, K. V. Rangaswami. *Rājadharma*. Madras: Adyar Library, 1941.

Amoghavarṣa. *Vimalapraśnottara Ratnamālā*. *Dri ma med pa'i dris lan rin po che'i phreng ba*. Sde dge bstan 'gyur, Toh. no. 4333, thun mong ba lugs kyi bstan bcos *ngo*, fols. 126a–27b.

Ārya ajātaśatru kokrīttya vinodananāma mahāyāna sūtra. *'Phags pa ma skyes dgra'i 'gyod pa bsal ba zhes bya ba theg pa chen po'i mdo*. Sde dge bka' 'gyur, Toh. no. 215, mdo sde *tsha*. Dpe sdur ma ed., vol. 62, 566–700.

Ārya bodhisattva gocara upāya viṣaya vikurvāṇa nirdeśa mahāyāna sūtra. *'Phags pa byang chub sems dpa'i spyod yul gyi thabs kyi rnam par 'phrul pa bstan pa'i theg pa chen po'i mdo*. Lha sa bka' 'gyur, no. 147, mdo sde *pa*, fols. 82a–141b.

Ārya saddharma smṛtyupasthāna sūtra. *'Phags pa dam pa'i chos dran pa nye bar gzhag pa*. Lha sa bka' 'gyur, no. 289, vol. 70, fols. 400b–41a.

Āryaśūra. *Garland of the Buddha's Past Lives*. Translated by Justin Meiland. 2 vols. New York: NYU Press for the Clay Sanskrit Library, 2009.

———. *Jātakamāla*. *Skyes pa'i rabs kyi rgyud*. Sde dge bstan 'gyur, Toh. no. 4150, skyes rabs *hu*, fols. 1b–135a.

Asaṅga, Ārya. *The Bodhisattva Path to Unsurpassed Enlightenment: A Complete Translation of the Bodhisattvabhūmi*. Translated by Artemus B. Engle. Boulder: Snow Lion, 2016.

"Asian Scholars at IsMEO," *East and West* 13, no. 1 (1962): 89.

Atiśa. *Mnyam med jo bo chen po rgya gar la phebs khar lha bla ma byang chub 'od la zhal gdams su btsal ba*. In *Legs bshad bstan bcos phyogs bsgrigs*, vol. 1, 367–74. Xining: Mtsho sngon mi rigs dpe skrung khang, 2006.

Bays, Gwendolyn, trans. *The Voice of the Buddha, the Beauty of Compassion*. 2 vols. Berkeley: Dharma Publishing, 1983.

Bhattacharyya, Deborah P. "Theories of Kingship in Ancient Sanskrit Literature." *Civilisations* 17, no. 2 (1967): 109–18.

Bloomfield, Maurice. "The Fable of the Crow and the Palm-Tree: A Psychic Motif in Hindu Fiction." *American Journal of Philology* 40, no. 157 (1919): 1–36.

Bod kyi khrims yig chen mo zhal lce bcu drug. Thimpu: Kunsang Topgyel and Mani Dorji, 1979.

'Brom ston rgyal bai 'byung gnas. *Mi chos gnad kyi phreng ba*. In *Blo sbyong nyer mkho phyogs bsgrigs*, edited by Cha ris skal bzang thogs med and Ngag dbang sbyin pa, 374–80. Lan kru'u: Kan su'u mi rigs dpe skrung khang, 2003.

Bstan 'dzin lung rtogs nyi ma. *Snga 'gyur rdzogs chen chos 'byung chen mo*. Beijing: Krung go'i bod rig pa dpe skrung khang, 2004.

Buddhaguhya. *Bod rje 'bangs dang btsun pa rnams la spring yig*, Sde dge bstan 'gyur, Toh. no. 4194, spring yig *nge*, fols. 387a–91b.

Buswell, Robert E., Jr., and Donald S. Lopez, Jr. *The Princeton Dictionary of Buddhism*. Princeton, NJ: Princeton University Press, 2014.

Cabezón, José Ignacio. "Bamda Gelek." *Treasury of Lives*. 2015. http://treasuryoflives.org/biographies/view/Bamda-Gelek/7272.

———. *The Buddha's Doctrine of the Nine Vehicles*. Oxford: Oxford University Press, 2013.

———. *Sexuality in Classical South Asian Buddhism*. Boston: Wisdom Publications, 2017.

Cakkavatti Sīhanāda Sutta. Digha Nikāya 26. In *The Dīgha Nikāya*, edited by T. W. Rhys Davids and J. Estlin Carpenter, vol. 3, 58–79. London: Pali Text Society, 1889–1904.

Campbell, W. L. *Shes-rab dong-bu*. Calcutta: Calcutta University, 1919.

Cāṇakya. *Rājanītiśāstra. Tsa na ka'i rgyal po'i lugs kyi bstan bcos*. Sde dge bstan 'gyur, Toh. no. 4334, thun mong ba lugs kyi bstan bcos *ngo*, fols. 127b–37b.

Chab 'gag rta mgrim. *Bod bstan po'i dus kyi rtsom rig*. Beijing: Mi rigs dpe skrun khang, 2009.

Collins, Steven. *Nirvana and Other Buddhist Felicities: Utopias of the Pāli Imaginaire*. Cambridge: Cambridge University Press, 1998.

Cowell, E. B., trans. *The Jātaka*. 3 vols. London: Pali Text Society, 1973.

Cuevas, Bryan J. "'The Calf's Nipple' (*Be'u bum*) of Ju Mipam: A Handbook of Tibetan Ritual Magic." In *Tibetan Ritual*, edited by José Ignacio Cabezón, 165–86. Oxford: Oxford University Press, 2010.

Cüppers, Christoph, ed. *The Relationship Between Religion and States (*chos srid zung 'brel*) in Traditional Tibet*. Lumbini: Lumbini International Research Institute, 2004.

Daśacakrakṣitigarbha sūtra. 'Dus pa chen po sa'i snying po 'khor lo bcu pa. Lha sa bka' 'gyur, no. 240, vol. 65, mdo sde *dza*, fols. 154a–371b.

Davenport, John T., Sallie D. Davenport, Lha-sa-ba Blo-bzang-don-ldan, and Sakya Khenpo Sangye Tenzin, trans. *Ordinary Wisdom: Sakya Pandita's Treasury of Good Advice*. Boston: Wisdom Publications, 2000.

Deegalle, Mahinda. "The Analysis of Social Conflicts in Three Pāli Canonical Discourses." Paper delivered at the 12th International Buddhist Conference on the United Nations Day of Vesak, May 28–30, 2015. www.undv.org/vesak2015/paper/analysis_social_conflicts.pdf.

Dhammika, S. "Kalinga Rock Edicts." *The Edicts on King Ashoka*, www.cs.colostate.edu/~malaiya/ashoka.html#KALINGA.

Dietz, Siglinde. *Die buddhistische Briefliteratur Indiens: nach dem tibetischen Tanjur herausgegeben, übersetzt und erläutert*. Asiatische Forschunden, Band 84. Wiesbaden: Otto Harrassowitz, 1984.

Dil mgo mkhyen rtse bkra shis dpal 'byor. *'Jam mgon bla ma mi pham 'jam dbyangs rnam rgyal rgya mtsho'i rnam thar gsol 'debs kyi 'grel pa mtsho byung dpal mo dgyes pa'i rgyud mang*. In *Dil mgo mkhyen rtse'i bka' 'bum*, vol. 15, 267–99. Delhi: Shechen Publications, 1994.

Dkon mchog 'jigs med dbang po. *Rgyal sras rgya mtsho 'jug ngogs*. Asian Classics edition. http://asianclassics.org/release6/flat/S0949E_T.TXT.

Dorji, C. T. *The Tree of Wisdom*. Delhi: Prominent Publishers, 2000.

Duckworth, Douglas. *Jamgön Mipam: His Life and Teachings*. Boston: Shambhala Publications, 2011.

———. *Mipam on Buddha-Nature*. Albany: SUNY Press, 2008.

———. "Mipam Gyatso." *Treasury of Lives*. 2013. http://treasuryoflives.org/biographies/view/Mipam-Gyatso/4228.

Dudjom Rinpoche, Jikdrel Yeshe Dorje. *The Nyingma School of Tibetan Buddhism*. 2 vols. Translated by Gyurme Dorje with Matthew Kapstein. Boston: Wisdom Publications, 1991.

Dunne, John, and Sara McClintock, trans. *The Precious Garland: An Epistle to a King*. Boston: Wisdom Publications, 1997.

Dutt, Manmatha Nath. *Kamandakiya Nitisara, or The Elements of Polity*. Calcutta: H. C. Das, 1896.

Emmerick, Ronald E. *The Sūtra of Golden Light: Being a Translation of the Suvarṇabhāsottamasūtra*. London: Luzac and Co., 1970.

Flick, Hugh Meredith, Jr. *Carrying Enemies on Your Shoulders: Indian Folk Wisdom in Tibet*. Delhi: Sri Satguru Publications, 1996.

Foucault, Michel. *Discipline and Punish: The Birth of the Prison*. Translated by Alan Sheridan. New York: Vintage Books, 1979.

Foucaux, Phillipe Edouard. *La guirlande précieuse des demandes et des réponses*. Paris: Maissoneuve et Cie, 1867.

Foucher, Albert. "Essai de classement chronologique des diverses versions du Ṣaḍdanta-jātaka." In *Mélanges d'Indianisme offerts par ses élèves a M. Sylvain Lévi*. 231–36. Paris: Ernest Lerous, 1911.

Freer, Léon. "Le Chaddanta-Jataka." *Journal Asiatique* (Paris) 9, vol. 5 (1895): 31–85, 189–223.

French, Rebecca Redwood. *The Golden Yoke: The Legal Cosmology of Buddhist Tibet*. Ithaca: Snow Lion, 2012.

Frye, Stanley, trans. *Nāgārjuna's a Drop of Nourishment for the People*. Dharamsala: Library of Tibetan Works and Archives, 1994.

———. *The Sūtra of the Wise and the Foolish*. 2nd ed. Dharamsala: Library of Tibetan Works and Archives, 2000.

Ganguli, Kisari Mohan, trans. *The Mahābhārata of Krishna-Dwaipayana Vyasa*. Vol. 3, bks. 8–12. Project Gutenberg ed. EBook #15476.

Gardner, Alexander Patten. "The Twenty-five Great Sites of Khams: Religious Geography, Revelation, and Nonsectarianism in Nineteenth-Century Eastern Tibet." PhD diss., University of Michigan, 2006.

Goodman, Steven D. "Mi-Pham rgya-mtsho: An Account of His Life, the Printing of His Works, and the Structure of His Treatise Entitled *Mkhas-pa'i tshul la 'jug pa'i mgo*." In *Windhorse: Proceedings of the North American Tibetological Society*. Vol. 1. Edited by Ronald Davidson, 58–78. Berkeley: South Asian Humanities Press, 1981.

Gupta, Sudhir Kumar. *Nitivakyamritam: 10th Century Sanskrit Treatise on Statecraft, original text with Hindi and English Translation*. Jaipur: Prakrita Bharati Academy, 1987.

Hahn, Michael. "The Indian Nītiśāstras in the Tibetan Tanjur." Unpublished English translation and expanded version of "Die indischen Nītiśāstras im tibetischen Tanjur." *Zeitschrift der Deutschen Morgenländischen Gesellschaft, Supplement VI, XXII Deutscher Orientalistentag vom 21. bis 25. März 1983, Ausgewählte Vorträge*, hrsg. von Wolfgang Röllig. Wiesbaden 1985: 227–37.

———. *Invitation to Enlightenment.* Berkeley: Dharma Publishing, 1999.

———. "Ravigupta and his Nīti Stanzas (I)." *Minami Ajia Kotengaku* [*South Asian Classical Studies*] 2 (2007): 303–55.

———. "Ravigupta and his Nīti Stanzas (II)." *Minami Ajia Kotengaku* [*South Asian Classical Studies*] 3 (2008): 1–38.

———. "The Tibetan *Shes rab sdong bu* and its Indian Sources (I)." Verses 1–110. *Minami Ajia Kotengaku* [*South Asian Classical Studies*] 4 (2009): 1–78.

———. "The Tibetan *Shes rab sdong bu* and its Indian Sources (II)." Verses 111–185. *Minami Ajia Kotengaku* [*South Asian Classical Studies*] 5 (2010): 1–50.

———. "The Tibetan *Shes rab sdong bu* and its Indian Sources (III)." Verses 186–260. *Minami Ajia Kotengaku* [*South Asian Classical Studies*] 6 (2011): 1–71.

Haksar, A. N. D., trans. *Subhāshitāvali: An Anthology of Comic, Erotic and Other Verse*. Gurgaon: Penguin Books, 2007.

Hartley, Lauran Ruth. "A Socio-Historical Study of the Kingdom of Sde-dge (Derge Khams) in the Late Nineteenth Century: *Ris-Med* Views of Alliance and Authority." Master's thesis, Indiana University, 1997.

"History of Ju Mohor Monastery." *Amnyi Trulchung Rinpoche*. www.amnyitrulchung.org/monastery/history/.

Hopkins, Jeffrey. *Nāgārjuna's Precious Garland: Buddhist Advice for Living and Liberation.* Ithaca: Snow Lion, 2007.

Huber, Édouard, trans. *Sūtrālaṃkāra*. Paris: Ernest Leroux, 1908.

Ingalls, Daniel H. H. *An Anthology of Sanskrit Court Poetry: Vidyākara's "Subhāṣitaratnakoṣa."* Cambridge, MA: Harvard University Press, 1965.

"Interview with Dzogchen Ponlop Rinpoche." *The Chronicle Project.* www.chronicleproject.com/stories_149.html.

’Jam dbyangs blo gter bang po. *Ston mchog thams cad mkhyen pa thub pa’i dbang po’i skyes rabs gsal bar brjod pa brgya lnga bcu pa nor bu’i phreng ba*. Beijing: Mi rigs dpe skrun khang, 2003.

Jamspal, Lozang, trans. *The Range of the Bodhisattva: A Mahāyāna Sūtra*. Edited by Paul G. Hacket. New York: American Institute of Buddhist Studies/Columbia Center for Buddhist Studies, 2010.

Jayaswal, K. P. *An Imperial History of India in a Sanskrit Text*. Lahore: Motilal Banarsidass, 1934.

Jenkins, Stephen. “Making Merit through Warfare According to the *Ārya-Bodhisattva-gocara-upayaviśaya-vikurvaṇa-nirdeśa Sūtra*.” In *Buddhist Warfare*, edited by Mark Juergensmeyer and Michael Jerryson, 59–75. New York: Oxford University Press, 2010.

Kale, M. R., ed. and trans. *The Nīti and Vairagya Śatakas of Bhartṛhari*. Delhi: Motilal Banarsidass, 2013 [reprint of the 7th ed. (1971)].

Kangle, R. P, ed. and trans. *The Kauṭilīya Arthaśāstra*. 3 vols. Delhi: Motilal Banarsidass, 2010.

Kornman, Robin, Sangye Khandro, and Lama Chönam, trans. *The Epic of Gesar of Ling: Gesar’s Magical Birth, Early Years, and Coronation as King*. Boston: Shambhala Publications, 2012.

Krug, Adam. “History, Ideology, and the Construction of a Tibetan Buddhist State Identity in ’Phags pa’s Advice to Prince Jibik Temür,” In *Kingship, Ritual, and Narrative in Tibet and the Surrounding Cultural Area*, edited by Brandon Dotson. *Cahier d’Extrême-Asie* 24 (2015): 117–144.

van der Kujip, Leonard. “Review of Oge Idan legs bshad.” In *Journal of the American Oriental Society* 106, no. 3 (1986): 617–21.

Lacôte, Félix. *Essai sur Guṇāḍhya et la Bṛhatkathā*. Paris: Ernest Leroux, 1908.

Lalitavistara. ’Phags pa rgya cher rol pa. Lha sa bka’ ’gyur, no. 96, vol. 48, mdo sde *kha*, fols. 1b–352a.

Mahāparinibbāna Sutta. Dīgha Nikāya 16. In *The Dīgha Nikāya*, edited by T. W. Rhys Davids and J. Estlin Carpenter, vol. 2, 72–78. London: The Pali Text Society, 1889–1904.

Mahāsannipāta ratnaketu dhāraṇī. ’Dus pa chen po rin po che tog gi gzungs. Lha sa bka’ ’gyur, no. 140, vol. 56, mdo sde *tha*, fols. 289b–432a.

Mahodaya, Kamayani, ed. and trans. *Bhartṛhari’s Śatakatrayaṃ*. Delhi: Chaukhamba Sanskrit Pratishthan, 2011.

Mañjuśrīmūlatantra. ’Jam dpal gyi rtsa ba’i rgyud. Lha sa bka’ ’gyur, no. 501, vol. 88, rgyud *tha*, fols. 53b–448b.

Masūrākṣa. *Nītiśāstra. Lugs kyi bstan bcos*. Sde dge bstan ’gyur, Toh. no. 4335, thun mong ba lugs kyi bstan bcos *ngo*, fols. 137b–43a.

Mātṛceta. *Mahārājakaniṣkalekha. Rgyal to chen po ka nis ka la springs pa’i spring yig*. Sde dge bstan ’gyur, Toh. no. 4184, spring yig *nge*, fols. 53a–56b.

Meiland, Justin, ed. and trans. *Garland of the Buddha’s Past Lives*. New York: New York University Press, 2009.

Mi pham rgya mtsho. *Lugs kyi bstan bcos lha dang dpal 'du ba'i nor bu*. In *Mi pham bka' 'bum*, vol. 7, 194–212. Chengdu: Gangs can rig gzhung dpe rnying myur skyobs lhan tshogs, 2007.

———. *Rgyal po lugs kyi bstan bcos sa gzhi skyong ba'i rgyan*. Leh, Ladakh: Gelong Jamyang, 1968.

———. *Rgyal po lugs kyi bstan bcos sa gzhi skyong ba'i rgyan*. Siling: Mtsho sngon mi rigs dpe skrung khang, 2006.

———. *Rgyal po lugs kyi bstan bcos sa gzhi skyong ba'i rgyan*. In *Collected Writings 'Jam mgon mi pham rgya mtsho*, vol. 3, 1–158. Gangtok: Sonam Tobgay Kazi, 1972.

———. *Rgyal po lugs kyi bstan bcos sa gzhi skyong ba'i rgyan*. In *The Expanded Redaction of the Complete Works of 'Ju Mi-pham*, vol. 1 (*oṃ*), 1–157. Paro, Bhutan: Lama Ngodrup and Sherab Drimey, 1984–1993.

———. *Rgyal po lugs kyi bstan bcos sa gzhi skyong ba'i rgyan*. In *Mi pham bka' 'bum*, vol. 7, 1–144. Chengdu: Gangs can rig gzhung dpe rnying myur skyobs lhan tshogs, 2007.

———. "The Treatise on the Modes of Being: 'The Jewel that Gathers Forth Divinities and Glory.'" Translated by the Ari Bhöd Translation Committee. http://aribhod.org/wp-content/uploads/2014/07/NORBU_CHOS-Web-021115.pdf.

"Mipham Rinpoche." *Rigpa Wiki*. www.rigpawiki.org/index.php?title=Mipham_Rinpoche.

Mitra, Raja Rajendra Lala, ed., and Sisir Kumar Mitra, trans. *The Nītisāra by Kāmandaki*. Kolkata: The Asiatic Society, 2008.

Mkhan po kun bzang dpal ldan. *'Jam mgon mi pham rin po che'i rnam thar snying po bsdus pa*. In *Mi pham bka' 'bum*, vol. 9, 551–648. Chengdu: Gangs can rig gzhung dpe rnying myur skyobs lhan tshogs, 2007.

Mohan, Pankaj. "Kingship." In *Encyclopedia of Buddhism*. Edited by Robert E. Buswell, Jr., vol. 1, 467–68. New York: Macmillan Reference, 2004.

Murty, K. Satchidananda. "Sanskrit and Philosophical Thought in the Vasco da Gama Epoch." *Annals of the Bhandarkar Oriental Research Institute* 58/59 (1977–1978): 785–98.

Nāgarājabherī gāthā. *Klu'i rgyal po rnga sgra'i tshigs su bcad pa*. Lha sa bka' 'gyur, no. 329, vol. 72, mdo sde *la*, fols. 314a–20b.

Nāgārjuna. *Jantupoṣaṇabindu* (or *Janapoṣaṇabindu*). *Lugs kyi bstan bcos skye bo gso ba'i thigs pa*. Sde dge bstan 'gyur, Toh. no. 4330, thun mong ba lugs kyi bstan bcos *ngo*, fols. 113a–16b.

———. *Prajñādaṇḍa*. *Shes rab sdong bu*. Sde dge bstan 'gyur, Toh. no. 4329, mdo 'grel *ngo*, fols. 103a–13a.

———. *Prajñāśataka*. *Shes rab brgya pa*. Sde dge bstan 'gyur. Toh. no. 4328, thun mong ba'i lugs kyi bstan bcos *ngo*, fols. 99a–103a.

———. *Rājaparikathāratnāvalī*. *Rgyal po la gtam bya ba rin po che'i phreng ba*. Sde dge bstan 'gyur, Toh. no. 4158, spring yig *ge*, fols. 107a–26a.

———. *Suhṛllekha*. *Bshes pa'i spring yig*. Sde dge bstan 'gyur, Toh. no. 4182, spring yig *nge*, fols. 40b–46b.

Nakamura, Hajime. *Indian Buddhism: A Survey with Bibliographical Notes.* Delhi: Motilal Banarsidass, 1987.

Nebesky-Wojkowitz, René de. *Oracles and Demons of Tibet.* Kathmandu: Book Faith India, 1996.

Ng, Zhiru. *The Making of Savior Bodhisattva: Dizang in Medieval China.* Honolulu: University of Hawaii Press, 2007.

Nobel, Johannes, ed. *Suvarṇabhāsottamasūtra = Das Goldglanz-Sūtra: ein Sanskrit-text des Mahāyāna-Buddhismus.* Leipzig: Harrassowitz, 1937–1950.

Norbu, Dawa, trans. *Khache Phalu's Advice on Art of Living.* Dharamsala: Library of Tibetan Works and Archives, 1986.

Oidtmann, Max. "A Case for Gelukpa Governance: The Historians of Labrang, Amdo, and the Manchu Rulers of China." In *Greater Tibet: An Examination of Borders, Ethnic Boundaries, and Cultural Areas.* Edited by P. Christian Klieger, 111–48. Lexington Books, 2015.

Okada, Yukihiro, and Michael Hahn. *Nāgārjuna's Ratnāvalī, Vol. 1, The Basic Texts (Sanskrit, Tibetan, Chinese).* Bonn: Indica et Tibetica Verlag, 1982.

Olivelle, Patrick, trans. *King, Governance, and Law in Ancient India: Kauṭilya's Arthaśāstra.* Oxford: Oxford University Press, 2016.

Pathak, Suniti Kumar. *Nītiśāstra of Masūrākṣa.* Shantiniketan: Viśva Bharati Research Publications, 1961.

———. *The Indian Nītiśāstras in Tibet.* Delhi: Motilal Banarsidass, 1974.

Pettit, John W. *Mipham's Beacon of Certainty: Illuminating the View of Dzogchen, the Great Perfection.* Boston: Wisdom Publications, 2002.

'Phags pa blo gros rgyal mtshan. *Rgyal bu ji big de mur la gtam du bya ba nor bu'i phreng ba.* In *'Gro mgon chos rgyal 'phags pa'i gsung 'bum.* Dpe sdur ma ed., vol. 4, 115–35. Beijing: Krung go'i bod rig pa dpe skrung khang, 2007.

———. *Rgyal bu mangga la la gtam du bya ba bkra shis kyi phreng ba.* In *'Gro mgon chos rgyal 'phags pa'i gsung 'bum.* Dpe sdur ma ed., vol. 4, 135–56. Beijing: Krung go'i bod rig pa dpe skrung khang, 2007.

Phuntsok, Karma. *Mipham's Dialectics and the Debates on Emptiness: To Be, Not to Be, or Neither.* London: RoutledgeCurzon, 2005.

Pitāputrasamāgama sūtra. Yab dang sras mjal ba'i mdo. Lha sa bka' 'gyur, no. 60, dkon brtsegs *nga*, fols. 85a–358a.

Poussin, Louis de la Vallee, French trans., and Gelong Lodrö Sangpo, English trans. *Abhidharmakośa-Bhāṣya of Vasubandhu: The Treasury of Abhidharma and Its (Auto) commentary.* 4 vols. Delhi: Motilal Banarsidass, 2012.

Rājadeśanāma mahāyāna sūtra. Rgyal po la gdams pa zhes bya ba theg pa chen po'i mdo. To Bimbisāra. Sde dge bka' 'gyur, Toh. no. 214, mdo sde *tsha*. Dpe sdur ma ed., vol. 62, 550–57.

Rājadeśanāma mahāyāna sūtra. Rgyal po la gdams pa zhes bya ba theg pa chen po'i mdo. To Udayana. Sde dge bka' 'gyur, Toh. no. 215, mdo sde *tsha*. Dpe sdur ma ed., vol. 62, 560–63.

Rangarajan, L. N., trans. *The Arthashastra.* New Delhi: Penguin Books, 1992.

Ravigupta. *Gāthākośa* (or *Āryākośa*). *Tshigs su bcad pa'i mdzod*. Sde dge bstan 'gyur, Toh. no. 4331, thun mong ba lugs kyi bstan bcos *ngo*, fols. 116b–22b.

Richardson, Hugh E. *A Corpus of Early Tibetan Inscriptions*. London: Royal Asiatic Society, 1985.

Ringu Tulku. *The Ri-Me Philosophy of Jamgon Kongtrul the Great: A Study of Buddhist Lineages of Tibet*. Translated by Ann Helm. Boston: Shambhala Publications, 2006.

Rje mi pham pa'i bla ma phyogs bsgrigs. Dar thang dgon pa, 2001.

Roy, Pratap Chandra, trans. *The Mahabharata of Krishna-Dwipayana Vyasa*. Vol. 8 (*Śāntiparva*). Calcutta: Oriental Publishing Co.

Samdong Rinpoche. "The Social and Political Strata in Buddhist Thought." *Tibet Journal* 2, no. 1 (1977): 1–9.

Sarkar, Benoy Kumar, trans. *The Sukranīti*. Sacred Books of the Hindus, vol. 13. Allahabad: Indian Press, 1914.

Śarma, Viṣṇu. *The Panćatantra*. Translated by Chandra Rajan. Gurgaon: Penguin Books, 1993.

Satyaka Sūtra. See *Ārya bodhisattva gocara upāya viṣaya vikurvāṇa nirdeśa mahāyāna sūtra*.

van Schaik, Sam. *Tibet: A History*. New Haven: Yale University Press, 2011.

Schiefner, Anton. "Carminis Indici '*Vimalapraçnottararatnamālā*' Versio Tibetica." In *Secularia Tertia*. Petra Poli: Academiae Jenesi, 1858.

———, trans. *Tibetan Tales Derived from Indian and Buddhist Sources*. Introduction by W. R. S. Ralson. Patna: Shri Publishing House, 1990.

Shastri, Losang Norbu. *Śatagāthā of Ācārya Vararuci*. Varanasi: Kendrīya Ucca Tibbatī Sikṣa Saṃsthāna, 2001.

Skilling, Peter. "King, *Sangha*, and Brahmans: Ideology, Ritual, and Power in Pre-Modern Siam." In *Buddhism, Power and Political Order*, edited by Ian Harris, 182–233. London: Routledge, 2007.

———. "A List of Symbols on the Feet and Hands of the Buddha from the *Bodhisatva-gocara-upāya-viṣaya-vikurvāṇa-nirdeśa-nāma-mahāyāna-sūtra*." *Journal of the Centre for Buddhist Studies Sri Lanka* 11 (2013): 47–60.

Smith, E. Gene. *Among Tibetan Texts: History and Literature of the Himalayan Plateau*. Edited by Kurtis Schaeffer. Boston: Wisdom Publications, 2001.

Snellgrove, David, and Hugh Richardson. *A Cultural History of Tibet*. Boston and London: Shambhala Publications, 1986.

Sternbach, Ludwik. *Cāṇakya-nīti-text Tradition*. 5 vols. Hoshiarpur: Vishveshvarananda Vedic Research Institute, 1963–1970.

———. *Cāṇakya-Rāja-Nīti: Maxims on Rāja-nīti Compiled from Various Collections of Maxims Attributed to Cāṇakya*. Madras: The Adyar Library and Research Centre, 1963.

———. "Ravigiupta and his Gnomic Verses." *Annals of the Bandharkar Oriental Institute* 48 (1968): 137–60.

———. "The Tibetan Cāṇakya-Rāja-Nīti-Śāstram." *Annals of the Bhandarkar Oriental Research Institute* 42, no. 1 (1961): 99–122.

———. *Subhāṣita, Gnomic and Didactic Literature*. Vol. 4, fasc. 1, *A History of Indian Literature*. Wiesbaden: Otto Harrassowitz, 1974.

Sternbach, Ludwik, et al. *Mahā-subhāṣita-saṃgraha: Being an Extensive Collection of Wise Sayings in Sanskrit.* 8 vols. Hoshiarpur: Vishveshvaranand Cedic Research Institute, 1974.

Strong, John S. *The Legend of King Aśoka: A Study and Translation of the Aśokāvadāna*. Princeton, NJ: Princeton University Press, 1983.

Suvarṇabhāsottamasūtra. 'Phags pa gser 'od dam pa mchog tu rnam par rgyal ba'i mdo sde'i rgyal po. Translated from the Chinese. Lha sa bka 'gyur, no. 513, rgyud *da*, fols. 1b–215b.

Suvarṇabhāsottamasūtra. 'Phags pa gser 'od dam pa mdo sde'i dbang po'i rgyal po. Translated from the Sanskrit. Lha sa bka 'gyur, no. 514, vol. 89, rgyud *da*, fols. 215b–405b.

Suvarṇabhāsottamasūtra. 'Phags pa gser 'od dam pa mdo sde'i dbang po'i rgyal po. Translated from the Sanskrit. Lha sa bka 'gyur, no. 515, vol. 89, rgyud *da*, fols. 405b–507a.

Tambiah, Stanley J. "King Mahāsammata: The First King in the Buddhist Story of Creation, and His Persisting Relevance." *Journal of the Anthropological Society of Oxford* 20, no. 2 (1989): 101–22.

Taylor, McComas. *The Fall of the Indigo Jackal: The Discourse of Division and Pūrṇabhadra's* Pañcatantra. Albany: State University of New York Press, 2008.

Tharchin, Geshe Lobsang, and Artemus B. Engle. *Nāgārjuna's Letter*. Dharamsala: Library of Tibetan Works and Archives, 1976.

Udānavarga. Edited by Franz Bernhard. 1965. *Ancient Buddhist Texts*. www.ancient-buddhist-texts.net/Buddhist-Texts/S1-Udanavarga/23-Atma.htm.

Udānavarga. Ched du brjod pa'i tshoms. Lha sa bka' 'gyur, no. 330, vol. 72, mdo sde *la*, fols. 320b–87b.

Vararuci. *Śatagāthā* (or *Gāthāśataka*). *Tshigs bcad brgya pa*. Sde dge bstan 'gyur, Toh. no. 4332, thun mong ba lugs kyi bstan bcos *ngo*, fols.122a–26a.

Wallace, Vesna A., and B. Alan Wallace, trans. *A Guide to the Bodhisattva Way of Life*. Ithaca: Snow Lion, 1997.

Wang, Francis. *Le Bodhisattva Kṣitigarbha en Chine du Ve au Xiiie siècle*. Paris: presses de l'École française d'Extrême Orient, 1998.

Weber, Albrecht. "Über die Praçnottararatnamālā, Juwelenkranz der Fragen und Antworten." *Monatsberichte der Königlich Preussischen Akademie der Wissenschaften zu Berlin* (1868): 92–117.

Wilkinson, Christopher. *Chogyal Phagpa: The Emperor's Guru*. Sakya Kongma Series, vol. 5. Concord, MA: Suvarna Bhasa Publishing, 2014.

Yamamoto, Carl. *Vision and Violence: Lama Zhang and the Politics of Charisma*. Leiden: Brill Academic Publishers, 2012.

Zimmermann, Michael. "A Mahāyānist Criticism of the *Arthaśāstra:* The Chapter on Royal Ethics in the *Bodhisattva-gocaropāya-viṣaya-vikurvaṇa-nirdeśa-sūtra.*" *Annual Report of The International Research Institute for Advanced Buddhology at Soka University for the Academic Year 1999* 3 (2000): 177–211.

———. "Only a Fool Becomes a King." In *Buddhism and Violence*, edited by Michael Zimmermann, 213–42. Lumbini: Lumbini International Research Institute, 2006.

Index